DNA and Property Crime Scene Investigation

Forensic Evidence and Law Enforcement

David A. Makin

Foreword by
Larry S. Miller

Routledge
Taylor & Francis Group
LONDON AND NEW YORK

First published 2014 by Anderson Publishing

Published 2015 by Routledge
2 Park Square, Milton Park, Abingdon, Oxfordshire OX14 4RN

and by Routledge
711 Third Avenue, New York, NY 10017

Routledge is an imprint of the Taylor and Francis Group, an informa business

First issued in hardback 2015

Acquiring Editor: Sara Scott
Editorial Project Manager: Marisa LaFleur
Project Manager: Punithavathy Govindaradjane
Designer: Matthew Limbert

Library of Congress Cataloging-in-Publication Data
Makin, David Alan.
DNA and property crime scene investigation / David Alan Makin.
pages cm

ISBN 978-1-4557-7553-8 (pbk)
ISBN 978-1-138-13721-9 (hbk)

1. Crime scene searches. 2. DNA fingerprinting. 3. Evidence, Criminal. 4. Forensic sciences. I. Title.
HV8073.5.M155 2015
363.25′2—dc23

2014014252

British Library Cataloguing-in-Publication Data
A catalogue record for this book is available from the British Library.

ISBN 978-1-4557-7553-8 (pbk)

CONTENTS

FOREWORD

Many years ago my first job in law enforcement was as an evidence technician for a small sheriff's office. We called it R&I (Records and Identifications) back then—before CSI or crime scene investigation was a household term. I was given an old 4 × 5 Speed Graphic camera, a flashlight, and a fingerprint kit. I had a few shopping bags and plastic sandwich bags in which to put any evidence I located. My only formal training was reading an FBI monograph on Collecting and Preserving Physical Evidence and working with an experienced criminal investigator. I learned a lot working with that investigator. We took great pains in documenting the scene, and locating and collecting physical evidence on those "serious" cases involving death or bodily injuries. But when it came to burglaries, larcenies, and vandalism we normally just made a report and, if any latent fingerprints were easily located, took a few dustings and a couple of photographs for the homeowner's insurance company and to pacify the victim. Those latent images were normally stapled to the report and filed away with no more time spent on the case. It was only if the perpetrator was caught doing another property crime that we could "talk him" into fessing up to the other unsolved property crimes.

Times sure have changed, but not by much. Yes, we have more knowledgeable and properly trained investigators. And we have more readily available and affordable technology in our crime scene investigation arsenal. The emergence of the Integrated Automated Fingerprint Information System (IAFIS) has greatly increased our ability to match latent prints at the scene with known prints in a national database. Digital cameras have replaced the old press cameras and 35 mm SLRs. The Alternate Light Source (ALS) and other forensic lights have supplanted the old three-cell flashlights we kept in our back pockets. Even the public is more aware of the advanced technology from watching crime scene television shows and motion pictures where evidence is located and tested in a laboratory within a matter of minutes. And, with increased public knowledge of crime scene investigation technology, there is increased accountability and expectation of police response and action at crime scenes. As many prosecuting attorneys will attest, if the jury feels the police did not do a proper job at the crime scene based on their advanced knowledge from watching crime television shows, it could lead to an acquittal. We have come to call this "the CSI effect."

Perhaps the most advanced crime scene investigation technology that has come about in the last few decades is DNA analysis. The public first saw the potential benefits and liabilities of DNA watching the O.J. Simpson murder trial on TV in 1995. Now, hardly a day goes by when someone is not either convicted on DNA evidence or exonerated by it. The technology for DNA analysis is constantly evolving and has become faster and cheaper. One could predict that within a few years DNA analysis will be as commonplace for CSI investigators as that old fingerprint kit I used to carry. It will be a portable, on-scene test.

This book contends that DNA evidence collection should be in commonplace use for property crimes and not just for personal crimes. Yes, there are backlogs of testing for serious personal crimes at many crime laboratories. And, yes, many crime laboratories restrict the testing to serious personal crimes due to cost and time. But that is not to say that collection at the scene should not be performed. When IAFIS went online, many a cold case was solved due to the collection of a latent print at a crime scene years ago by some conscientious R&I officer. Already we have seen nonviolent and property crime cases solved using DNA technology in cases such as illegal tree harvesting, narcotics manufacturing, stolen livestock, counterfeiting, and game poaching. To not collect DNA evidence at the scene of even nonserious property crimes may now be seen as negligence, even if the crime lab doesn't do an analysis. Perhaps we may just staple the swabs to the report like we did with those latent prints until the day when DNA analysis will be commonplace, cheap, and fast. Yes, times sure have changed—but not by much.

Larry S. Miller, PhD
Professor & Chair
Department of Criminal Justice & Criminology
East Tennessee State University
Johnson City, TN, USA

ACKNOWLEDGMENTS

I have been working on this book, or more specifically the broader connections between technology and criminal justice, since I started pursuing criminal justice research nearly 15 years ago. Specific to this book, it is a culmination of 3 years' worth of research. As typical, I should work through the exhaustive list of people and institutions supporting and enabling me to dedicate time to this book. While I will do that, I want to highlight specifically the patrol officers, detectives, command staff, forensic technicians and experts, and prosecutors who allowed me to step into their word and view forensic technology through their eyes. Thanking them for the participation seems routine. However, I do not merely value their participation. Rather, each shared their frustration, hopes, and even questionable ethical behavior involving forensic evidence. Their openness to this study introduced new concepts and valuable insight into the challenges, successes, and opportunities to refine our forensic practice. The trust they placed with me is something that I will never forget and truly, without them, this book would not exist and its contribution to the field would be minimal. I also want to thank the individual officers that completed the survey providing remarkable insight in their responses to the open-ended questions on the survey. Anyone who conducts survey research is aware of how rare are these questions completed and many of the officers took considerable time to share policy, procedure, and again their frustrations. To continue highlighting the practitioners involved, I want to highlight Chief Gary Jenkins for his contributions to this book, specifically the two chapters he wrote speaking to the challenges and opportunities of expanded genetic processing. I have been fortunate to collaborate with Gary on multiple projects over the years and his insight on police practice is immensely beneficial. I have worked with many police officers over my career, but Gary is one of the most research-oriented, which speaks to his eagerness to learn more about practices around the nation and even the world adapting them into his agency.

I am indebted to those mentors who helped me refine my research skills and supported me throughout my academic career. Not forgotten were their support, contribution, and confidence in me, and that of my research agenda. In no specific order, I want to thank, Otwin "Otto" Marenin, Toni Dupont-Morales, Thomas "Tad" Hughes, William "Bill" Walsh, Faith Lutze, David Brody, and Jennifer Marchand-Reilly. While it is difficult to measure the influence of a person, I want to highlight specifically a few of those who have been instrumental in my career. I have known Toni for the last 15 years, starting at Pennsylvania State University, and she has provided me with countless advice, support, and criticism over these last years to see me develop from an uncertain undergraduate to a confident academic. While I will always consider her a mentor, I am proud to be able to call her both a colleague and friend. Without her advice early in my career and her belief in my ability, I would not be writing this section, nor would there be a book. Otto provided invaluable guidance and his honest, albeit brutal questions and comments, taught me the value of an inquisitive research question, one where the answer is important but the value of the question progresses the entire field. Faith has been my "book writing" compatriot. We both worked on writing our books over the course of the last few years and our conversations truly helped push through those periods of writers block. I also want to thank both Tad Hughes and Bill Walsh of the Southern Police Institute. Their mentorship early in my career came to influence the direction of my research. Critical thinking, analytical reasoning, statistical analysis are vital core attributes of a scholar, but to do so with no practical application is to fail to step outside of the ivory tower. In part to them, I learned how to work with agencies, to collaborate with agencies, and specific to this research, speak to cops, and more importantly get them to talk back.

I also wish to acknowledge Washington State University and the Washington State Institute for Criminal Justice Research, where I serve as faculty and research fellow. Additionally, I want to highlight the entire team at Anderson Publishing, including Marisa LaFleur my Editorial Project Manager, and the Acquisition Editor Sara Scott. I also want to acknowledge Larry Miller for his introduction, which speaks to the importance of this work.

I owe immeasurable gratitude to my family. Long were the hours, the discussions, and even the missed opportunities of interaction with my wife and children. In what has been an intense 3 years of research, writing, interviews, and focus groups, I have missed much of them. Holding a full-time job, completing my doctoral degree, and finishing this book has meant that my time with them has been brief and while what time we spent was valuable, I realize that it should have been more. It is with deep gratitude that I thank them for all the support, patience, and love. To my wife Danielle, I offer the deepest of recognitions. In over 13 years of marriage, and three universities, you have always been the person in most support of me. To my son Ryleigh, my fishing partner, whose equal love of fishing forced me out of my office and onto the shore, without you, I would have never taken a moment to enjoy those summers. To Esabella, my inquisitive daughter, I cannot begin to thank you for all the questions on what I was writing. You do get the first signed copy as you asked. I also want to thank my closest of friends who listened to me express my frustrations with the process and who provided support, encouragement, and always a source of inspiration. Thank you.

CHAPTER 1

A Series of Questions

The costs are there, really you can never really get away from the costs but I believe it is important and if there is evidence, our task is to collect it.

Police Chief

While unorthodox, I start this book with a series of questions. What if ~250,000 criminal cases existed where forensic evidence was present but remained uncollected? The cost of this crime nationally exceeded 14 billion dollars. However, what if processing evidence could improve, on average, an agency's identification rates, arrest rates, and conviction rates by twofold? What reasons, rationalizations, or, potentially, excuses would be offered? What if the costs could be offset? What reasons exist for ignoring evidence? What if the costs still presented an issue, but still some agencies vigorously aimed for high volume processing? What explanations and what insight would those stakeholders offer for continuing to analyze this evidence?

The key to this puzzle of questions is to narrow the unit of focus, and transition the historical lens on forensic technology to the individual officer level. To understand the connection between officer and forensic technology is to gain an accurate understanding of the current state of forensic technology. A skeptical reader has likely remarked, "Those cases receive the lowest priority," and this book does not challenge that claim. Instead, we must reflect on why, despite knowledge of the benefits of expanded processing, these cases still receive limited forensic treatment. Why, despite three decades of research within forensic technology, have few peered into the black box of forensic evidence practice?

This book is about social, organizational, and individual change. Specifically, how technology through a forensic evidence lens, has come to influence the police service. It highlights the experiences of patrol officers, command staff, detectives, and chiefs who navigate the expectations of forensics and the forensic technicians who support them. As the investigative continuum exceeds police officers and forensic technicians, I include interviews with prosecutors to understand the influence this technological innovation has had on criminal investigations. The objective of this book introduces the relationship between the investigative process and forensic technology, using property crime scene evidence as a narrowing frame. An analysis of forensic technology offers insight into the social construction of this technology that has placed high value on the use of forensic technology—if only in limited application (that is high-level crime).

The broader objective of this book is to explore how technology has come to shape organizations and individuals. As a book on forensic technology, this book addresses many similar topics covered within other books. However, this book departs from the norm by examining technology beyond the abstract. Technology influences people and therefore it is important to highlight the experiences of those who use this technology, to place them at the center of the analysis. Exploring the forensic experiences, attitudes, and views of those involved in the investigative process allows for both a practical and theoretical analysis into the current state of forensic technology within modern police services.

A BRIEF HISTORY

The history of forensic technology has long been a core feature of modern policing, institutionalized just over a century ago in American policing by August Vollmer. However, it was not until the Crime Commission met that a systematic examination into technology and policing would occur. In 1967, the Crime Commission would offer several commonsense recommendations that would introduce technology to address the most routine of police practices. Formed as a response to the likely criticism that President Johnson would have received for the increase in crime, this science and technology commission sought to understand how technology could aid police. While the commission accepted that technology was not a cure to crime, it was the first foray into the study of technology and its influence on the criminal justice system, specifically police organizations.

Since this report, scholars have tried to understand the role of technology within the criminal justice system. Early research by Anderson (1967) and Wolfe (1967) explored the inner workings of the Crime Commission offering unique perspectives for understanding technology within the organizational context and not merely applied to solve crime. As each warned, we must not forget how advanced technology may not overcome low-tech determination (in referencing the Vietnam War). Technology in this capacity is not the solution; rather it is but a part of the solution.

With each decade, new research explored emerging technology but still largely unexamined was the influence technology had on the organization, the officers, or society. In the 1990s, research emerged examining information technology; specifically the work of Postman (1992) and Manning (1992), offering that information technology had come to alter the structural, symbolic, and social organization of police. Nearly a decade later, Chan (2001) would offer insight into this area, research that has influenced this work and has come to benefit both academic and practitioner.

The research in the 1990s introduced researchers and practitioners to the complex relationship between technology and the police organization. While a small subunit of focus within the field of criminal justice research, scholars have tried to understand how technology has shaped police practice. Early research was theoretical, highlighting the likely benefits of recent technology developments. As technology integrated into the police organization, researchers focused on key measurements (effectiveness and efficiency). This research proved valuable, but only across the theoretical and the quantitative measures of effectiveness that developed. Something was missing. Specifically, missing from this conversation was ethnographic and strong mixed-method research approaches introducing the practitioners to add their experiences to the history that is police technology.

While the state of forensic technology has been a focus of research, largely missing was the influence on the individual officer. Despite improvements in our overall knowledge on forensic technology and practice, details on the evidence backlog, and the current state of technology developments, largely unexamined has been the individual officer level. Without this perspective, it is difficult to provide answers to the complex questions involving forensic technology. For example, how and in what ways have police practices changed in the last decade? What role do first responders or detectives have in forensic collection? What knowledge do they have, what training have they received, what influences their decision to collect? Now, we have answers to some of the questions. However, many answers concern only the collection and analysis for compulsory processing of sexual assault incidents and homicides, crimes with clearly described protocol. What we lack is an understanding of decision-making at the lowest forensic level, specifically property crime scenes. This book provides answers to these questions. Sharing officer experiences affords the unique opportunity to understand how forensic technology has come to influence the daily tasking of officers and how these taskings have come to influence the use of forensic technology.

WHERE IT STARTED

As with any intellectual effort, some pinnacle experience captivates an interest, fostering the pursuit of understanding the complexity and nuances for a given topic. My fascination with technology, specifically police technology, emerged one fateful morning when walking to my car to drive to my university; I discovered my car was missing the stereo. I called the police to report the incident, something I had never previously needed to do, and in what could not have been an hour later, a patrol car arrived. Having spent a decade studying policing, I realize how uncommon was my experience but more importantly, that event and what occurred influenced my primary field of study.

When the officer arrived, he began writing down the model of the car and details of the stereo; he inquired if I had locked the doors and what other valuables I noted as missing. There were several valuable items, mostly reflecting various criminal justice and statistics books, but they remained untouched, the only missing item being the stereo in the empty dash of a Dodge Neon. As the officer walked around the car writing down the details, I inquired into how likely it was that they would recover my stereo. Having some familiarity with the criminal justice system, I knew the answer, but the victim in me wanted my stereo back. The answer came quickly and the response "*Rather unlikely.*"

In what was nearly 30 minutes, the officer provided suggestions on how *I* could prevent this in the future. He expressed that because of the neighborhood, I needed to be more cautious. In addition, he provided tips that I should park closer to my home and should install a car alarm (something I did that first weekend). However, when I inquired about potential fingerprints on the windows, the potential for genetic evidence in the car, the officer's response was "*We don't do that.*" I never asked why, something I deeply regret. However, that statement came to influence and foster a research agenda including a national study on the influence of technology on police practice, the focus of this book.

Thinking back on the statement from the officer, the theoretical interpretation would reflect the following:

1. The officer could have lacked the specific knowledge (training).
2. The agency lacked the technological capacity (resources) or the officer was unable to perform the collection (a combination of the former).
3. The officer was unwilling to use the resource, with the latter an expression of apathy.

In one of the first explorations into police technology, Manning (1992) came to offer that technology rarely transforms an agency; technology is merely adapted to reproduce traditional police practice. Technology did not have the capacity to transform police practice; it was a tool, one reserved to solve specific crime problems and its ability to aid all levels of the organization were rarely achieved.

THE BROADER AIM

Human history contains examples of how technology has come to shape the world around us. Technology has the capacity, and the proven ability, to alter the social world in which we live. Technology intertwines the way we interact and the methods by which we gain knowledge. The continued integration of technology into the fabric of life has had a deep impact on culture, politics, economics, and communication. Technology growth across all sectors of society, from manufacturing, to media, from communications to organizations, alters the world. However, this marked statement on technology does not reduce or ignore the potential effects that this integration has had on, society or, by extension, organizations. Emerging new crime, new costs, and new ways to control, for all the benefits there are unintended results.

Within the police service, we have witnessed a "technological arms race," one reflecting technology gain to display technological modernity. The increasing organizational and personal pressure to display technological modernity is ever-present. At a forensic level, gaining the personnel and resources necessary to collect and process forensic evidence displays achieving a threshold of technology professionalism, a threshold easily achieved. However difficult is the effective and efficient use of that technological professionalism, which is to say, gaining the technology is but a matter of costs, making use of that technology involves a different set of issues.

WHY PROPERTY CRIME SCENES?

The decision to use property crime scenes as a framing lens reflected the lack of knowledge at this level. Clear protocol exists for violent crimes, including sexual assault and homicides. However, understanding influences on those within the investigative continuum needs focus on crime scenes that contain forensic evidence but lack standard operating procedure (SOP). The National Institute of Justice (NIJ) study on property crime scene evidence detailed clear benefits expansion provided. However, limited research existed explaining the personal, organizational, and external influences on the decision to collect. As property crime scenes have historically received lower priority, it was an apt moment to explore this level. To understand the reasons associated and the best practices within agencies that process property crime scene forensic evidence is to transition the police force into one more forensically oriented.

THE STUDY

To conduct an analysis of these parts needed an extensive method. A survey of officers alone would not be enough. Moreover, a qualitative research design of interviews and focus groups would provide insight into collection practices but research would merely provide microlevel signs.

Fortunately, I could use a mixed-method research design, a design incorporating a national survey of police officers, interviews, and focus groups to provide a macro- and microlevel trends analysis. This design would enable me to exceed much of the research available by highlighting the experiences of those stakeholders within the investigative continuum. The cumulative effect of this design would prove valuable to practitioners and academics.

Interviews

With over a decade of experience researching police and valuable contacts across the investigative continuum, I could interview participants who reflected the entire range of stakeholders, including police officers, detectives, police executives, forensic technicians and forensic experts, and prosecutors. While a reader is likely to be cautious about the use of 12 interviews for an ambitious study, it is important to remember that this is a mixed-method research design. Therefore, the results of the national survey and focus groups are used in unison. The qualitative and quantitative parts all seek to answer the same question, so when they all reveal the same information, the confidence in the results is improved. This becomes known as triangulation—to answer the same question through several different research approaches. The duration of the focus group interviews ranged from an hour to several hours. The transcriptions were analyzed within the qualitative method of Interpretative Phenomenological Analysis (discussed in a later chapter).

National Survey

The sample for the survey stemmed from a training database. The survey contained 37 questions sectioned into four category items: Agency Information (12 Close-Ended Questions), Lab Information (3 Close-Ended Questions), Officer Perspective (10 Close-Ended Questions and 1 Open-Ended Question), and General Information (11 Closed-Ended Questions). Four hundred and sixty surveys were completed.

STRUCTURING A THEORETICAL AND PRACTICAL ANALYSIS

The book structure should appeal to both practitioner and academic. Therefore, the arrangement of chapters combines prior works in a way to provide the foundation for the present analysis within the treatment of forensic evidence and the influence on the police organization. Considering the financial reality, the practical orientation toward property crime scene evidence, the skepticism levied at expansion recommendations, the first several chapters disclose the importance of this unit of focus, why a lens is vital, providing a foundation for the research study. Chapter 3 examines the current state of genetic evidence in the police service, highlighting the current use and the associated issues in forensic evidence. As technology use is a social, organizational, and individual construction, Chapter 4 explores the history of forensic evidence and technology, specific to the police service. These chapters frame the genealogy of forensic evidence and technology implementation, providing a detailed summary of the history through the investigative lens. Chapter 4 also includes a comparative synthesis of the current state of research within property crime scene genetic evidence. It includes the National Institute of Justice study on the efficacy of expanded property crime scene evidence, analysis of studies conducted by the Home Office in the United Kingdom, and research from New Zealand.

Chapter 5 discusses collection of genetic forensic evidence, a brief how-to. Chapter 6 includes the methodology of the research study. Chapter 7 provides the results of the national survey of police officers across the nation, including excerpts from interviews with police officers, police executives, forensic technicians and experts, and prosecutors. I close with a comprehensive analysis, an analysis written in the prospective of "future thinking" about genetic evidence and police practice. This chapter has two aims. First, to examine whether the past and present state of forensic practice does a disservice by not offering the reader the potential for expansion. Vital remains the point that the recommendations provided within are not a cure, there is no formula, no silver bullet provided to practitioners or academics. The implementation strategies present challenges, challenges that need dedication and commitment to transitioning the organization into one that is more technology-oriented. However, a transition should not promote adoption of a philosophy within the organization that is technology-focused. The philosophical alignment of oriented versus focused becomes the secondary focus of the chapter. To be technology-oriented is to align the agency within the problem-solving model while upholding the community-oriented policing process. Recognizing that this work is aimed at both academics and practitioners and that this work owes a debt to those practitioners and experts who have allowed me access to their world, Chapter 9 is a reflection on this book by a Chief of Police, Gary Jenkins of the Pullman Police Department.

CHAPTER 2

Transition the Lens

> *Being honest, a large issue for us is prioritization, we devote forensic resources to serious personal crime, and then there is the issue that we have no one to go out and collect and process—budget is an issue, there's no money to investigate the case or send out an evidence tech. In some instances, we take property calls over the phone.*
>
> **Detective**

To argue that property crime scene forensics is worthwhile to the criminal justice system is to take on deeply rooted and engrained attitudes on the realized worthiness of these crimes. This attitude is pervasive across the criminal justice process, credited in part to the war on crime—a war represented and dominated by an extreme focus on violent interpersonal crime both in the prevention of crimes through criminalization of precursors (opinions of dangerousness, drug use, etc.) and the increase in penalties associated with precursors (possession offenses). The dominant policy and features within this war are the identification and neutralization of sources of danger. So dogmatic is this focus that all resources come to highlight this keen focus on the identification and neutralization of sources of danger, and with forensic science as a narrowing lens, the sole purpose of forensic evidence is to lessen the threat to society, threats specific to violent interpersonal crime.

Property crime scenes receive some of the fewest resources within the crime hierarchy. This determination is not solely borne out of the perception of worth (property vs. violent); rather it is compounded by the realization that these crimes often lack witnesses and evidence, making finding suspects much more difficult. Also, there often exists a third party (insurance providers) able to address the loss of property. This effect has produced a current state in which some agencies have stopped responding to automobile thefts, have resorted to a report practice communicated over the phone, and in a change of practices, have used point systems in which certain characteristics must be met to send an officer to the scene.

To introduce the war on crime may seem out of place, but it is a core feature displaying the importance of narrowing focus on property crime scenes, or specifically, why this focus is necessary and timely. The last decade has witnessed agencies seeing reduced budgets but the requirement and evaluation mechanism of clearance rates pressured to increase and subsequently the expectation that crime rates must decrease were preserved. Command staff and officers are required to do more with less, to adopt, implement, and uphold their professional status (technological modernity), while seeking out grants, technology, and training, often with no assessment of the relative worth. This has promoted a technology arms race, in which the myopic implementation of forensics focuses on violent interpersonal crime.

The resulting response is rather expected. Violent victimizations produce an immediate visceral reaction; they are crimes anyone can experience. These cases create media inquiry, notoriety for the offender, and the responding agency when using forensics displays professionalism. There is worth, clear benefits, and a guarantee on the return on investment when violent interpersonal crime becomes the inherent beneficiary of forensic practice. However, explaining the limiting use of forensics may reflect the fiscal reality within the organization, but it fails to understand the criminology of crime and also why the decisions of the state limiting forensic expansion undermine the social contract between citizens and the state.

PHILOSOPHICAL JUSTIFICATION

To argue for increased focus on property crime scenes, a high volume crime, is problematic. First, to argue for forensics is to argue for increased resources, in which the expense inevitably requires a decrease in resources within other areas of the agency. These discussions have traditionally focused only on the practical explanations, undertaken within a pragmatic reality. However, brought to the forefront of this discussion must be the philosophical connections. To argue for expanded processing is to offer that this expansion is the duty of the state and by extension the agency. An agency that ignores evidence violates the social contract.

A Kantian interpretation of the state proposes the purpose of the state is to "Do no one injustice." Therefore, it is the responsibility, the sole purpose of the state to mediate conflict, promote a successful resolution to conflict, to intervene, and use resources to create justice. While justice is relative and normative to each individual, injustice is created when the state ceases to intervene and rightfully ignores (directly or indirectly) evidence that potentially holds the key to resolving that specific conflict and preventing later conflicts. When the state fails to intervene, there is injustice (Weinrib, 1992). Holding a state accountable is the only way to ensure that justice occurs (Garland, 1990). To offer forensic expansion is to offer a modified interpretation, one critical of a state that fails to protect a citizen from victimization when the state holds the necessary means. The state violates "Do no one injustice" when it willfully ignores property crime scene forensic evidence.

To provide a figure to the injustice, consider the research of Strom and Hickman (2010), which noted that between the years of 2003 and 2007 potentially, 5,126,719 unsolved property crime cases, 27,595 unsolved rape cases, and 3,975 homicides containing forensic evidence went unrequested for forensic analysis (p. 391). While the research explored unrequested analysis comprising all forensic types, it shows a notable issue. A later analysis by Goulka, Matthies, Disley, and Steinberg (Goulka et al., 2010) calculated roughly 563,939 property crime cases containing forensic evidence but remaining unanalyzed, using the 11% DNA recovery rate reported by the Home Office (2005).

Tragic is any victimization, be it property or personal. However, more tragic is the unfortunate reality to read of incidents in which a victimization could have been preventable, had evidence recovered in a property crime scene been tested. In some cases victims endured horrific experiences, trauma they will carry with them forever, and evidence identifying the offender was not recovered or analyzed. Policy limiting collection and analysis must change to see equal treatment in the collection and analysis of forensic evidence.

The philosophical connection reflects the narrow vision of forensic evidence. Despite the glorified, misunderstood, and often scientifically inaccurate portrayal of forensic science within popularized crime dramas, there remains a keen interest to see forensic science evolve. However, it has seemingly evolved with a dualistic role, as an investigative tool and as a preventive mechanism. This dualistic role has produced a philosophical and practical disconnect. This narrow vision has again been co-opted by the war on crime to create a system that is unbalanced; one in which the benefits granted to forensic collection are limited.

Consider the NDIS system, containing ~10 million offender samples and continuing to expand as states have continued to pass laws requiring DNA samples be collected and cataloged across the entire crime continuum (arrests and convictions from misdemeanor to felony). The resulting focus has sought to maximize offender collection at the expense of scene samples (a topic of Chapter 3). To return to the philosophical connection, treatment of forensic evidence can take two paths: (1) forensic evidence tries to link individuals to scenes or (2) forensic evidence tries to link scenes to individuals. The fundamental difference in the treatment of forensic evidence has an influence in success rates. To highlight how the co-opting of the forensic database for political purposes promoted a narrowing use of forensic evidence, and limited property crime scene utilization, consider the following. In 2006 there were 3,977,433 offender profiles in the system and 160,582 forensic profiles from crime scenes (Federal Bureau of Investigation, 2011), myopic at best, and an unbalanced approach that would perpetuate. In 2008, the offender profile submission rates exceeded 6,500,000 and forensic profiles within the system increased to only 249,000, a paltry increase in comparison to the offender profile submission rate (Federal Bureau of Investigation, 2011). The present reality is a current strategy designed to maximize offender processing with a narrow focus on violent interpersonal crimes.

Despite a clear determination to increase offender collection, this clear demarcation is convenient. Also, familial DNA typing introduced the ability to search for markers indicative of family members (a topic within Chapter 4) and continued development reveals the emerging use for DNA, including generating phenotypical expression of a person's characteristics (eye color, hair color, etc.). Transitioning into high volume processing advantages the existing unbalanced system to provide increased clearances and over time the potential for general deterrence.

Forensics within property crime scenes becomes not the goal but the standard, to maximize what has been a tremendous expenditure of resources. From a philosophical perspective, equal treatment in the processing of forensic evidence ensures that even those crimes that some may offer are insignificant (i.e., property crime) are analyzed and processed to improve the likelihood there is an arrest and that resulting victimizations are prevented or unsolved cases see a successful resolution. It is not the intent to argue that one is any more worthy of processing but rather, that understanding the reasons associated with the decision to collect and analyze property crime scene evidence is necessary to transition the police agency into one more forensically oriented, producing improvement across the forensic evidence process.

PRACTICAL JUSTIFICATION

To offer for the expansion into property crime scene processing is to balance the philosophical with the practical, which is to say, philosophically it is the responsibility of the state to use *all* evidence. However, to offer that a practical justification exists, it is important to exceed the philosophical. To inject the practical importance to this expansion is to revisit a prior point, specifically President Johnson and the Crime Commission. In 1965, then President Johnson issued a special message. He appealed to the American people, criminal justice institutions, and Congress to identify ways to reduce what was a significant increase in crime. Specific to the police service, he called on agencies to become more efficient and effective across issues of training and investigations.

Noting with great precision how the "average citizen" is concerned with "street crimes" the police would need to adapt to the changing environment. The landscape had changed, the population marked by an increasing transient nature, rising crime and associated fear, and the burden on the police to adapt practice vital to the success of the nation. To provide agencies with specific recommendations, he formed the Commission on Law Enforcement. While the recommendations were many, at the core, President Johnson and the Commission put forth that the police service had to adapt technology to the organization. As not the best of mechanisms to reform practices, the Commission heavily criticized the police, specifically within the use of technology to address the organization's primary problems. Most critical was the finding that while police practice had successfully integrated science (technology) into the investigative process, the resulting integration had stopped diffusing throughout the organization. The outcome of the integration was an organizational apparatus specific to violent crime investigations that enjoyed marked success to resolve crime. However, those adaptations were so specific to violent crime problems that at a general level, it was offered the organization had avoided implementation of technology across the entire organization; rather the use of technology (science) was marred by a narrow use, which should be a familiar statement on the application of technology.

Continuing an examination into the practical benefits is to introduce not only the historical but also the future of the police service. Mirroring many of the key points from the Commission on Law Enforcement, police scholar David Bayley (1994) in his work *Police for the Future* offered that police organizations could not merely reproduce their tasks using old practices. To improve, police organizations must adapt to an ever-changing environment. To ignore this requirement, to continue a predetermined path, to rely on the same processes, ignoring recent developments was to remain antiquated. In what was a scathing critique, Bayley (1994) argues that agencies must seek new ways and adapt old practices to solve crime and create order. While an equally important work within policing literature, the point relevant to this line of thought is the promising benefits awaiting agencies that sought the expanded use of forensic evidence, that to meet the demands of an ever-changing environment was to seek out and incorporate one of the fastest evolving investigative tools, forensic science.

The resulting literature has produced an impressive and growing body of work by police scholars and practitioners expressing how vital is this transition. A transition must diffuse technology across the organization to encompass all activities, embracing technology to prevent crime, adapting existing approaches to use, when suitable, the most current and effective technologies, to see a marked improvement in the successful resolution of crime incidents. However, while diffusion is vital to the future of policing, and the alignment of the organization to adapt to a changing environment, diffusion must assimilate into the organizational culture (Chan, 2001; Manning, 1992).

The historical and modern resistance to technology implementation and thus a lack of focus on property crime scene evidence is also credited to its innovatory capacity, which is to say that, while an innovative practice, its implementation when undertaken is often sporadic, resulting from a lack of training and resources, promoting an implementation that rarely meets the expectations as imagined. In addition, the expectations often narrowly attribute success within those specific cases, lacking the typical recognition that comes from higher crime incidents, and lacking is an understanding of how the practice provides clear benefits across the police mission (Manning, 1992).

Therefore, to offer that a narrowing lens is important, which is to say this work is important, is to convince police officers and academicians that clear benefits exist, benefits that have far-reaching impact on society, culture, criminal justice institutions, communities, and individuals. David Lazer (2004), in a remarkable book on the history of forensic technology, specifically DNA, and the criminal justice system, offered that no other scientific advancement held the potential for benefits to the criminal justice system and society. A nation that approaches the diffusion, continued development and refinement, and targeted use of forensic science is one that maximizes justice. A nation that ceases to adapt, to improve practices, to seek out and effectively and efficiently use new tools to address its primary mission is one relegated to the delivery of poor services, which specific to the police service is lessening public trust, confidence, and support, all of which are necessary to improve police practice.

While it is easy to state that agencies should position their organization to be more forensically oriented, it is not forgotten how important the budget is, and how complicated it is to try to undertake what is an expensive practice. Now police agencies are experiencing budgetary shortfalls, in part due to the economic decline, forcing cities to make spending cuts, and unfortunately partly a result of a crime policy focusing on addressing crime through increased staffing. The resulting reality is one in which agencies are forced to make difficult decisions on how best to assign resources and as discussed previously, some agencies have made the unfortunate, but practical, decision to reduce shares to property crime scenes.

From a resource perspective, I offer the National Institute of Justice study, one of several case studies discussed in a later chapter. Roman et al. (2008), in a pilot study examining the benefits of high volume processing, identified a return on investment that was unanticipated for agencies undertaking this routine practice. In fact, in the Denver study, Ashikhmin (n.d.) identified a cost saving of more than $5 million in police costs and $36.8 million in property loss prevented by the expansion in processing of forensic evidence within property crime scenes. Identification of these cost savings is also reflected in studies from the United Kingdom and New Zealand.

To exceed the financial is to connect to a deeply rooted and widely held belief in the police service; specifically, that the police exist to fight crime. While some have used this belief despairingly, crime fighting is a marked feature driving officers to solve crimes, to identify suspects, and to prevent victimization. While this belief has aligned forensics to focus on violent crime, consider the resulting victimizations that could have been prevented for Joseph Cave, also known as the "flashlight rapist." Cave was convicted in 1991 for burglary, and went on to commit several more crimes including five rapes. In part due to the dedication of a detective, Cave's DNA was submitted and resulted in a "hit" with the Combined DNA Index System (CODIS), leading to his conviction on eight counts of burglary, five counts of rape, four counts of sodomy, three counts of sexual abuse, and one count of attempted rape (Lovrich et al., 2004). Cave is not an isolated case. Numerous examples exist in which evidence testing at property crime scenes could have prevented later victimizations at the property and violent interpersonal crime levels.

It is important to note that not all scenes will have forensic evidence suitable for collection. The current estimate is that 11% of property crime cases will yield evidence suitable for processing (Home Office, 2005). To put this into perspective, there were 2,199,125 burglaries as reported by the UCR in 2009 (Federal Bureau of Investigation, 2009). This would suggest there exists potentially 241,904 property crime cases with forensic evidence suitable for collection and processing, evidence with the potential to aid in early identification, arrest, and conviction preventing additional crimes and resulting victimizations and clearing potentially unsolved cases.

While the sections above have addressed the philosophical and practical reasons for expanding the role of forensics within property crimes scenes, there is potential skepticism present in any work proposing a realignment of what is standard practice specific to violent crime. Therefore, in support of such an expansion in forensic evidence, I introduce four key reasons as to why agencies should adapt their policy and states should expand their funding: (1) public safety, (2) transitioning the police organization into a more technology-oriented organization, (3) public confidence in the police, and (4) justice for victims.

Public Safety

Property crime cases suffer from one of the lowest clearance rates. From a public safety perspective, expansion of forensics within property crime cases can aid in improving clearance rates, incapacitating those responsible for these invasions, and preventing more victimizations experienced by the community. In 2009, the clearance rate for burglary was 12.5% (Federal Bureau of Investigation, 2009). While this is appallingly low, it is important to remember that this is partially a result of prioritization of violent crime, which has more resource allocation, coupled with the lack of eyewitnesses. Because of low clearance rates, these offenders have some of the longest and most pervasive criminal careers before incarceration. Moreover, this population experiences higher recidivism rates and many of the offenders reflect criminal nonspecialization, meaning they transition between violent and property crimes across their careers and some may escalate from property to violent offenses (McCue, 2007; DeLisi, 2006).

To expand on the offender point, and to inject some empirical evidence, consider the life course criminology literature on career criminals. Specifically, the literature indicating that a small percentage of individuals commit more than half of all crimes (DeLisi, 2005; Shannon, 1980; Peterson et al., 1980; Collins, 1977). Routine forensics within property crime scenes provides an early evidentiary source for linking an offender to a scene intervening in their subsequent offending cycles. Moreover, consider the lengthy offending cycles for career burglars. A series of research projects conducted in the 1980s revealed astonishingly high rates of offending, research that is still held to be valid. Visher (1986) uncovered an average of 98.8 burglaries per year among inmates arriving at a penitentiary. Chaiken and Rolph (1985) discovered slightly more elevated rates with an average of 114.6 burglaries, and Chaiken and Chaiken (1982) uncovered a range of between 116 and 204 burglaries among prison inmates. Offending cycles have a considerable impact on the tangible and intangible costs of crime. The resulting low clearance rates facilitate these offending cycles, maintaining on average 100 burglary offenses. Improving forensic study of these crimes will improve public safety by identifying offenders early and linking them to prior unsolved cases. Current research suggests that identification, arrest, and conviction rates often double when agencies undertake forensic practice.

While the empirical evidence is important, it is useful to look at case studies, as often a myopic focus on the numbers undermines the personal experience of being a victim of crime. In a section dedicated to case studies, Lovrich et al. (2004) identified a substantial incidence of preventable crime including thirteen rapes that likely could have been prevented had the forensic evidence from earlier incidents been processed. In addition to the sexual assault cases, the importance of scene and offender sample processing is obvious in a robbery incident. In this case, a further seven robberies and five rapes could have been prevented had the sample been processed. At a property crime level, the researchers identified multiple cases where further sexual assaults and property crimes need not have occurred had the property crime forensic evidence been processed. While these cases are a brief introduction into the public safety benefits, there is no denying that expanding forensic collection and analysis practices within agencies will improve public safety both in the short and long term.

A comparative perspective offers that of all the tasks of police officers, the two most prominent, which is to say those universal tasks that all police officers undertake, are law enforcement and order maintenance. To minimize forensic expansion is to reduce public safety through the inability to effectively identify and efficiently arrest criminals. While the above section is but a brief review of a later detailed analysis, it is important to state that improved processing can only improve public safety.

Transitioning the Police Organization

While easy to misinterpret as a philosophical benefit, transitioning the police organization into one more forensically oriented is, at a practical level, clearly valuable. The future of policing will be marked by a continued alignment of technology to the police mission. Proliferation of on-officer video recording, the slow diffusion of unmanned aerial vehicles, the increase in crimes involving digital evidence, and the "technification" of policing in which policing tasks become increasing connected and dependent on technology (i.e., issuing citations, verifying identity, etc.) warrant an agency organizationally able to adapt.

To transition the police organization is to overcome its most daunting barrier to change, that of the organizational culture. As both Chan (2001) and Manning (1992) suggest, the police organizational culture is resistant to change and variation or alteration of traditional police practice is increasingly difficult. Crank (2004) echoes this point, noting how changes to organizational culture or by proxy police practice are not done easily or trivially.

To reform police practice at an organizational level is to appeal to the organizational traditions. As presented earlier, technology is often seen as a threat to traditional police practice (Chan, 2001; Manning, 1992). When organizations implement technology, they do so in a manner that both produces and reproduces traditional police practice (Manning, 1992). With the increasing role of forensic evidence collection and thus responsibility placed on the police agency, there is likely going to be resistance. Expansion warrants skepticism as it is clearly an added responsibility on what is an already task heavy profession. However, expanding the police role in evidence collection simply reproduces traditional police practice and only further aligns to the organizational goal of being a "crime fighter" (Crank, 2004).

The reason for resistance is understandable; in undertaking the research for this book, the frustrations were clear, the explanations offered, rather justifiable, but a clear point within the interviews was officers and technicians will make use of any tool that will enable them to solve a crime. A common expression surfacing was "if there is evidence, we collect the evidence," but whether it was processed was an entirely different discussion. Originally, the assumption was that individual officers were skeptical of expanded technology use, and that the evidence lacked benefit specifically for property crime scenes. However, as discussed here, that is simply not the reality. The reality is that officers are not in need of convincing. Rather, the organization must transition to positioning technology as an important addition to the individual officers' investigative toolkit and a valuable resource to aid the organization.

As a final point, transitioning the organization aligns the entire organization, all roles and responsibilities, to one not just forensically but technology oriented. Gaining the technical skills, the necessary knowledge, and the ability to improve protocol, policy, and technology use produces a more efficient and effective organization and forensic process. The current costs of processing have remained high and for some agencies prohibitively high. Agencies that lack the equipment, personnel, training, and capacity will undoubtedly experience similar outcomes as technology diffuses across the criminal justice system.

Public Confidence in the Police

Producing trust and confidence in the public has become increasing important within the police service as a means of addressing crime and disorder. Some have gone as far as to argue that in the absence of some level of public support an organization cannot be effective (Loader and Walker, 2007). When the community lacks confidence in the police they are less willing to participate, more likely to be skeptical of police action, and in the absence of trust, more likely to contribute to a growing divide between the police and community. All of these promote lower clearance rates, more expanded resources, and can foster increasing resentment, reproducing the cycle.

As Warr (1980) discovered in surveying the public about crime, while the view of crime is distorted, more often than not a community member's outlook on crime reflected the actual conditions. The reality is that unsuccessful resolutions to crime incidents have a negative impact on police image. To experience an unsuccessful resolution has the propensity to influence a negative view, particularly if the precursors for a negative view exist. As opinions of the police often develop vicariously (Rosenbaum et al., 2005) each unsuccessful case can have an overall detriment to public confidence. In addition, when the expectations exist that all cases should experience forensic treatment, a perspective perpetuated via popularized crime dramas, this inability to explain why evidence is not present (training) or why collection is not undertaken when evidence exists (again, training) can promote a decreased state of public confidence.

Improving clearance rates is the most obvious benefit. However, it should be added that confidence in the police and thus the criminal justice process is also about accountability. An unfortunate reality is the criminal justice system, at the local, state, and federal levels, has a long history of distrust, a distrust borne from policing practice, court proceedings, and correctional policy and practice, which in many ways was misguided and in some unfortunate instances unjust. In fact, in 1996, then Attorney General Janet Reno declared, "Our system of criminal justice is best described as a search for the truth" (Pyrek, 2007). To search for the truth was to use all available means to treat everyone fairly and equally, and to make the criminal justice process accountable, specifically when mistakes occur.

Current research suggests that between 0.5 and 2% of the imprisoned population is innocent (Clear and Cole, 2000; Scheck et al., 2000; Radelet et al., 1992; Huff and Rattner, 1988; Radin, 1964). While some would argue that is an acceptable error level for a nation processing millions of cases a year, to be one of those thousands incarcerated but innocent would certainly change that perspective. When incidents arise, it undermines public confidence and at the policing level, the reality is that both individual officers and organizational culture have helped in the false arrest and conviction of individuals. As Sherman (1978) and Manning and Van Maanen (1978) identified, officers may resort to unethical means to see a case closed. These unethical means, though rare, have fostered a view of distrust in the police and in some areas have undermined the word of the officer and by extension the agency.

Expanding forensic collection and analysis affords an extra layer of accountability to ensure the individual suspected of a crime is the person responsible. Forensic science has long existed as an accountability mechanism for the police (Miller, 2003) and via expansion, it affords a scientific means of establishing a connection beyond that of the officer's word, which is of importance within communities that lack confidence in the police. However, the current state of forensic sciences within the system is such that there are continued criticisms levied against agencies for manufacturing evidence or not voicing concern when evidence is improperly handled. While some instances of criticism are unwarranted, there are clear cases in which officers, agencies, and forensic labs have made mistakes, undermining the trust in the agency and the forensic process. Using forensic evidence is not merely an action one-sidedly imposed. Rather, successful use of forensic evidence, necessities accountability and transparency, predicated on trust.

Often trust is the measurement by which the police are evaluated in terms of the community perception, which is to say, the value of trust is how positive the attitude of the community is towards the police. However, it should be added that increased levels of forensic processing have the potential to improve the working conditions, relationships, and most importantly foster more trust between the officer and the community. The degree to which an officer responds can be dictated by the personal, organizational, and external influences they experience. While police scholars have often described cold and callous interactions between the police and the community, the reality can be quite different (White, 2007; Crank, 2004; Manning and Van Maanen, 1978). Most often officers want to help but cannot do so because they are constrained, constrained by a lack of resources (time constraints, personnel, and other budgetary issues), evidence, or community participation. While improving public trust is multifaceted, improving an officer's toolkit in their ability to do their job effectively can not only improve the personal successes but also the officer's reputation.

Last, to improve public trust is to display both efficiency and effectiveness through not only improved clearance rates, but through an improvement in the investigative process. There is an opportunity to help reduce processing times, decrease processing costs, promote better interagency collaborations, and improve the overall image of the police agency as a professional and modern police force. While clearance rates and accountability are key to improving public confidence, the reality is that members of the community are concerned with the allocation of *their* money, which is an important perspective that administrators are conscious of.

The National Institute of Justice Field Experiment which looked at high volume processing of DNA for property crimes found that it cost an extra $1,400 to collect and analyze DNA evidence, $4,502 to identify a suspect, and $14,169 to arrest a suspect (Roman et al., 2008). It should be added that the latter two figures represent identification and arrest of a suspect who would not have been identified otherwise (Roman et al., 2008). In addition, in the Denver study, Ashikhmin et al. (n.d.) noted a saving of more than $5 million in police costs and $36.8 million in property loss prevented by an increase in forensic processing. In what is the most astute statement on processing of forensic evidence recovered from property scenes in a "best case" scenario, Roman et al. (2009) states "it is probably fair to characterize spending $3,679 to arrest a burglary suspect who would otherwise never have been caught, and who averages three prior felony convictions, as a small cost" (p. 365). While this experience is identified as a "best case" scenario, research suggests similar benefits across the studies conducted. From a community perspective, there would certainly be a willingness to assign funding, should this type of return be achievable.

Justice to Victims

Despite being relative, normative, and individualistic, justice is an all-encompassing reason to adjust any criminal justice process. While academics and practitioners may argue if the institutions of the criminal justice system (police, courts, and corrects) reflect a system or a non-system—an argument typified by working towards common goals or individual goals,—the fundamental principle to any democratic system is justice—or at the most basic level fairness. Ignoring evidence or avoiding standardization of forensic practice is an injustice.

It is suggested that the collection and analysis of forensic evidence from property crimes scenes will increase the successful resolution of cases of victimization and offer the possibility that future victimizations will be less likely to occur, a result of police officers having the necessary resources needed to link crime scenes to offenders ensuring that victims receive proper closure from the police. In over a decade of study of police services, both domestic and international, a common theme in my discussions, interviews, and other interactions with officers was the drive to help. While scholars may argue over the variations and the fact that these are isolated incidents, the practical reality remains that officers want to see a successful resolution to the crimes to which they respond, and while the mechanisms by which they respond are shaped by their interactions, perceptions, and the organizational culture, to equip them with new tools is to positively shape these mechanisms. This statement should not in any way be taken as fact, as there are considerable influences on the police and rarely is the technology adaptation able to transform an organization and by association its officers. However, if the fundamental activity of what it means to police is to solve crime, equipping officers with the necessary conditions to use new tools undoubtedly creates justice for victims.

Greater collection and analysis of forensic evidence from property crime scenes potentially increases the chances of successful resolution of the crime and offers the possibility that future victimizations are less likely to occur. This is the result of police officers having the necessary resources needed to link crime scenes to offenders ensuring that victims receive proper closure from the police. In fact, the Denver DNA Burglary Project determined that when DNA evidence was analyzed in burglary cases, the average prison term of those found guilty increased from 1.4 years to 14 years. In addition, DNA evidence coupled with the investigative process helped increase prosecution filing rates to roughly 42%, which was more than eight times the rate of filings in cases without DNA evidence (Denver DNA Burglary Project, 2004). The presence of DNA evidence ensured that significantly more cases made it to trial. Moreover, in many of those cases, the resulting sentence was significantly higher, maximizing justice for victims who would have seen their case dismissed or a reduced sentence applied and reaffirming the importance of such evidence collection.

Expanding on the justice perspective, I would add that improved analysis might aid those wrongly convicted, whose victimization is a by-product of the criminal processing system. The last decade has experienced an increasing number of exonerated individuals who have been released from prison, including death row, with the assistance of DNA testing (Leo, 2008; Pyrek, 2007; Lazer, 2004). Greater collection of forensic evidence could help to identify those wrongly imprisoned, prompting their exoneration, and bring those responsible to justice.

It is important to include the enormous number of unsolved cases that continue to amass across the United States, spanning all crime types, and compounded with each passing year. Increasing evidence processing has the potential to improve the likelihood of getting a "cold hit," i.e., the successful identification of an arrestee or offender in a "cold case," a case that has exhausted all possible investigative leads.

CONCLUSION

In sum, to argue for expansion within forensics recovered from property crime scenes, there must be clear identification that at a practical level changing and expanding the police role in forensics is both worthwhile and warranted. Current literature suggests that increasing such analysis is worthwhile (Dunsmuir et al., 2008; Roman et al., 2008; Briody, 2004; Lovrich et al., 2004; Walsh et al., 2002). However, today a large evidence backlog has emerged from property crime scenes and what remains unclear is what influences forensic analysis in these cases and under what situations. I wrote this book with the belief that a more forensically oriented police force is capable of being more effective and efficient and also more accountable to the communities that it serves.

CHAPTER 3

Forensic Science and the Criminal Justice System

> *The more tools, the more effective, the better at it and the quicker we get at using this evidence type, the more we are able to obtain justice. The office will just have to adapt and how we adapt will matter for the community.*
>
> **Prosecutor**

Before detailing the current state of forensics and the associated literature on high volume processing, it is important to shift the lens to the historical, which is to understand the important role forensic science (technology) has held in developing professional policing. To offer here that forensic orientation and thus technology orientation will transition police agencies and by extension individual officers and their respective organizations into a more efficient and effective organization is to provide a genealogy of forensic science within the investigative process. Scholars agree that this alignment and use promoted the advancement of police science; an alignment fostering the creation and manifestation of a modern and professional policing organization, equipped to address crime and disorder. If we can agree that alignment produces positive benefits then we may overcome one of the barriers to implementation toward high volume processing.

EARLY HISTORY OF FORENSICS WITHIN THE POLICE SERVICE

The application of genetic-based forensics within the criminal justice system began more than a century ago, with the discovery of the human ABO blood type by Karl Landsteiner in 1900 (Rudin and Inman, 2002). This groundbreaking discovery created the opportunity for investigators to collect and compare scene samples and blood collected from suspects to aid in linking them to crime scenes or providing exculpatory evidence. In fact, it can be said that genetic-based forensics entered the investigative process at a mainstream level in a rather short period of time, when Lattes developed a portable antibody test for blood groups around 1915 (Rudin and Inman, 2002). While these kits were seldom used within the police service, these developments are important to understanding the history of forensics within the police service, which would seek out new scientific technologies to solve crime. In fact, groundbreaking scientific discoveries and technologies originated within the creation of the first crime laboratories and resulting development of the Locard Exchange Principle. In concert, they established the foundational link between science and criminal investigations.

Examining these developments shows that while the forensic science existed, there was no mechanism, no organizational framework to include the science within police practice. In fact, while fingerprinting had been around for centuries, it would not enter the police service until the early 1900s (Rudin and Inman, 2002). The forensic science existed but there was no mechanic, no drive to incorporate the science into the investigations (Evans, 2007; Lazer, 2004; Rudin and Inman, 2002; Soullière, 1999). As Rudin and Inman (2002) note, development of forensic science and its inclusion into the police service is built on a scientific means to connect suspects to crime scenes but needed a catalyst, which had to exceed simply solving crime.

In many regards, if it were not for Edmond Locard and August Vollmer, it may have taken decades for forensic sciences to enter policing (Rudin and Inman, 2002). This emphasis on using forensic science marked an era similar to that of criminology that would look to science and its seemingly objective evidence as a means of discovering guilt or innocence. It was a decision to move beyond the subjective interpretations of crime scenes and suspect behavior. Edmond Locard, whose theoretical principle has guided development of all forensic sciences, would introduce forensic science to the police service. The principle states that:

> *... whenever two objects come into contact, a mutual exchange of matter will take place between them. Linking suspects to victims is the most important and common type of linkage accomplished by physical evidence in criminal investigations. Linking victims and suspects to objects and scenes can also be accomplished by use of the physical evidence.*
>
> ***(Miller, 2003, p. 116)***

On this seemingly simple observation, Locard would come to influence forensic science within police services around the globe. In addition, to this principle, Locard is responsible for creating the first crime laboratory, in Lyon, France, that would bring forensic science and that of the scientific method to the investigation process. Locard, like Landsteiner, believed that forensics had the capacity of not only aiding in identification of suspects, but also had the ability of clearing individuals at a scientific level in which reproducibility, objectivity, and validation would mark this investigation tool (Rudin and Inman, 2002; Soullière, 1999).

Using science to identify criminals is not a new phenomenon. In the early 20th century, criminologists tried to identify with "scientific methods" those predisposed toward criminal leanings. While Lombroso and those of his ilk were later discredited as scientific methods improved (Rafter, 1997), there is no discounting the role of science in identifying criminals. It was the merging of the objective science with that of the subjective process of criminal investigations that caught the eye of August Vollmer. To Vollmer forensic science, and by extension technology, was but one of the many changes the police service needed to become more professional.

August Vollmer, held as the "Father of Modern Policing" and by extension the "Father of Technology Implementation within Policing" (Soullière, 1999), was heavily influenced by the work of Lombroso and the accounts of science aiding in apprehending criminals reported by Locard. Vollmer, inspired by the early work of those criminology pioneers, and with Sylvester and Wilson, brought forth the modern professionalism movement within policing. Vollmer was ambitious in his decisions to advantage science and technology within the police force. He recognized that education and professional training alone could not create the skilled professionals he envisioned; rather higher education coupled with the inclusion of "science" would create a modern police force ready to perform duties and accomplish tasks as skilled professionals (White, 2007; Soullière, 1999). Note the following key points within Vollmer's tenure as chief of police in Berkeley (White, 2007):

- **1909:** Vollmer, named the chief of police in Berkeley, institutes a Bertillon expert and purchases fingerprinting equipment, and creates the first *modus operandi* file system.
- **1919:** Vollmer begins testing delinquents and using psychology to predict delinquent behavior; he implements a juvenile program to reduce delinquency.
- **1921:** Vollmer guides the development of the first "lie detector" and begins developing radio communications between patrol cars; he also initiates handwriting analysis.

During his tenure, Vollmer introduced fingerprinting, evidence collection, graphology, and rudimentary database design, within file system storage (hard files). He petitioned Congress to create a national fingerprinting bureau and implemented a crime laboratory similar to what Locard had designed (White, 2007). Today, research has discredited graphology, and the state of lie detectors is severely questioned (Alder, 2007). However, there is no discounting the vision that Vollmer had to create a truly modern police force by leveraging technology across all levels of the police organization and that of its tasks.

Today, numerous police agencies around the world have come to collect and analyze forensic evidence across fingerprints, blood typing, ballistics, and DNA. The acquisition of the technical skills and required budget have come to mark agencies as being highly professionalized and often highlighted as the "gold standard" in modern agency capabilities (Lazer, 2004; Soullière, 1999). To be able to process forensic evidence, including the latest technology developments, is to exceed the standards and represent the "best" of what police agencies are capable (Lazer, 2004). To offer a comparative perspective, consider the work of Saxena (1997), who in describing the state of policing in India, noted how the inclusion of forensics marked an agency as truly "modern" and indicated a state of professional police service. While the "gold standard" in forensic evidence has transitioned over the years as new tools and techniques evolve, there is no discounting the importance of forensics to the investigative process and that of the agency.

From ABO Typing to DNA

For nearly a century, ABO blood typing had remained the primary genetic based forensic evidence, which had widespread use within the investigative process (Rudin and Inman, 2002). Serology, as it would become known, used the unique markers present within blood to identify the presence of antigen and antibody systems. These markers would represent the blood types – type A, type B, type AB, type O – and in addition had the capacity to indicate the presence of rhesus (RH) factors (positive or negative). The identification of these markers had the potential to link individuals, but not unequivocally identify an individual. The first known criminal case using the ABO genetic marker system occurred in 1902, a relatively brief period following the discovery by Landsteiner in 1900 (Bell, 2008).

As a source of genetic evidence, blood was relatively easy to identify and in many of the cases in which it was collected was in ample supply (i.e., violent crimes). However, the tests of the time required fresh samples and considerable volume, which limited its utilization. Recognizing this limitation, Leone Lattes developed a procedure for ABO testing of bloodstains on cloth using a saline solution, which was capable of restoring the dried blood (Bell, 2008). However, there were still issues within the procedure and it was not until the late 1920s that Franz Joseph Holzer developed an improved typing system that was capable of yielding results within smaller, older, and dried samples (Bell, 2008).

As police specialization evolved within investigations, subsequent cases took on a more specific focus. In some instances, investigators encountered cleaned crime scenes, cleaned to mask the presence of the crime. Forensic science would evolve its techniques and tools to deliver to investigators a means of identifying the presence of blood. In 1937, Walter Specht would suggest that agencies utilize Luminol as a preliminary test to identify the presence of blood (Bell, 2008). Over the next several decades, the tools and techniques expanded to provide investigators with the means of linking individuals to crimes, such as cases of sexual assault via the ability to conduct a serology assessment on semen stains and saliva. As challenges emerged within investigations, the scientific community would develop techniques and tools that would prove instrumental to clearing what were horrible cases and often in circumstances in which the forensic evidence provided was key to the prosecution's case.

However, ABO typing was not without its faults. While seemingly highly beneficial to investigators of violent crime, it required additional resources and adaptations within the agencies' standard operating procedures (SOPs), and in some regards many officers found its inclusion provided no additional benefit to the investigative process for the vast majority of crimes the agency was involved in (Stevens, 2011). It should be added that one particular point of reluctance in its application was its conclusive power. As Garrett (2011) notes in discussing the case of Gary Dotson, while it was true that only 11% of the Caucasian population shared the type B blood type and that Dotson in fact possessed this blood type, it in no way should have provided evidence of his guilt (p. 87). Nevertheless, the evidence was used to convict Dotson in 1979. It was not until DNA analysis was conducted that Dotson was exonerated and released in 1989 (Garrett, 2008).

Scholars have argued that it was the expansion in the investigative utilization and the subsequent inclusion by prosecutors of ABO typing that would bring about its demise as a forensic tool (Stevens, 2011; Garrett, 2011). During the peak of its use throughout the 1970s and 1980s, primarily within cases of sexual assault, issues within evidence collection, improper testing protocol, and expert testimony that was misguided and in some instances false, undermined the forensic evidence as a tool (Garrett, 2011; Lazer, 2004; Radelet et al., 1992). As more incidents of misconduct and falsehoods became associated with the forensic practice, prosecutors and agencies became much less inclined to incorporate ABO blood typing into their standard operating procedures (Garrett, 2011; Lazer, 2004). In fact, the documentation of misuse of forensic science is vast (see Garrett, 2011; Baumgartner et al., 2008; Gould, 2007; Lee and Tirnady, 2003) and few offer an in-depth work as conducted by Garrett (2011). In fact, Garrett (2011) uncovered numerous examples of individuals falsely incarcerated because of ABO typing and with police policy in the 1980s often not retaining evidence after a conviction, an untold number of individuals remained incarcerated with no mechanism to overturn their conviction. Police practice, coupled with incidents of prosecutorial misuse, facilitated a negative perception of blood typing as a means of identification.

Criminal cases require a high standard of proof and while blood typing provided a means of linking individuals to incidents, there needed to be a more powerful method. As such, there would come to exist a forensic gap within investigations wherein forensic science would again evolve to offer to the investigative practice a more reliable tool – deoxyribonucleic acid or, as it is more commonly known, DNA.

THE SCIENCE OF DNA

As Derksen (2010) states, DNA is a universally accepted scientific means of identification. It is universally accepted because DNA is contained in nearly every human cell and unique markers present within the genetic code allow identification to occur. From an investigative perspective, DNA is contained most readably within samples recovered from scenes. It can be found within blood, bone, mucus, tissue, skin cells, teeth, saliva, semen, sweat, and human excrement: feces and urine (Lazer, 2004). Most people possess within each cell 23 pairs of chromosomes (46 in total), half from the paternal source and half from the maternal, which, when examined at a genetic level, reveal a sequence of nucleotides that represent DNA. The DNA structure is aligned in a double-helix configuration, which contains four base types (adenine, thymine, cytosine, guanine) that in concert make up the DNA molecule. As the pairing of the bases are specific, adenine (A) may only bond with thymine (T) and cytosine (C) may only bond to guanine (G). Understanding the base pairings and the sequences within segments of the DNA molecule allows for a means of distinguishing one individual from another (Calladine, 2004; Lazer, 2004).

While the above description of DNA is rather simplistic, it is important to stress that the human genome contains billions of base pairs, which are nearly identical (Calladine, 2004). The ability for DNA to uniquely identify a person relies upon key differences as contained within a segment of DNA known as "junk" DNA (Calladine, 2004). "Junk" DNA contains short tandem repeats (STRs), which are short repeating segments of DNA that differ among people (Calladine, 2004). Analyzing these segments across the chromosomal regions (loci) allows a sequence to be completed to determine the alleles present in the sample. These short sequences vary in length but because they repeat in tandem at different intervals from person to person, it is possible to identify a particular person based on this unique pattern with extreme precision. For example, when matching across 5 or 6 loci, the probability of a random person's profiling matching a suspect is said to be 1 in 100 billion (US Department of Justice, 2000).

Most beneficial within the STRs is that the short sequence can be replicated, meaning that a smaller sample can be amplified to produce a desired amount for comparison purposes (US Department of Justice, 2000). Because DNA degrades at a significantly slower rate and is constantly discarded as a natural process (i.e., skin shedding) it provides a scientific means to link an individual to a scene by the presence of DNA. However, it must be noted that DNA does not provide a timeframe, nor does it explain how DNA arrived at the scene. As the body easily discards DNA, it is quite possible to leave DNA at a scene and not to have committed the crime.

While the Locard Exchange Principle is vital to the investigative process, this fundamental principle also works against investigators as DNA can be discarded even via fingerprints. Subsequently, it should be noted that also of importance is the issue of sample contamination. The greatest weakness of this investigative tool is that of its sensitivity (Calladine, 2004). Improper handling of a sample could potentially transfer DNA between samples, effectively matching the scene sample to the scene sample and not the offender's sample. While processes have been developed to limit this potential error (discussed later in the literature review), nevertheless there are opportunities for contamination and deception via DNA to occur.

Equally beneficial, but controversial, is the ability for DNA profiles using the STR sequencing to identify siblings or close relatives. The process, termed familial DNA typing, affords police officers the ability to compile searches that are close, but not identical to the DNA evidence to identify potential suspects. At present, familial DNA is capable of revealing parents, children, and full siblings of the person matched within the system. In fact, the use of this technique made national news when the serial killer known as the "Grim Sleeper" was discovered via the technique (Rubin, 2010).

The "Grim Sleeper" was responsible for the deaths of at least 10 women in Los Angeles since 1985 (Rubin, 2010). The LAPD working with the Department of Justice had been conducting ongoing analysis on the samples hoping to find a match within the Combined DNA Index System (CODIS), but throughout the years there had been no such luck. It was not until the Department of Justice undertook a familial DNA search that there came a break in the case. The police had arrested a young man who matched the samples recovered from the crime scenes but who was also too young to be the killer. Further testing revealed that the partial DNA match reflected a parental relationship and the allele match was that of a paternal source (Rubin, 2010). While legal and privacy issues were being addressed, investigators undertook surveillance and evidence collection from recovered pizza crust and on July 7, 2010, the LAPD arrested 57-year-old Lonnie Franklin Jr. This marked one of its first uses within the United States, but is not the world's first as the United Kingdom utilized the technique in 2004 to identify a killer (Bhattacharya, 2004). It should be added that the use of the technique is not limited to violent crime. Denver became the first state to utilize the technique for property crime, when detectives linked Luis Jaimes-Tinajero to two car thefts based on familial DNA (Griffin, 2009). With increasing use of this technique and both investigative successes and exonerations based on this technique, the inherent benefits are being recognized and implemented. For example, in 2011, Virginia Governor Bob McDonnell indicated that agencies in the state would begin using familial DNA typing.

The discriminatory power of DNA to link individuals to crime scenes is clearly one of the most important forensic tools to investigators. There is no other universally accepted means of identification than DNA and its investigative benefits continue to expand. Most recently, even the most "unsolvable" case (that of identical twins) has now become solvable. Prior to the discovery that there are genetic variations within identical twins, a case involving twins could not rely upon DNA evidence. Bruder et al. (2008) discovered that there was in fact variation. With this discovery, a technique was developed to determine which twin's DNA matched the scene sample. While such a case would be extremely rare and often reserved for the fictional stories of crime television programming, there is no denying that the science of DNA is an asset to the criminal investigative process.

HISTORY OF DNA IN CRIMINAL JUSTICE

In many respects, the history of DNA in the investigation process has sought to aid in the identification of criminals for violent offenses. In fact, the very case that resulted in its widespread adoption was that of a rape and subsequent homicide of two young girls on November 21, 1983, and July 31, 1986, in Leicestershire, England. The case involved Colin Pitchfork, a husband, father of two, and local baker who subsequently raped and then killed via strangulation Lynda Mann and Dawn Ashworth both at the young age of 15. The first victim, Lynda Mann, was abducted while walking on a footpath and was raped and then strangled by Pitchfork. The investigation yielded valuable evidence via semen recovered from the victim. However, with no investigative leads, the case stalled. It is important to note that during this period Pitchfork was arrested for indecent exposure and sentenced to probation.

Several years later, Pitchfork would assault, rape, and murder Dawn Ashworth. The investigation discovered that the cases had identical modus operandi and blood typing matched the semen recovered from the scenes, but blood typing alone could not provide any additional help in the investigation. The investigation uncovered a lead to a local man, Richard Buckland, who was subsequently arrested and confessed to the second murder. Seeking to link Buckland to the first murder, the agency sought out the assistance of Alec Jeffreys, a Leicester University professor. Peter Gill, Alec Jeffreys, and Dave Werett had recently developed a technique capable of extracting DNA from samples containing human cells, which could be analyzed to produce a profile capable of identifying individuals at a unique level (Gill et al., 1985). Using this new technique, Jeffreys revealed that there was one person responsible for the rapes and murder of those young girls and that Buckland could not have been that person (leading to the first exoneration because of DNA profiling).

With this new forensic technique, the agency undertook a mass screening of all of the men in the area, some 5,000, which yielded, after 6 months of analysis, no profile matches. It was not until the agency received a report from a woman who overheard a man bragging about providing a DNA sample for a friend that the agency had their lead. Pitchfork was arrested. His DNA profile matched the semen samples recovered from the two rapes and murders and he was subsequently convicted on both charges.

The importance of the Pitchfork case within the history of DNA in Criminal Justice is how the inclusion of this new forensic technique resulted in several of the world's firsts. This new forensic technique resulted in the exoneration of Buckland for a crime he did not commit, mass DNA screening, a preventable rape and homicide (if there had been DNA collection for low-level offenses), and the introduction of DNA profiling into the criminal justice system. The discovery by Jeffreys and his colleagues and its use by the police agency would come to mark a new era within the investigative process with a forensic tool that was capable of identifying individuals at a genetic (unique) level from material easily discarded as a natural human process (skin, saliva, blood, and semen). With this forensic investigative tool, skin underneath a victim's nails, saliva on a cigarette found outside a home, saliva left on a soda can discarded within the house, the presence of pubic hair when semen was no longer present, and countless other examples, now yielded valuable forensic data that became capable of identifying and linking a person to the scene. However, there were no standards, no mechanism for collection, retention, or comparison. As such, within the United States, the CODIS was created to allow for the comparison of DNA samples at the national, state, and local levels.

Creation of CODIS

The CODIS is a hierarchical, combined system of three interlinking systems: the Local DNA Index System (LDIS), State DNA Index System (SDIS), and National DNA Index System (NDIS). It was authorized by the DNA Identification Act of 1994. In creating CODIS, the Federal Bureau of Investigation selected 13 STR loci as the forensic standard for comparison of samples. The decision to employ the 13 loci as the forensic standard relied upon the current forensic knowledge and capacity of laboratories to participate and cooperate based on current technical standards (US Department of Justice, 2000). As noted prior, the discriminatory power of the 13 loci is extremely high. As DNA variations differ across racial background types, the probability of a match between two unrelated persons that are Caucasian American is 1 in 575 trillion

Table 3.1 CODIS

Local Laboratories (LDIS)	State Laboratories (SDIS)	National Laboratories (NDIS)
The Local DNA Index System (LDIS) installed at crime laboratories is operated by police departments or sheriffs' offices. DNA profiles originated at the local level can be transmitted to the state and national levels.	Each state has a designated laboratory that operates the State DNA Index System (SDIS). SDIS allows local laboratories within that state to compare DNA profiles. SDIS is also the communication path between the local and national tiers. SDIS is typically operated by the agency responsible for implementing and monitoring compliance with the state's convicted offender statute.	The National DNA Index System (NDIS), the highest level of the CODIS hierarchy, enables qualified state laboratories that actively participate in CODIS to compare DNA profiles.

Source: *DNA Initiative, May 2011: http://www.dna.gov/solving-crimes/cold-cases/howdatabasesaid/ldisndissdis/*

(US Department of Justice, 2000). To offer a more common scenario as to a match between two unrelated persons from a highly heterogeneous population, such as the United States, the probability match for the 13 core loci would be 1 in 10 billion (US Department of Justice, 2000). Offered another way, DNA recovered at a crime scene and matched to an individual has a 1 in 10 billion chance of being that of another person.

Using 13 STR loci as the forensic standard, the Federal Bureau of Investigation created a computer software system capable of comparing DNA samples across the national, state, and local levels. To date, the system has assisted in more than 137,000 investigations, producing over 142,700 "hits" (Federal Bureau of Investigation, 2011). As Table 3.1 displays, the CODIS system was designed to be hierarchical with three separate systems comprising the overall CODIS system. While the system is capable of comparing samples across all levels, the database reflects local (i.e., city or county) and state submission rules, which is to say there is great variation in what is submitted and available for comparison with the CODIS system based on eligible qualifying offenses.[1] This was an intended characteristic designed to meet minimum legal thresholds, most specifically that of privacy concerns (Goulka et al., 2010). The system, housed at the FBI Laboratory, allows agencies across the nation to compare samples across four levels: Convicted Offender Profiles, Forensic Profiles, Arrestee Profiles, Suspect Profiles,

[1]See Table 3.2 for an overview of the current statutory requirements for qualifying offenses.

Unidentified Human Remains, Missing Person, and Relatives of Missing Person Profiles.

Convicted offender profiles constitute the most common profile submitted to the system. As of April 2011, the National DNA Index (NDIS) contained over 9,635,757 offender profiles (Federal Bureau of Investigation, 2011). As of March 2011, when the Idaho legislature passed a bill to expand DNA analysis for "all convicted felons" (Associated Press, 2011), all states now include statutory provisions to allow for the collection and retention of DNA samples from convicted offenders. *Forensic profiles* (also known as scene samples) refer to collected DNA evidence obtained from unsolved cases. Evidence profiles are submitted to the system in hopes of obtaining a "hit" to match a known offender or to generate investigative leads; as of April 2011, the CODIS system contained 370,875 forensic profiles (Federal Bureau of Investigation, 2011). *Arrestee profiles* are the most recent addition to the NDIS system, as arrestee samples were ineligible for comparisons at the NDIS level until a revision to the federal law in 2006. These profiles reflect individuals arrested for offenses and differ greatly across state statutes. Currently, 12 states allow for the collection and retention of DNA for all felony arrests. *Suspect profiles* reflect DNA samples collected from suspects in criminals cases and the policy differs greatly from state to state. The current legal and privacy concerns have limited its inclusion into the NDIS system. The last profile within the system that agencies may compare against is that of *Unidentified Human Remains, Missing Person, and Relatives of Missing Person Profiles.*

DNA Statutes

All federal and state laws permit DNA collection for individuals convicted of a felony. In addition, several states have expanded their collection to misdemeanor convictions and those arrested for certain criminal offenses, including all felony arrests (Gordon Thomas Honeywell Governmental Affairs, 2010). According to the latest collation of statutes provided by Gordon Thomas Honeywell Governmental Affairs (2010) and noted in Table 3.2, Alabama, Alaska, California, Colorado, Florida, Kansas, Louisiana, Ohio, South Carolina, and South Dakota have the most inclusive laws in the country. These states

Table 3.2 State Statutes

State	Statutory Inclusion
Alabama, Alaska, California, Colorado, Florida, Kansas, Louisiana, Ohio, South Carolina, South Dakota (10)	All felony convictions, juvenile adjudications, jail and probation, sex crime misdemeanors, all felony arrests (including murder, sex crimes, and burglary arrests)
Alabama, Alaska, California, Colorado, Florida, Kansas, Louisiana, North Dakota, Ohio, South Carolina, South Dakota, Vermont (12)	All felony arrests (including murder, sex crimes, and burglary)
Alabama, Alaska, Arizona, California, Colorado, Florida, Kansas, Louisiana, Maryland, Minnesota, Missouri, New Mexico, North Carolina, North Dakota, Ohio, South Carolina, South Dakota, Tennessee, Texas, Utah, Vermont, Virginia (22)	Burglary arrests
New Jersey, New York, Oklahoma, Utah, Washington (4)	Misdemeanor convictions (exceeding sex crime misdemeanors)
Source: *DNA Resource (2010), http://www.dnaresource.com/documents/statequalifyingoffenses2010.pdf*	

permit DNA sampling for any individual who meets any of the conditions noted below:

1. Convicted of a felony
2. A juvenile adjudicated delinquent (including provisions for certain violent and nonviolent crimes) or adjudicated not delinquent by reasons of insanity
3. A probationer or parolee[2]
4. Convicted of sex crime misdemeanors (i.e., indecent exposure or solicitation of a prostitute)
5. Persons arrested for any felony (Gordon Thomas Honeywell Governmental Affairs, 2010)

Of importance to this discussion is that of arrestee samples, originating in the DNA Fingerprint Act of 2005, which authorized collection of DNA samples from persons arrested or detained under federal authority (Biancamano, 2009). With the passage of the act, many states passed

[2]Requires DNA samples from offenders placed on probation or parole. Variations as noted in survey research undertaken by the Interstate Commission for Adult Offender Supervision (2005) includes Alabama, which requires DNA samples from all offenders placed on probation or parole; Missouri requires DNA samples from every probationer or parolee convicted of a felony and under supervision by the Board in Missouri; New Hampshire includes a retroactive provision of anyone incarcerated or under probation or parole for sexual assault; Nebraska requires any person convicted of a sex offense, including those adjudicated via probation to submit DNA samples; and New Mexico allows for DNA samples if stated in the conditions of probation (Interstate Commission for Adult Offender Supervision, 2005).

similar legislation authorizing DNA collection within the arrestee designation (Biancamano, 2009). Currently, 12 states include conditions requiring samples be collected from a person arrested for any felony. Interestingly, while only 12 states have included the designation for "any felony" arrest, 22 states have expanded collection from individuals arrested for the crime of burglary. As Biancamano (2009) noted, there has been an increasing focus at the legislative level to expand DNA collection to the arrestee level for all felony offenses and some states have even gone as far as expanding their collection to misdemeanor convictions, though not arrests (extending beyond misdemeanor sex crimes). As for 2010, New Jersey, New York, Ohio, Utah, and Washington include provisions for the collection of DNA samples from individuals convicted of certain, but not all, misdemeanors (i.e., gross misdemeanors).

As noted above, there has been a clear trend within states to expand their statutory requirements (Biancamano, 2009; Fender, 2007) and there is little reason to believe that states will slow down their expansion and refinement of existing laws (Biancamano, 2009). There is also clear evidence that DNA bills have continued to mark legislative sessions. In fact, in 2007, there were 42 bills put forth in relation to DNA samples from arrestees and 57 proposed in 2008 (Biancamano, 2009). As of March 2011, 86 bills have been put forth concerning DNA, often expanding DNA collection, refining costs, or clarifying processes for expungement (Gordon Thomas Honeywell Governmental Affairs, 2011). Despite many of the bills and amendments failing to pass committee or failing a vote, DNA testing bills continue to occupy a prominent place within police policy during legislative sessions. Consider the 2011 legislative session in Georgia, which put forth the following proposed amendment to *Code Section 17-6-1 of the Official Code of Georgia*. The amendment reads as follows:

> *(k)(1) A person charged with any offense which is bailable only before a judge of a superior court as provided in subsection (a) of this Code section shall be required, as a condition of bond, to have an oral swab or a sample obtained from a noninvasive procedure taken for DNA (deoxyribonucleic acid) analysis to determine identification characteristics specific to the person. Prior to the person's release from custody on bond or recognizance, the law enforcement entity responsible for releasing such person on bond or recognizance shall be responsible for collecting a DNA sample in accordance with rules and regulations established by the Division of Forensic Sciences of the Georgia Bureau of Investigation and notifying the person of his or her right to petition to exclude his or her DNA from the data bank in accordance with paragraph (4) of this subsection.*

Under this amendment, persons charged with any offense that is eligible for bail would be required to submit to a DNA sample. Similar amendments have been proposed across the nation and while as of yet, no clear scholarship has revealed a considerable movement, anecdotal evidence suggests that the movement to expand collection into arrestee sampling is occurring. Most recently, New Mexico approved a bill (A-2594) expanding DNA arrestee sampling within the state by requiring DNA samples from anyone arrested on suspicion of a violent crime. The 2011–2012 legislative sessions in Washington State witnessed the introduction of the Katie Sepich Enhanced DNA Collection Act of 2011, which looks to expand DNA samples from arrestees. However, while there has been a movement to expand collection, there are examples of bills failing to pass committee or failing to pass either a senate or a house vote. Recently, a bill expanding DNA collection to arrest offenses failed to move out of committee in Nevada (Ryan, 2011).

While, no state has yet passed legislation to expand DNA collection and retention across all felony, misdemeanor, and arrest categories, it is important to recognize the financial burden that states endure as they expand DNA collection statutes. As one clear factor associated with the decision to process property crime scene evidence relates to the budget, it is vital to examine the current funding initiatives and associated costs of testing. It is the intent of the following section to highlight the initialization of CODIS and examine the current funding initiatives and the relevant backlog research to provide the reader with a more comprehensive background into those financial factors.

Initialization of CODIS

The initialization and subsequent utilization of CODIS, while authorized in the DNA Identification Act of 1994, would not see a significant increase in utilization until 2004. It was not until the passage of the Justice for All Act of 2004 that there existed a legislative goal and more specifically a substantive funding source to ensure efficient and effective processing of DNA evidence. Scholars and practitioners have long marked the passage of this act as a commendable and indispensable source of legislation. It was perhaps Rago (2005) who offered one of the most succinct statements on the act, "*The Justice for All Act and its treatment of the information science of DNA represents the most significant piece of criminal justice reform legislation, perhaps in our lifetime*" (p. 47).

The act was designed across seven key points (Rago, 2005):

1. Eliminate the backlog of DNA samples collected from crime scenes and convicted offenders
2. Expand the Combined DNA Index System
3. Improve and expand the DNA testing capacity of federal, state, and local crime laboratories
4. Increase research and development of new DNA testing technologies
5. Develop new training programs for the collection and use of DNA evidence
6. Extend the statute of limitations for crimes where the suspect is linked to the crime through DNA evidence
7. Provide post-conviction DNA testing and the preservation of biological evidence

While the application of DNA forensics into the criminal justice process originated within the case of *Andrews v. State* (1988), up until the passage of the act, there existed limited utilization of DNA forensics within the police service. Much of the limitations originated out of needs to refine and evaluate the scientific methods and procedures within forensic testing (Peterson and Leggett, 2007), inclusion of forensic protocol within the investigative standard operating procedures (Lovrich et al., 2004), alignment of the laboratory and agency, and effective resource sharing to distribute the costs of processing, which arguably has still not occurred (Williams and Hammond, 2009).

By many accounts, the generous funding allocations that are available to states has greatly facilitated the use of the CODIS system. As would be expected, providing a funding source facilitates greatly the adoption of technology. Consider the example of the in-car camera and its significant adoption by the police service. To address increasing complaints and allegations of racial profiling, the Department of Justice's Office of Community Oriented Policing Services (COPS) created the In-Car Camera Incentive Program (IACP, 2004). This program created funds for agencies to deploy the in-car camera within patrol vehicles. A 2000 National Institute of Justice report noted that, prior to the COP funding initiative, 3,400 (11%) of state police and highway patrol vehicles were equipped with in-car cameras (IACP, 2004). The IACP (2004) found that in the 3-year period following the funding, there was a considerable increase in implementation of the in-car camera. With over 21 million dollars in grants dispersed to agencies, the implementation as of 2004 was over 17,500, which represented nearly 72% of total state patrol vehicles (IACP, 2004). It is clear that agencies embraced the mobile video system, in part due to the substantial financial resources attached to the technology and the benefits that the technology delivered to the agency (IACP, 2004).

While this is but one example, it provides a valid point concerning technology inclusion that, unless there exists a funding source *and* an organizational focus on its relevance, there is considerable resistance to this inclusion. In the case of the in-car camera, there was an organizational push to counter allegations of racism during traffic stops and the considerable funding allocations supported its nearly complete integration into police agencies. In the case of DNA forensics, there was resistance to its inclusion. However, the establishment of a dedicated funding source and subsequent training, would see it become gradually integrated into the police service.

Backlog Research

Stated simply, a backlog occurs when there are more forensic samples collected than the laboratory can process. While no universal definition exists, the National Institute of Justice defines a backlog as a sample remaining untested after a period of 30 days once submitted to the laboratory (Nelson, 2011; Williams and Hammond, 2009). Of interest within this operationalization of the backlog is the criterion of "once submitted to the laboratory." It is possible for samples to be collected but not submitted to a laboratory, excluding them from being considered a backlog sample. To date, considerable research has attempted to explain the amount of criminal cases that contain unanalyzed forensic evidence or the total offender backlog (reflecting individuals convicted of a crime).[3] While the intent of this book is to examine the factors associated with DNA scene processing within property crimes, it is of importance to highlight the backlog for offender samples. It must be remembered that currently the philosophy within the treatment of forensic evidence has myopically focused upon offender samples (Goulka et al., 2010). As of 2007, the estimated backlog in offender samples waiting for analysis was 708,706 according to the National Institute of Justice (NIJ) or 599,622 according to the Office of the Inspector General (Office of the

[3]Please see Goulka et al. (2010) for an analysis into the research that has been completed.

Inspector General, 2009). As of April 2011, there were 9,635,757 offender profiles (Federal Bureau of Investigation, 2011). In comparison, the total forensic samples as of April 2011 included 370,875 forensic profiles (Federal Bureau of Investigation, 2011) and recent research by Goulka et al. (2010) suggested nearly 563,939 property crime scenes with untested DNA forensic evidence (p. 9).

To date, there have been eight research projects conducted to ascertain the crime scene evidence backlog (see Goulka et al., 2010). Peterson and Hickman (2005) conducted the first crime scene backlog research of forensic laboratories and discovered approximately 50,000 scene samples submitted to a lab facility that remained unanalyzed. Lovrich et al. (2004), in a national survey of police agencies, discovered approximately 221,000 personal and 264,000 property crimes that contained forensic evidence but were not submitted to laboratories, and over 57,000 cases that had been requested but were not analyzed. Pratt et al. (2006), using the survey research conducted in Lovrich et al. (2004), further identified 48,324 homicides, 154,649 rapes, and 253,931 property crimes that contained forensic evidence but had not been submitted and 57,349 homicide and rape cases that had been submitted but were unanalyzed. Hurst and Lothridge (2010) discovered 68,543 unanalyzed crime scene samples that had been submitted to DNA laboratories, which is a significant increase on prior research by Durose (2008), who noted 38,227 unanalyzed cases. However, most noteworthy is the official rate reported by Nelson (2011), indicating approximately 100,000 unanalyzed crime scene samples. Keteyian (2010), in an investigative report for CBS News, focused on sexual assault kits within 24 states and discovered approximately 15,500 untested kits.

Of importance in the prior research is the focus on DNA forensic evidence. In the research of Strom and Hickman (2010), a national survey of police agencies with specific emphasis on untested forensic evidence (comprising all forensic types) was undertaken. The researchers noted that between 2003 and 2007 potentially 5,126,719 unsolved property crime cases, 27,595 unsolved rape cases, and 3,975 homicides contained forensic evidence that wasn't requested for forensic analysis (p. 391). Using the results from Strom and Hickman (2010), Goulka et al. (2010) calculated approximately 563,939 property crime cases, using the 11% DNA recovery rate reported by the Home Office (2005). To put this into perspective, there were

2,199,125 burglaries as reported by the UCR in 2009 (Federal Bureau of Investigation, 2009). Using the conservative estimate of 11% of property crime cases yielding DNA evidence suitable for testing, this means potentially 241,904 of those cases would contain DNA evidence.

Reducing the Backlog

Recognizing that there is a significant backlog and that states continue to expand their DNA testing conditions, there have been considerable attempts to reduce the backlog. The most prominent method has focused upon increasing the availability of funding to states to facilitate improving process mechanics to streamline DNA testing. Under rare circumstances, some states, despite having expanded collection practices, have limited evidence collection within certain crimes to reduce the backlog. With the availability of federal funding and improvements within DNA technology, it is important to highlight the current funding programs and improvements that have occurred within forensic testing to decrease the backlog and streamline forensic testing. The following section addresses the status of federal funding, which has greatly influenced both the expansion and utilization of forensic testing, and the recent technological advancements.

DNA Backlog Reduction Program

The DNA Backlog Reduction Program assists states and units of local government with reducing their existing forensic backlog, improving their forensic throughput and overall turnaround time within DNA laboratories, and analyzing forensic DNA samples. The Attorney General is responsible for preparing a report to Congress including the aggregate amount of Debbie Smith DNA Backlog Grant Program grants, which are contained in abstract form at the National Institute of Justice. As is typical within federal funding programs, states (or agencies) are required to submit funding proposals and while there is a predetermined funding allocation assigned to each state, the proposals have an influence on the appropriation to each agency

Prior to 2011, there existed two separate funding sources, namely the Forensic DNA Backlog Reduction Funding and Convicted Offender/Arrestee Grant Program Funding. In 2011, these combined into a single program requiring one solicitation by agencies. As noted prior, the NDIS system did not contain arrestee samples prior to 2005 and the funding awards to states did not begin until 2005. However, between 2005 and 2010, the Convicted Offender/Arrestee Grant Program awarded states over $35 million (DNA Initiative, 2010).

In 2004, the initial federal funding allotment to states exceeded $65 million and over the next 7 years would average $56 million in funding allotments. In total, the program has provided, as of 2010, nearly $400 million dollars in assistance to states to reduce backlogs and improve their efficiency within DNA forensic collection and analysis (Nelson, 2011). As Table 3.3 shows, as of May 2011, 8,263,688 offender profiles and 366,918 forensic samples have been approved and stored within the CODIS system, which has resulted in 136,567 investigations being aided. As of 2011, there are now currently 194 laboratories capable of analyzing and submitting samples to the CODIS system. As expected, recipients of greater federal funding have predominately been those with significantly higher index crimes including California ($51,589,194), Florida ($33,585,401), New York ($21,122,133), and Texas ($35,742,680).

DNA Backlog Reduction Program Abstracts

Granting of federal funding is contingent upon submitting an abstract and meeting the required federal program guidelines. From a property crime perspective, the Fiscal Year 2009 and 2010 abstract submissions contained many references to increasing property crime processing. In 2009, Kern County was awarded $245,810 to improve their DNA analysis capability and in part to increase their capacity to process property crime forensic evidence (US Department of Justice, 2009). Miami-Dade received $1,084,501 to increase their in-house DNA analysis and to fund outsourcing of property crime and cold cases to a commercial laboratory. Palm Beach County Sheriff's Office specifically noted in their abstract their intention to improve the collection of crime scene evidence from minor property crime cases and received $427,775. The trend continued in the 2010 abstract submissions with the Los Angeles County Sheriff's Department receiving $1,561,300 to address their sexual assault kit backlog and analyze approximately 462 property crime cases (US Department of Justice, 2010a). Colorado, one of the case studies in the high volume property crime experiment, received $580,593 to improve their workflow process and continue with their property crime scene evidence collection practices. One particular recipient stood out in the abstract submission report—

Table 3.3 Backlog Reduction Funding Awards and CODIS Descriptive

State/Jurisdiction	Total Federal Funding in US$ (2004–2010)	Offender Profiles (2011)	Forensic Samples (2011)	Investigations Aided (2011)	Number of CODIS Labs (2011)
Alabama	6,328,056	192,431	7,062	3,747	4
Alaska	1,383,329	21,795	911	332	1
Arizona	8,296,640	201,036	10,399	4,189	7
Arkansas	3,618,244	117,336	4,378	1,492	1
California	51,589,194	1,340,553	34,169	12,777	22
Colorado	5,615,625	138,225	6,485	2,204	6
Connecticut	2,963,701	80,798	2,582	907	1
Delaware	1,391,284	4,214	388	24	1
District of Columbia	1,807,266	0	229	0	1
Florida	33,585,401	754,729	32,528	15,328	12
Georgia	12,360,127	214,944	10,494	3,250	4
Hawaii	775,789	19,238	472	174	1
Idaho	1,172,894	5,292	262	16	1
Illinois	20,562,603	396,051	23,118	12,253	10
Indiana	7,085,345	167,291	6,190	2,057	5
Iowa*	601,355	65,875	3,371	795	1
Kansas	3,366,021	74,234	4,033	1,381	5
Kentucky	4,166,746	27,824	3,552	623	1
Louisiana	8,457,994	110,303	6,024	2,238	7
Maine	973,843	15,609	1,967	73	1
Maryland	9,012,726	93,751	6,356	2,052	6
Massachusetts	8,293,464	87,467	5,342	1,701	2
Michigan	18,999,705	295,586	10,508	4,594	3
Minnesota	4,815,870	105,578	7,218	2,310	2
Mississippi	3,162,277	56,739	460	145	1
Missouri	8,481,284	211,764	11,997	5,082	7
Montana	950,649	16,558	410	84	1
Nebraska	1,752,878	7,690	752	48	1
Nevada	4,495,190	62,948	4,127	1,655	2
New Hampshire	897,671	3,392	831	72	1
New Jersey	6,690,784	226,803	10,424	4,502	2
New Mexico	2,753,574	54,761	2,813	1,264	3
New York	21,122,133	365,647	33,403	11,680	9
North Carolina	11,666,738	192,962	5,319	1,663	2
North Dakota	757,848	8,783	534	167	1

(Continued)

Table 3.3 (Continued)

State/Jurisdiction	Total Federal Funding in US$ (2004–2010)	Offender Profiles (2011)	Forensic Samples (2011)	Investigations Aided (2011)	Number of CODIS Labs (2011)
Ohio	13,845,696	385,883	21,563	6,243	11
Oklahoma	5,248,285	97,408	2,193	215	3
Oregon	3,296,355	133,772	6,953	3,107	1
Pennsylvania	14,358,979	247,318	9,098	3,575	3
Puerto Rico	2,216,641	12,527	143	23	1
Rhode Island	941,717	13,204	452	46	1
South Carolina	9,388,599	155,343	7,595	3,203	2
South Dakota	1,038,295	23,874	383	117	1
Tennessee	4,131,490	128,152	3,158	394	3
Texas	35,742,680	558,338	28,880	7,499	16
Utah	1,742,238	57,627	479	57	1
Vermont	732,608	12,757	385	99	1
Virginia	7,375,666	326,042	13,459	6,672	4
Washington	7,909,951	198,947	3,235	1,295	6
West Virginia	1,537,907	14,203	604	87	1
Wisconsin	4,760,613	143,772	8,993	3,030	3
Wyoming	650,658	16,314	237	26	1
Total	394,872,626	8,263,688	366,918	136,567	194

**Idaho received no funding between the years 2006 and 2009.*
Source*: DNA Initiative website, http://www.nij.gov/topics/forensics/lab-operations/capacity/backlog-reduction-funding.htm & Federal Bureau of Investigation website, http://www.fbi.gov/about-us/lab/codis/ndis-statistics*

Pinellas County, Florida, was one of the few recipients that specifically noted an "*increased focus on property crime*" as a reason for the funding. Unlike other recipients who either noted an increase in property crime evidence as the source of their backlog or sought to outsource this evidence, Pinellas County noted intent to become better at processing evidence recovered in these cases. Despite being only a brief abstract, the county received $333,220.

While a theme emerged among the abstracts concerning property crime scene evidence, several states have sought to focus specifically on addressing their backlog by reducing collection of DNA evidence from these cases by placing a limit on how many cases would receive testing. North Carolina in its funding request from the Department of Crime Control and Public Safety specifically included this provision, which explicitly limits processing for this evidence type (though exceptions exist). The decision was made to improve turnaround times by limiting the analysis of property crimes and other minor crimes (US Department of Justice, 2000).

It is important to note that agencies must demonstrate improvements within their forensic process to continue to be eligible for funding. As noted in the *Solicitation: FY 2010 Forensic DNA Backlog Reduction Program*, any laboratory that receives federal funding must demonstrate, by the end of the project period, improvements within their forensic process. Expected results include (US Department of Justice, 2010a):

- A reduction in the average number of days between submission of DNA evidence samples to the applicant's forensic science laboratory (or laboratories) and delivery of DNA test results to the requesting office or agency
- An increase in the number of forensic DNA samples processed per analyst per month
- A reduction in the applicant's backlog of forensic DNA casework

When a facility is unable to demonstrate improvements, they must include the following in their final report: (1) descriptions of any observed increases in evidence submissions; (2) explanations of issues which have negatively impacted project goals; and (3) approximate quantities for the increase in the forensic DNA casework backlog that would have occurred had the activities funded under this program not been performed (US Department of Justice, 2010b).

In the case of North Carolina, in both 2009 and 2010 abstract submissions, they noted a considerable backlog and one mechanism of reducing the backlog was to improve efficiency and synergy between the laboratory and the agency and to reduce the number of eligible cases for DNA testing. The importance of this subsection within funding mechanisms is that while substantial funding is made available to agencies, there is an accountability mechanism that places considerable external pressure on the organization to become efficient in their processing of forensic evidence. While many agencies have expressed intentions to improve process mechanics, a few states have yielded to both internal and external pressure resulting in a reduction in forensics. The end result is an agency that seeks to modernize their testing procedure by ignoring an entire range of cases. However, several agencies expressed an interest in progressing their antiquated testing platforms by incorporating robotic testing equipment.

FORENSIC TECHNOLOGY: GENERATIONAL IMPROVEMENTS

As with any scientific process, the more it is used, the more efficient and effective it becomes. Originally, collecting fingerprints proved burdensome because of the additional steps involved in recovering latent prints from a crime scene, a chore in patience. However, with training, institutional knowledge transfer, and improved technology, collection practices became routine, the costs reduced, and the turnaround time for processing cut down to minutes (Komarinski, 2005). Each technological generation brought with it improvements. What started with messy ink and modified index cards transitioned into messy ink cards and a digital scanner. As the technology improved, index cards were replaced with desktop digital scanners. Over time, intake processing became streamlined and the technology took on portability, allowing officers to process prints in the field (Komarinski, 2005). At a practical level, consider the Livescan rapid identification project, conducted in Minnesota, in 2008. The nearly $10 million project brought the technology to agencies across the state, which allowed fingerprints to be collected and analyzed within a few minutes, including notifying the agency if the prints were not accepted (CriMNet Program Office, 2008). This project also delivered portable fingerprinting devices to squad cars for field processing. What previously could have taken hours was reduced to mere minutes as the technology improved.

While this is but one example, it demonstrates how generational improvements within forensic testing have brought efficiency and effectiveness. It was not long ago that agencies raised concerns over the expansion of fingerprinting collection practices. However, with training and most importantly financial assistance, the implementation of the Automated Fingerprint Identification System (AFIS) became systemic and an important source of forensic evidence within the investigative process.

Over time, DNA technology has improved and with it the ability to process samples at a more efficient and effective rate. As with the

AFIS, it would see nearly identical generational improvements. With each technology generation, the systems improved their capacity and their accountability (reducing error), but the system could not account for the expansive and mandated collection practices resulting in overburdened laboratories plagued with incidents of testing protocol violations. While the latter is of importance (and discussed in detail toward the end of this chapter), the former has seen considerable improvements to reduce costs, improve accuracy (reducing error), and streamlining processing.

FORENSIC TECHNOLOGY: THE COSTS OF PROCESSING

In 2000, the average DNA profile cost \$100 (Watson, 2000). However, this does not take into account the criminal justice system costs in processing a sample, which include the necessary chemicals and reagents and salaries of forensic technicians. Today, depending on the laboratory used (private or public), costs vary but as technology improves, the costs have been reduced. The DNA Field Experiment yielded a weighted average cost of a CODIS entry at \$74, preliminary testing at \$374, and another \$135 to generate a DNA profile (Roman et al., 2009, p. 361). However, within the experiment, Los Angeles and Phoenix utilized private facilities, significantly increasing their expenditures. For example, the Los Angeles facility spent \$980 on preliminary testing and \$167 on the CODIS entry (Roman et al., 2009, p. 361). It is important to note that use of private facilities not only increases costs, but also a surcharge may be levied by the facility. In the RAND report completed by Goulka et al. (2010), it was noted that private DNA labs often placed a premium on expediency, including a \$600 surcharge for a 15-day turnaround, an \$800 surcharge for a ten-day rush, and a \$1,000 surcharge for a five-day rush (p. 8). These private vendors also had contractual agreements for costs, which often exceeded (two to four times as much) the in-house costs for a confirmation sample analysis (one of the last steps in the process). Los Angeles paid \$400 per confirmation sample, which is significantly higher than the \$108 paid in Topeka or \$280 in Phoenix (Roman et al., 2009, p. 360).

Collating all of the costs, Roman et al. (2009) noted that the average cost per suspect identified was approximately \$4,500, ranging from \$1,466 in Denver (the most efficient) to as much as \$8,147 in Los Angeles (p. 360). It should be noted that these rates relate to processing property crime and as agencies become more familiar with the DNA process, these costs will be reduced. In the Denver labs, deemed the most efficient and effective in their processing, the costs were relatively close to the estimated costs of rape kits, which hospitals and agencies are very familiar with (criticisms notwithstanding). According to Lovrich et al. (2004), the estimated cost of a rape kit is approximately $1,100. Equally important within the costs perspective is the associated issue of suspect identification and arrest. Under the best cost-benefit scenario, including DNA collection, suspect identification, and successful conviction, Roman et al. (2009) states "*it is probably fair to characterize spending $3,679 to arrest a burglary suspect who would otherwise never have been caught, and who averages three prior felony convictions, as a small cost*" (p. 365).

FORENSIC TECHNOLOGY: FROM TECHNICIAN TO ROBOT

As forensic testing expands, the commercial market has responded to improved forensic testing products. Most notable has been the introduction of robotic testing platforms, which are fully automated and capable of processing considerable amounts of evidence. Murphy (2006) offered in 2006 that it would be feasible, with the improvements within forensic testing technology, to see analysts able to process up to 800 samples in a day (p. 9). Discounting the magnitude of what 800 forensic samples equates to at a financial level, the possibility of an agency that has forensics efficiency is staggering, but is attainable.

When the United Kingdom initialized the DNA expansion program in 2000, it witnessed an increase of nearly 300,000 new samples per year, including evidence recovered from crime scenes (Kemp and Pinchin, 2007). At first the police came under harsh criticism when it was reported that up to 10% of DNA matches were not pursued, and of those crimes most related to car theft and burglary cases (Smith Alling Lane, 2000). This external pressure, coupled with the increasing internal focus to maximize the use of the NDAD system, would see a significant increase in the number of evidence samples recovered at the scene, which placed a considerable strain on the system (Goulka et al., 2010). However, through robotic automation, improved sample processing, and improved evidence collection training, the system is currently capable of processing in excess of 12,000 subject samples and 1,000 scene-of-crime samples a week, while maintaining the capability of processing evidence within

24 hours under exigent circumstances (Kemp and Pinchin, 2007). While this is impressive, it should be noted that processing labs within the United States are capable of a similar turnaround time under exigent circumstances. However, in the United Kingdom, it takes on average 3.5 days to analyze a suspect sample and 2 weeks to analyze the crime scene, while maintaining *no* backlog (Goulka et al., 2010). Currently, the turnaround for a case in the United States can exceed 90 days, with the average being 60 days (Goulka et al., 2010). According to Kemp and Pinchin (2007), the Forensic Science Service (FSS), one of the forensic DNA testing providers within the United Kingdom, is currently capable of processing in excess of 1,000,000 forensic DNA samples per year, which is an astonishing feat.

FORENSIC TECHNOLOGY: ISSUES OF ACCOUNTABILITY

In addition to the reduced costs and increase in processing, the movement to robotic platforms affords an increase in accountability to reduce error. As Soullière (1999) eloquently stated, police and technology have entered an era marked by the politicalization of forensic technology. Forensic technology has come to mark the era with an increasing utilization and reluctance to question forensic findings. In likely what is the best account of the power given to forensics is this quote from defense attorney David Baugh "*If you put God on the witness stand ... and God's testimony conflicted with the DNA evidence, everyone would automatically say, 'Why is God lying like this?'* " (As cited by DiFonzo, 2005).

Hyperbole notwithstanding, the belief in forensic science, specific to DNA, is absolute to juries. In a multivariate path analysis into the CSI effect, Kim et al. (2009) discovered that the most important feature is the acquisition of beliefs favorable towards forensic evidence, which is to say that those who were exposed to CSI programs containing scientific evidence had higher expectations of the evidence than what the prosecutor presented as valid. Today, juries and the community view DNA forensics as absolute and while the exclusionary power is remarkable, there have been considerable errors within labs.

While no statistical assessment exists as to the total number of cases completed in error, strong anecdotal evidence certainly suggests that there is a problem and one that most certainly will grow as states and agencies expand their collection statutes. Starting in 2001, reports began to emerge citing more than 100 DNA tests at the FBI Laboratory that were in error when a lab technician had not performed a "negative control" to isolate DNA profiles from crime scene samples (Willing, 2003). A series of failures discovered in Minneapolis yielded a contamination rate of 2% or one out of every 50 cases (Chanen, 2005 as cited by DiFonzo, 2005). Of interest within the Minneapolis incident is that the samples were accidently mixed into other crime samples. Even my state of Washington was not immune to profound error. In a news report for the *Seattle Post-Intelligencer*, Ruth Teichroeb (2004) highlighted 23 major crime cases conducted in error over a 3-year period.

As DiFonzo (2005) points out, there have come to exist considerable errors in forensic analyses performed by "untrained, underpaid, and overworked forensic technicians" (p. 2). In addition, within many of these facilities technicians have come to represent police in "lab coats" rather than objective scientists seeking the truth. The uncomfortable reality is that, despite nearly a decade of news accounts highlighting considerable errors, which should have marred our faith in forensics, its popularity and belief in its certainty continue to grow.

Not forgotten in this discussion of forensic technology and accountability is the reality that false convictions exist and while DNA has resulted in numerous exonerations, it exists as the last line of defense and the movement to robotic platforms is essential to reducing error. Uncomfortable as it has become, there exists a considerable number of individuals "*Convicted by DNA and exonerated by science.*"[4] As the cases above denote, DNA has been used to convict many people only to be used later to exonerate them because of technical error, improper testimony, or outright fraud. The movement to robotic platforms is necessary to reduce the potential of error and to provide safeguards to identify sampling error resulting from hands-on sample handling, which is one of the leading reasons for errors. In addition, the redundancy and safeguards within the robotic platforms should afford additional protection compared with the lab

[4]In reference to the National Institute of Justice report, "Convicted by Juries, Exonerated by Science," detailing numerous cases of error.

where opportunity for misconduct decreases. Not forgotten is the highly conservative estimate by Huff and Killias (2008), who state an error rate of 0.5 to 1% within criminal convictions. It is vital that *if* agencies pursue enhanced processing of property crime scene evidence, there must be safeguards in place to ensure that error is reduced. Staley (2005), in collating research for GeneWatch UK, highlighted a UK National Criminal Intelligence DNA Database report stating that internal and external quality assurance assessments on the system require an error rate below 0.05%.

A recent evolution has taken place within robotic platforms in the creation of the HID EVOlution System. A recent test of the system detected that the rate of contamination within the system is 0.00 during automated liquid-handling operations. The system was designed with multiple subroutines to safeguard evidence and to run a fully automated analysis. As the researchers discovered, the system is capable of reducing errors within hands-on sample handling, minimizing pipetting errors, and improving both throughput and processing consistency (Fang et al., 2010).

CONCLUSION

Discourse on forensic evidence has occurred throughout the last century. The application of scientific evidence has brought closure to victims and exonerations to those victimized by the criminal justice process. The investigative process has uniquely benefitted from these inclusions to see resolution to some of the most prolific crimes. For example, the Green River serial killer eluded capture for decades to only later be identified by DNA recovered from one of his calling cards. While these crimes are few in number, their notoriety has resulted in states increasingly passing legislation requiring forensic testing for an entire range of individuals (offender and arrestee). Such expansion has created a forensic backlog that continues to plague states and agencies around the nation. Adding to the burden are the complications within property crime scene evidence, which often remains uncollected or collected and unanalyzed (Strom and Hickman, 2010).

This chapter aimed to introduce forensic testing within the investigative process, to ensure that the reader is acquainted with the history and contemporary issues surrounding DNA forensics. In addition, it was important to outline the funding mechanisms and statutes associated with DNA testing, including the current literature involving the backlog and improvements in technology that have occurred. If forensic analysis has become intrinsically linked to the criminal justice process, it is of importance to understand how engrained it has become specific to the institution of focus within this book, namely that of the police. The following chapter explores the benefits of DNA expansion within property crime scenes. I include the criminal nonspecialization literature to help frame the argument that expansion of forensic analysis within these scenes is beneficial and warranted.

CHAPTER 4

The Police Organization, Forensics, and the Investigation Process

We do not pay for evidence processing, I can send off as much as I want to the lab, we pay for my kits but evidence costs us nothing and yet the Chief still is resistant to allowing me to submit evidence for processing.

Forensic Expert

Bayley and Nixon (2010) offer that, of the many facets within the changing environment of policing, DNA forensics poses a considerable benefit and challenge within the organization. It is important to remember that over a decade prior Bayley (1994) offered a similar finding. The reality is that the inclusion of DNA forensics, or that of forensic evidence including fingerprints, met with resistance. While early research revealed that the investigative process did not enjoy considerable benefit via forensic evidence (Greenwood et al., 1975), later research would come to highlight the benefits that "tangible evidence" could produce within the investigative process and that of the adjudication process (see Briody, 2004; Peterson, et al., 1984; Forst et al., 1977). The discovered benefits included improved clearance rates, improved collection and analysis rates via application of institutional knowledge to forensic evidence detection (including training), improved prosecution filing rates, and increases within the length of incarceration (see Roman et al., 2009; Denver DNA Burglary Project, 2004; Briody, 2004; Walsh et al., 2002; Peterson et al., 1984; Forst et al., 1977).

While the discovered benefits were considerable and well documented, agencies were still hesitant to incorporate forensic analysis into police practice. Research would later highlight that, despite considerable expansion of forensic analysis within the criminal justice process, the utilization of forensic evidence within the investigative process was severely limited. In fact, Horvath and Meesig (1996) offered that investigators viewed this evidence as complementary to the interview process (a value add) to advantage during interrogations or, as often was the case, the forensic analysis was conducted to support the prosecution. Stevens (2011) would later offer using survey research that currently many officers still view forensic evidence as disconnected from the investigative process.

At a comparative level, research within Australia, New Zealand, the United States, and the United Kingdom have demonstrated clear benefits that forensic evidence brings to the investigative process (see Dunsmuir et al., 2008; Roman et al., 2008; Briody, 2004; Home Office, 2005; Lovrich et al., 2004; Walsh et al., 2002). However, as Horvath et al. (2001) noted in their analysis within the history of the investigative process, few changes have occurred and most unfortunate is that forensic evidence has not become inexplicitly linked to the investigative process. As Roman et al. (2008) stress, while DNA evidence is a widely accepted investigative tool and has become routinely collected and analyzed in homicide cases (p. 12), its extension into property crime scenes has proven of interest but has not become widely utilized. Despite the availability of this evidence indicating high recidivism rates for these offenders, abysmal clearance rates, and the high probability that many of these offenders will escalate over time, the expansion of DNA forensics within property crimes had been hindered.

THE INVESTIGATIVE PROCESS WITH DNA EVIDENCE

As detailed in Figure 4.1, the investigative process involving forensic evidence includes six primary steps from evidence collection to generation of a matching report (Goulka et al., 2010). Specific to the DNA process, Bond et al. (2008) express that there are five primary stages reflecting: (1) Recover, (2) Profile, (3) Match, (4) Arrest, and (5) Solve (p. 798). Of importance within this process is the involvement of additional stakeholders, which may slow down the investigative process. Unlike the involvement of latent fingerprints, which can be collected, analyzed, and matched often at the agency level (Komarinski, 2005), DNA forensics often requires assistance of an outside agency or private facility, and while some agencies are capable of in-house processing of evidence, most require external assistance.

The Decision to Collect

Most important within the initialization of the investigative process is that of the decision to collect evidence, closely followed by the detection and recovery of forensic evidence. Concerning the decision to collect evidence, research conducted by Griswold and Murphy (2010) suggests that the investigator's discretion guides the determination to

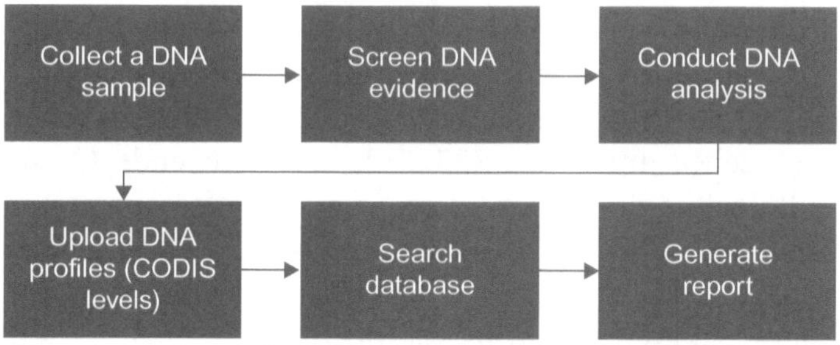

Figure 4.1 Overview of the investigative process involving forensic evidence (adapted from Goulka et al., 2010).

collect DNA for potential analysis. While the research specifically sampled PERF members, the research does support much of the prior research indicating that officer discretion plays a significant role in the utilization of forensics (Horvath and Meesig, 1996). The results of the PERF survey (n = 216) noted that 85% of agencies indicated that investigator discretion influenced the decision to collect DNA evidence. Forty-four percent of agencies specified that the determination to process forensic evidence occurred at the request of the prosecutor, 32% of agencies having a formal written agency policy, 30% utilizing an informal policy, and 18% describing that there were other factors influencing the determination (Griswold and Murphy, 2010, p. 31). Of importance to note within the "other determination" category is the role of the victim in determining if an officer collected DNA evidence. Within forensic cases such as rape, victims have a considerable role in determining the collection of evidence from their person.

Despite having a limited sampling frame of PERF members, the research does support much of the prior research on factors that influence an officer's decision to collect forensic evidence, and in speaking with Griswold (2011), the researchers discovered in follow-ups with officers the surprising influence that the prosecutor has within the decision to process DNA evidence. Despite being anecdotal, it does reflect in prior research, noting again the involvement of the prosecutor within the decision-making process specific to the investigative process and forensic evidence (Horvath and Meesig, 1996).

Collection of Evidence

As with any process, the quality of the output is dependent on the quality of the input. The ability for DNA evidence to generate a profile match with sufficient evidentiary weight is dependent on the quality of the sample. In conducting research on the value of DNA material recovered from property crime scenes, Bond et al. (2008) noted that numerically the largest sources of DNA recovered from these crime scenes are saliva (33.3%), cigarette ends (30.0%), blood (17.4%), cellular (i.e., offender touching an item leaving a skin sample), and chewing gum (3.5%) (p. 798). This is similar to the research of Roman et al. (2008), indicating that blood and saliva samples are significantly more likely to yield usable profiles, so much in fact that biological evidence had a higher probability matching than fingerprints. In addition, the research by Walsh et al. (2002) within New Zealand

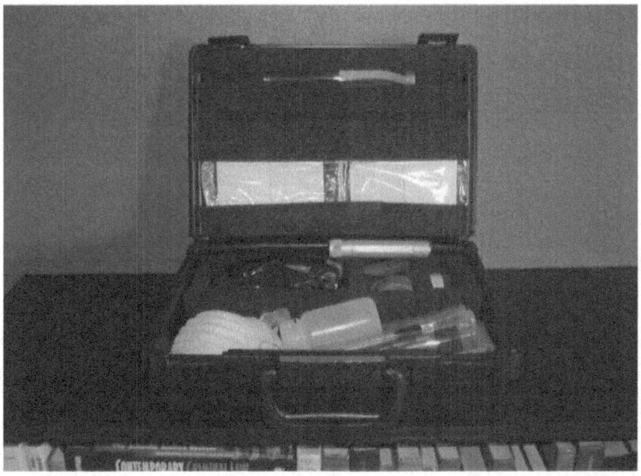

Figure 4.2 Personal forensic kit.

yielded nearly identical ratings. This was an unexpected finding within the research and speaks volumes towards the effectiveness of biological evidence. Within the DNA Field Experiment, Roman et al. (2008) noted that 16% of the biological evidence recovered yielded identification of a suspect, with 9% yielding an arrest (p. 359). Equally, important within the research, specific to the identification and collection of forensic evidence, is that the quality of the sample is nearly identical between forensic technicians and officers that have received training. In fact, within the DNA Field Experiment, Roman et al. (2008) noted that as the experiment continued, more officers began to collect evidence for analysis. Their resulting submissions were accepted at nearly the same rate. Equally important is that the forensic evidence kits are capable of processing multiple scenes and are easily procured at a significant discount. The kit shown in Figure 4.2 was procured during my duration as Chair within the School of Criminal Justice at a prior college. They were purchased for students within the program for utilization during criminal investigation and forensic courses and cost approximately $100.00.

OFFICER TRAINING

While the science of DNA analysis requires specific training to interpret, improvements in training have eased transference of the skills necessary for collection. In fact, the federal government provides a free self-paced training course concerning collecting DNA evidence at property crime scenes. The training is available to anyone who registers at the website (http://www.dna.gov/training/property-crime/) and covers four modules:

1. Types of Evidence
2. Crime Scenes
3. Evidence Collection
4. Combined DNA Index System (CODIS)

Having registered and completed the training course, I found it contained a wealth of information addressing many of the fundamental collection practices and providing considerable assistance in what to look for as potential sources of DNA evidence at a property crime scene. The training was immensely helpful in developing the survey instrument and better understanding the investigative process. As detailed in the interview analysis within the findings section, several officers noted how helpful the training was to become better acquainted with identification of DNA evidence and more importantly how to preserve the evidence and maintain integrity. While simply the impression of this author, the training would certainly prove beneficial to a seasoned detective or to a patrol officer looking to better detect and handle DNA evidence at property crime scenes.

While the investigative process is a relatively straightforward process because of the limiting structure of the CODIS architecture (LDIS, SDIS, NDIS) and the limitations placed upon private labs (unable to upload profiles to CODIS), the system experiences delays. In addition, inhibitors emerge within the decision to collect evidence with regard to how useful the evidence is to the officer. The reality is that police officers exist in a reactive world. Research on technology inclusions into agencies suggests that officers may view it as a burden, hassle, or a resource expenditure that could be better spent elsewhere. The challenge in moving forward is to balance the inclusion, to highlight what awaits agencies that expand into such collection practices. Technology does not need to reform an agency; it needs only assist the agency in progressing it to become a better agency in how it delivers its services. When speaking to officers, as detailed in the interview section of this book, it has come to light that agencies exist that have resorted to handling burglary calls over the phone.

To complement this section on the relationship between police practice and forensic science, it is important to provide a brief history of technology within the police organization, to highlight the four key eras that have come to encompass the implementation and development of technology within the police service. It is the intent of this subsection to provide the reader with a more thorough understanding as to how technology has come to influence the organization and the power of the police organization to resist technology inclusion by modifying the technology to fit the organization's goals.

TECHNOLOGY DEVELOPMENT AND IMPLEMENTATION WITHIN THE POLICE SERVICE

There are three schools of thought concerning the use of technology within an organization: (1) technology is modifying police practice, (2) technology is simply a ploy in power by administrators to demonstrate "professionalism" regardless of how the technology is actually used in the agency, and (3) technology is simply used to replicate traditional police practice and has not brought about any substantive changes. Manning (2008) likely offered the best explanation for the interaction between police and technology when he noted that it reproduces traditional police practice. Rarely does the organization implement technology in a manner that drastically changes the daily tasks of officers. If officers are likely to encounter additional tasking, the implementation either will fail or be utilized in rare circumstances when it is advantageous to the organization/officer (Chan, 2001). The purpose of this section is to highlight the relationship between technology and that of the police to demonstrate how, traditionally, organizations have embraced technology and what factors have come to influence technology implementation and associated practices. The development of police technology exists across four stages, as developed by Soullière (1999).

First Stage: 1881–1945

The first stage began in the late 1800s and ended in 1945. This stage signified the implementation of the core organizational technology that would reflect the professionalization of policing. I should note that Vollmer (mentioned earlier in the review of the literature) is credited with the creation of, or implementation of, many of the organizational practices and technologies that would mark this stage, including evidence collection, crime analysis, and development of a crime laboratory. In an era of policing marked with a lack of professionalism (training, education), Vollmer would progress the field by merging science with institutional practice and knowledge.

It began with the creation of the red light signal system in 1907 that allowed for agencies to contact officers on patrol. What is important to remember is that these systems were not used to convey incidents to officers (i.e., incident directing) but rather were used to increase accountability and oversight within the rank and file. In essence, this was the first technology to increase a supervisor's span of control. Vollmer would later institute a records management system, which included the collection of offenders' *modus operandi* (the groundwork for modern criminal investigative analysis). Vollmer would also initiate the entrance of policing into forensics through fingerprinting. What is important at this level is that forensics epitomizes the focus on improving clearance rates.

A last item of importance was in 1917 when Vollmer transitioned the entire Berkeley police agency into the first fully motorized police force in the country and would introduce radio communications into the patrol car to improve agency-to-officer communication, and officer-to-officer communication. This improved officer safety and allowed agencies to more efficiently and effectively respond to calls for service within the community. It should be noted that the automobile is often referred to within technology literature (see Soullière, 1999) as being the first and only "transformative" technology. This type of technology refers to those capable of changing how organizations operate. In essence, the technology transforms the organization and in the context of the police service, the automobile changed how services were delivered—from quasi proactive to entirely reactive. However, one technology in over a hundred years does not provide enough evidence to suggest that technology shapes police culture.

The first stage witnessed the foundational technology that would enhance the delivery of police services and reinforce the professional image of the police force as crime fighters. By the end of the first stage in 1945, police agencies had a mobile police force that could respond to calls for service from the community and could be held accountable by supervisors who had the ability to contact officers and issue commands. Lastly, the technology facilitated the development and utilization of the hierarchical organizational structure and specialized police units that we see today via the knowledge specialization and focus on forensics to solve specific crimes (Soullière, 1999).

Second Stage: 1946–1959

The second stage of technology integration was signified by the bureaucratization of the police agency. While short-lived from a technology perspective, between 1946 and 1959 the technology that was sought and embraced highlighted the challenges the organization faced. With prohibition ending about a decade before and with the end of WWII, police agencies found themselves with an increase in the number of motorists and, more importantly, a population that witnessed an increase in utilization of alcohol. What the police lacked was a scientific means of assessing the speed of cars and levels of intoxication. It was not until 1954 that Dr. Borkenstein, a police captain, developed the first Breathalyzer. This technology provided the final means of addressing a mandate to address particular crimes (focus on alcohol intoxication), police agencies witnessed the development of techniques that could assess speed (shadowing) and assess levels of intoxication (field sobriety tests). The technology during this stage provided an efficient and effective means of addressing the majority of police encounters.

Third Stage: 1960–1979

The third stage (1960–1979) showed a complete reluctance of police agencies to implement technology. The reluctance was noted in President Johnson's Commission in 1967, which criticized the police for not using technology to address the organization's primary problems. The report noted that science and the police organization had been linked since the creation of the modern police force but the organization had become reluctant to embrace technology with the exception of specific crime problems and those were primarily violent crime related. Also of importance is the historical context. During this time, the police were increasingly organizationally introverted in dealing with their internal conflict. The "Us vs. Them" mentality and subsequent police community cleavage was becoming increasingly noticeable; police organizations found themselves cited for civil rights violations, brutality, and racism. There was so much internal conflict that looking to embrace technology to accomplish their mandate was furthest from their sights.

Recognizing the criticisms, the police embraced technology at the end of this stage to address the criticisms they faced (the police did not care about the communities' problems). Most notable within this stage was the creation of the 911 system, computerized record management systems, and computer-aided dispatch; all of which reinforce the ability to respond to calls for service (reactive policing) and keep a record of those calls as a means of meeting any external requests for information from watchdog groups or other police agencies (Chan, 2001).

From a police culture perspective, 911 likely had the most influence on reinforcing the working class personality. A report arranged by the Seaskate Corporation for Congress highlighted 911 as a key technology implementation that had great benefit to the organization and to communities. As portrayed to police officers, 911 would exist as a mechanism for community members to seek assistance to address emergencies; this would reinforce the image of police officers as crime fighters. However, the reality was quite different. What was meant to be used for emergency calls for service would predominately be used for nonemergency calls. A technology that was intended to produce the image of a crime fighter, only exacerbated the cleavage that was forming as officers responding to calls for service found themselves in nonemergency situations. Thus, 911 as a technology did not shape the police culture but only strengthened the police culture that saw the community to blame for their victimization.

Fourth Stage: 1980–Present

The fourth stage identified by Soullière (1999) began in 1980. This stage is signified by the "politicalization of forensics" including the development, implementation, and increasing utilization of forensic databases. These databases included the Automated Fingerprint Identification System (AFIS), the CODIS, and the National Integrated Ballistics Information Network (NIBIN). In addition to these networks, the fourth stage brought networked interfaces within the patrol car, via the mobile data terminal, allowing access to local, regional, and national databases. Examples include the National Crime Information Center (NCIC) and administrative access to other databases, including the National Law Enforcement Information Exchange (NDEX) and the National Precursor Log Exchange (NPLEX).

Of importance within this discussion on the eras of technology implementation and policing is the importance of context. Each technology era responded to the current challenges within policing. Thus, police technology implementation reflects the unique context of the era.

The fourth stage is signified by the "politicalization of forensics," which has come to rely upon forensics across all levels of the criminal justice system. With expansive collection programs in place across the nation, it is clear that DNA forensics has become commonplace within the criminal justice system and databases and processes have evolved to store evidence for process. While the original assessment from Horvath et al. (2001) still holds true, in many regards there is clear indication that the investigative process has incorporated DNA forensic evidence. However, what remains unclear are the practical benefits that come from increasing property crime scene processing. Obvious are the improvements within clearance rates, but to what degree? In addition, it is of vital importance to discuss the role of forensics within the COMPSTAT and community policing paradigms. How an agency responds to DNA forensics within its existing model is as important as the use of DNA forensics.

If "intelligence-led" policing does come to influence police practice, by the inclusion and reliance upon information utilization and sharing, it does become of importance to understand what benefits potentially await agencies that expand their evidence collection practices into property crime scenes. The following section provides the academic literature concerning criminal nonspecialization and the associated comparative case studies that have indicated clear agency benefits.

CRIMINAL NONSPECIALIZATION AND SEX OFFENDERS

Early use of forensic evidence was predominately used to solve violent crimes, often specific to sexual violence. Subsequently, the expansion of DNA statutes (i.e., offender and arrestee sampling) and treatment of forensic evidence recovered at crime scenes relied upon the belief that sex offenders had elevated rates of recidivism and specialized in their criminal behavior, which was perpetuated by the political and social climate concerning sex offenders (Harris et al., 2009; Harris and Hanson, 2004). While their crimes are heinous and some offenders a threat to public safety, the evidence suggests that sex offenders are *not* more likely to recidivate than nonsexual offenders (Harris et al., 2009). Prior to this research, Sample and Bray (2006) noted that sex offenders, despite the assumptions, did not display homogeneity. Rather, sex offenders are a heterogeneous group with varying recidivism rates. Harris et al. (2009) discovered that those most likely to commit a sexual offense often had prior criminal histories (often reflecting property or violent crimes). Despite later research, several studies reported connections resulting in fallacies concerning sexual offenders. Consider the following *USA Today* article as referenced by Smith Alling Lane (2000):

> *"Study: Many rapists were thieves first Results may lead to taking." USA Today, July 10, 2000.*
>
> *A recently released Virginia study concludes that 40 percent of men arrested for rape began their criminal careers in property crime, such as burglary and petty theft. The study is expected to prompt more calls for expansion of DNA databases. The Virginia study supports a study in Britain that found that three-quarters of all rapists started off as burglars, and an ongoing study in Florida is finding that half of their rapists were burglars first.*

As Sample and Bray (2003) argue, it is of great importance to note that burglary is not a "gateway" offense to sexual offending. It has been common for policy to utilize this assumption, which has resulted in the creation of sex offender registries and additional requirements (Harris et al., 2009; Sample and Bray, 2006; Harris and Hanson, 2004; Sample and Bray, 2003). However, current research suggests that many of those who commit these offenses vary in their criminal offending transitioning between property and personal, violent and nonviolent crimes (Sample and Bray, 2003). This heterogeneity within offending creates the illusion that burglary is a gateway to sexual offending; rather, burglary is just one of the many offenses that these individuals commit, including rape. Most important is that early research noted those descriptive characteristics, but few researchers gave attention to the relationship (see Pokuchek et al., 1997; Southey et al., 1994; Grubin and Gunn, 1990; Scully, 1990). At a comparative level, writing on New Zealand, Walsh et al. (2002) noted that 82% of violent offenders had prior convictions, with 56% of those having prior property crime offenses (p. 213). When Virginia implemented its point-of-arrest DNA collection program, it discovered that, within the 1,000 "hits" the system produced, 37% of the violent crime matches linked to offenders whose only previous convictions were property offenses (Murphy, 2006).

Currently, research suggests that new sex offenses are more likely to be committed by people with nonsexual offense histories or by people with no criminal history (Harris et al., 2009, p. 42). Likewise, in the sex offender recidivism research of Harris and Hanson (2004), the researchers state that "Most sexual offenders do not re-offend sexually over time ... this finding is contrary to some strongly held beliefs. After 15 years, 76% of sexual offenders had not been charged with, or convicted of, another sexual offense. The sample was sufficiently large that very strong contradictory evidence is necessary to substantially change these recidivism estimates" (p. 17).

Important within this subsection is the recognition that sex offenders, specifically those who commit rape, often have prior nonsexual offense histories, including burglary. While research has revealed that burglary is not a gateway offense, it suggests that for many of these offenders they do possess heterogeneity within their offending histories. Factoring in the results of both Hanson and Bussiere (1998) and Smallbone and Wortley (2004) that "adult sexual offenders are twice as likely to be convicted for nonsexual offenses as they are for sexual offenses, both before and after being convicted of a sexual offense" (as cited in Harris et al., 2009, p. 1), suggests that expanded processing within property crime scenes is advantageous toward early identification of sex offenders. The claim is predicated on the results of the Home Office (2005) report noting an 11% success rate in the recovery of evidence suitable for forensics within property crime scenes. Consider the following two cases as reported by Smith Alling Lane (2006):

> *"DNA match brings charges in 1994 St. Louis killing." Associated Press, September 6, 2006.*
>
> *In Missouri, a man already serving time for a burglary was charged in the 1994 rape and killing of a woman thanks to a cold hit on the DNA database. The 68-year-old grandmother was found raped and strangled in her bedroom with a vacuum cleaner cord. The DNA match came from seminal fluids recovered from the victim's body. The man's prior record includes convictions in 1997 and 1998 for burglary, tampering, and stealing credit cards.*
>
> *"Rape of Alameda woman". Contra Costa Times, September 12, 2006.*
>
> *In California, a cold hit on the DNA database has resulted in a guilty verdict for a 1995 rape. The victim was raped in her home after the man broke in for a burglary and was surprised to find her there. The man admitted to the crime when police approached him in prison. He now faces a sentence of up to 25 years in prison. He was initially included on the database due to a burglary conviction.*

Additionally, consider the recent case of the "Twilight Rapist," whose varied offending history underscores the brutality of his offenses. As reported by KWTX News 10 (2011), Billy Joe Harris, a Texas prison system employee, is alleged to be the rapist, linked to nearly 20 cases of home invasion, burglary, and sexual assault. The case summary as collated by KWTX News 10 (2011) is denoted below.

Case chronology:
January 21, 2009: Home invasion, rape in Yoakum
*February 27, 2009: Home invasion, rape in Yoakum *DNA*
July 3, 2009: Home burglary in Marquez (evidence recovered)
*July 20, 2009: Home invasion, rape Marquez *DNA*
August 14, 2009: Home invasion, rape Zabcikville (evidence recovered)
August 2009: Home burglary in Falls County
September 5, 2009: Home invasion and assault Marquez
*September 11, 2009: Home invasion, assault Bell County *DNA*
*October 10, 2009: Home invasion, rape Falls County *DNA*
October 24, 2009: Home invasion, assault, Centerville
*November 9, 2009: Home invasion, assault Yoakum *DNA*
November 24, 2009: Attempted home burglary Yoakum
November 24, 2009: Home invasion, fondling, Luling
December 24, 2009: Home burglary in Moody (evidence recovered)
March 1, 2010: Home invasion, assault, Moody
December 4, 2010: Home burglary in Edna (evidence recovered)
January 8, 2011: Attempted burglary Yoakum

While these are but a few cases indicating the link between property crimes and sexual assaults and arguably anecdotal at best, they are used as context to connect the academic literature suggesting heterogeneity or nonspecialization within many sexual offenders to the reality. From a property crime scene evidence perspective, consider the following case:

"DNA links man to 1992 rape," Miami Herald, June 11, 2008.

In Florida, a match through the DNA database led to an arrest in a 1992 kidnapping, rape, and armed sexual assault. The man had a criminal history for domestic battery and battery on an elderly person, and was in the convicted offender database from previous arrests. His DNA sample was matched with crime scene evidence.

(Smith Alling Lane, 2008a)

It is obvious to note that increasing forensics within property crime scenes is advantageous to improving clearance rates specific to property crimes. However, it should be added that increasing processing has proven a reliable method to increase detection of violent offenders (Roman et al., 2008). As noted prior, the movement to expand forensics within property crime scenes reflects the current trend within research noting that those most likely to commit sexual offenses are those with nonsexual offense histories or those with no criminal history

(Harris et al., 2009; Smallbone and Wortley, 2004). While sex offenders may specialize (pedophiles and child pornographers), recent research has revealed that this class of offender is versatile in their criminal behavior (Harris et al., 2009). These offenders are referred to as nonspecialized criminal offenders and their criminal histories vary across personal and property incidents. Understanding the current recidivism rates and offender patterns is an important element within expansion of genetic treatment. Currently, the misconceptions surrounding recidivism and offending patterns have fostered an attitude within the community that is misplaced and dangerous.

Intervening in Offending

A second benefit to expanded forensic analysis within property crime scenes is that of offending intervention. Early onset offending has been an ongoing and critical research topic within criminology; in fact, it was Moffitt's (1993) theory that would distinguish between early and late onset offending, denoting how those most likely to continue in their offending would reflect those who started early in their criminal behaviors. In fact, in their pinnacle study, Krohn et al. (2001), reviewing 19 criminal career studies conducted over the last half century, noted that early onset criminals committed between 40 to 70% more criminal acts than those who took up crime later in their life course (p. 92). In addition, these offenders were significantly more likely to develop into chronic criminals and display nonspecialization. DeLisi (2006) discovered similar results, noting how early onset offending (denoted by the age 14 years), was a significant predictor for chronicity, dangerousness, offending frequency, career span, and violence specialization (p. 24). While the research findings further validated the early onset offending and career criminality literature, an important discovery was the considerable delay in arrest for those early onset offenders.

As DeLisi (2006) noted, 62% of the habitual offenders were not arrested until age 18 and an additional 25% not until the age of 21. While DeLisi (2006) comments on a potential methodological issue within these rates (sample frame), it is important to highlight that the career burglary research conducted in the early 1980s (still considered valid) has supported the finding of lengthy careers by these offenders, originating from early onset offending (DeLisi, 2005; Peterson et al., 1980; Shannon, 1980; Collins, 1977). In fact, on average, the offending histories ranged from 98.8 (Visher, 1986) to a high of 204 burglaries per year, per offender (Chaiken and Chaiken, 1982).

Early interventions are an important first step in deterring further criminality, and while there are arguably several points of discussion within the desistance and treatment literature on the current effectiveness of interventions (see Pycroft and Gough, 2010), it is accurate to state that early and effective criminal justice intervention can have an influence on an offender's desistance from criminality (Skinner, 2010). However, in many of the crimes that these offenders engage in, specific to burglary and other property crimes, the likelihood of arrest is low and therefore there is less chance that this intervention can occur. Instead, many of these offenders continue to commit crimes, across various crime types, and increase their criminal capital (DeLisi, 2005). Recognizing that most burglary offenders are juveniles and young male adults, intervention in their offending histories by early detection is of vital importance (Cromwell et al., 1991). With the expansion of scene processing within property crime scenes, Webb et al. (2005) discovered that the average number of days from an active case to a solved case fell from 89 to 45.

The Name of the Game: Clearance Rates

Of interest within this literature on intervention and identification of violent offenders is the importance of clearance rates and timeliness of case resolutions. Clearance rates have remained a de facto unit of measurement within agencies, as the mechanism by which they evaluate performance and the public judges them. Predominately, clearance rates reflect at the violent crime level, and while there is no discounting the reality of how heinous these crimes truly are, it is of importance to highlight how beneficial expanding forensics within property crimes can truly be for an agency.

Historically, burglary offenses have maintained consistently low clearance rates, a factor of resource expenditures, low leads, and jaded investigators who see little benefit in solving these cases. Therefore, at a pragmatic level, what awaits agencies that expand their forensic testing into property crime cases? The answer is improved clearance rates. Research within the United Kingdom revealed that, within their DNA Expansion Program, with the recovery of forensic evidence, suspect identification occurred in 41% of cases (Asplen, 2004). Within New Zealand,

Walsh et al. (2002) highlighted resolution rates for burglaries containing forensic evidence at 24.8%. Those agencies that invested heavily within DNA databanks also witnessed the highest crime-to-person matching, at 42% (p. 212). In fact, the overall resolution rates increased from 14.3% to 17.2% and, demonstrating the importance of submission rates, if agencies were to increase burglary submissions by 10%, the national clearance rate would rise ~3% equating to 1,000 solved burglaries (p. 212). The results of the NIJ DNA experiment, as conducted by Roman et al. (2008), yielded identification rates of 31%, arrest rates of 16%, and conviction rates at 19%. Most important within these rates is that identifications, arrests, and convictions all doubled at the testing sites. These mirror by many accounts the results in the United Kingdom and New Zealand. Also of importance is the recognition that suspects identified through DNA forensics had more felony convictions than those identified conventionally (three times as many). While agencies may seem reluctant because of the media portrayal of these "trivial" crimes, consider these two news stories.

> *13. "Fast-Track DNA Thwarts Crooks." Birmingham Evening Mail, March 8, 2003.*
>
> *In an area of the UK, a new "fast tracking" of DNA evidence from property crimes is slashing the time it takes for DNA analysis to just seven days. Operation Safer Homes is a forcewide initiative to tackle house burglary, and many burglars are winding up in jail only days after committing the crime. Year-to-date figures show that since April offenses have fallen by almost 15 per cent compared to the same period last year, from 29,098 to 24,796 break-ins, leading to 4,302 fewer victims.*
>
> ***(Smith Alling Lane, 2003)***

> *25. "Burglary DNA Project Update." Denver District Attorney and Denver Police Department Joint News Release, June 10, 2007.*
>
> *Denver's participation in a federal study regarding use of DNA in property crimes is showing significant dividends. The project has identified over 40 prolific burglars since the project started November 1, 2005. (A prolific burglar commits an average of 243 cases per year.) For burglary cases where DNA is recovered, the prosecution rate is 5 times higher than cases without DNA. The average sentence for burglars linked to DNA is over 12 years in prison (compared to 6 months without DNA evidence). In a recent case, after police arrested one man – who later admitted to over 1000 burglaries – the burglary rate in the neighborhood dropped about 40%.*
>
> ***(Smith Alling Lane, 2007)***

Recognizing that there are clear benefits to expanding evidence collection within property crimes scenes, it is important to highlight how common evidence remains at crime scenes. While most research depicts the 11% recovery rate as noted by the Home Office (2005), it is important to recognize that in the DNA Field Experiment, offenders with prior felony arrests were significantly more likely to leave evidence behind at a scene. Factoring in that many of the offenders are young, nonspecialized (therefore lacking knowledge of how to avoid detection), and are unfamiliar with DNA, it is quite common for DNA evidence to be left at a scene. Therefore it is important to highlight a few cases demonstrating how common evidence is discovered in these incidents. Consider the following cases as reported by Smith Alling Lane:

> *"Chicken bones traced to burglary suspect." The Times, January 6, 2008.*
>
> *In Kansas City, Missouri, DNA evidence left on chicken bones at a burglary scene have now been matched with a man who was already serving time in a Kansas jail on an unrelated crime using the national DNA database. Investigators at the scene found chewed-up chicken scattered around the residence – leftovers authorities believe were stolen from a refrigerator at the earlier burglary. The suspect had stolen firearms from several different residences. He has 16 prior felony convictions for second-degree burglary, stealing, tampering, receiving stolen property, automobile theft and resisting arrest.*
>
> ***(Smith Alling Lane, 2008b)***

> *"Man charged in church burglary after DNA match." The Associated Press State & Local Wire, November 18, 2004.*
>
> *In Wisconsin, a man has been charged with a church burglary after a cold hit on the DNA database. Authorities say they matched his DNA with some recovered from a saliva-laced cigarette butt found at the scene. The church building is a smoke-free facility. Investigators say they had no suspect in mind when the butt was sent to the crime lab last winter, and a suspect in the church break-in probably would not have been found without the DNA match.*
>
> ***(Smith Alling Lane, 2004a)***

> *"Street Beat: Burglary Suspect's Modus Operandi: Snacking, Entering." The Oregonian, November 16, 2004.*
>
> *In Oregon, police detectives arrested a sixth member of the so-called "Dirt Crew," a ragtag cast of men suspected of burglarizing some 120 East Portland homes during the summer. While burglarizing homes, the man helped himself to whatever was in the cupboards, leaving his DNA on unfinished food and soda cans. Bio-evidence from cigarette butts left at several houses tied the other five suspects to the burglaries, he says. In fact, it appears they were behind scores of other break-ins that had gone unsolved. The total number of burglaries is edging toward 150. Investigators also uncovered DNA samples that don't belong to the current gang of suspects. "There could be some more arrests coming."*
>
> ***(Smith Alling Lane, 2004a)***

"Fruit Snack Snares A Burglar." Daily Post (Liverpool), August 23, 2005.

In England, a man who took a bite out of a pear during a burglary was caught after his DNA was found on the fruit. The man was given a 12 month suspended sentence after admitting burglary. DNA analysis of the remains proved the suspect had been in the house.

(Smith Alling Lane, 2005)

"Prolific Burglar Jailed For Four Years." Express & Echo (Exeter), January 22, 2004.

In England, a prolific burglar who admitted raiding 17 homes in three counties and stealing £20,000 of property has been jailed for four years. The court heard that the 18-year-old was caught after police found his DNA on a carton of apple juice at the scene of a burglary.

(Smith Alling Lane, 2004b)

"DNA link to burglaries 2 years on." Canberra Times, July 27, 2004. In Australia, a man, whose DNA was traced to the scene of seven burglaries nearly two years after they were committed, has appeared before the Supreme Court. The man has pleaded guilty to the burglary of seven commercial premises committed between March 2001 and July 2002 but he was not charged until this year. It was not until advances in DNA technology, coupled with the fact that DNA samples were taken from the man after his arrest in 2003, that police were able to link him to the earlier offences. On different occasions, blood stains, a cigarette butt, part of a latex glove, and a partial fingerprint were all left behind.

(Smith Alling Lane, 2004c)

While but a series of news accounts, these cases again demonstrate how common DNA can be recovered at burglary crime scenes. Likewise, as DNA is recovered and processed, it becomes engrained as a standard operating procedure to be included when suitable evidence is detected. As described above, there are clear improvements within clearance rates, but that is not the only factor that influences decision-making. Arguably, the factor most commonly reported as limiting DNA forensic analysis is that of costs and while the costs of testing are discussed in-depth in Chapter 3, it should again be noted that in comparison, the cost of crime significantly outweighs the financial burden placed upon the agency that processes forensic evidence within these crime scenes.

Clearance Rates and Costs: The Pursuit of the Bottom Line

As reported by Kleiman (2009), currently, the police receive 60% of the overall criminal justice budget in the United States, which was $200 billion (p. 27). The reality is that the police receive a considerable allocation but the bulk of the costs reflect in personnel costs and equipment upkeep. From a forensic perspective, only a few studies have attempted to estimate the cost of processing and until recently, few provided updated estimates concerning the cost of crime. With the economic recession and hiring reductions that have occurred, it is important to highlight the costs of processing and the costs of crime to demonstrate how the pursuit of evidence processing within property crime scenes clearly fits within the "bottom line" mentality.

As McCollister et al. (2010) and Kleiman (2009) point out, the cost of crime runs to trillions of dollars. To demonstrate the "bottom line" to the police, it is important to recognize the politicalization of technology inclusion within the police service. As Garland (2001) and others have discussed, politics drives policy, and as denoted within this literature review, there have been considerable resources allocated to DNA forensic testing and analysis.

To frame this for an agency, in what is the crudest but most effective visual way, consider that in the most recent cost estimates for crime, McCollister et al. (2010) denote the tangible and intangible[1] cost of burglary at $6,170 and $321 (p. 104). In 2009, there were 2,199,125 burglaries as reported by the UCR (Federal Bureau of Investigation, 2009), and using the conservative estimate of 11% of property crime cases yielding DNA evidence suitable for testing, there were potentially 241,904 burglary cases containing DNA evidence suitable for collection. The total tangible and intangible costs of burglary exceeds $14,210,745,750 as calculated by the total reported incidents of burglary and the reported cost estimates of McCollister et al. (2010) of $6,462. To further break down those rates using the McCollister et al. (2010) victim cost rates of $1,362, the total cost of burglary to victims in 2009 was $2,995,208,250. It is important to note that this rate reflects tangible costs; the intangible costs (risk of homicide costs) would add another $705,919,125. The calculated criminal justice system costs include costs at the federal, state, and local levels reflecting police, prosecution, legal and adjudication, and corrections costs. According to McCollister et al. (2010), these costs were $4,127, resulting in $9,075,788,875 in criminal justice system costs. See Figure 4.3.

[1]According to McCollister et al. (2010), tangible costs include crime victim, criminal justice system, and crime career costs; intangible costs include pain and suffering and risk of homicide costs.

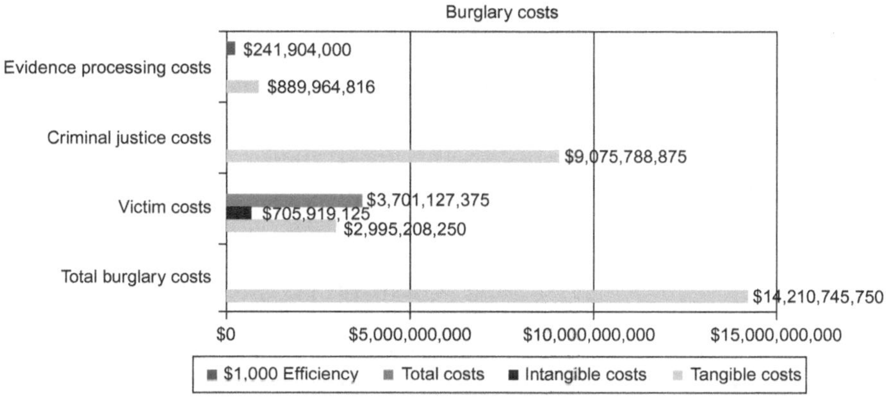

Figure 4.3 Burglary costs.

Factoring in the DNA costs at the most efficient level as reported by Roman et al. (2009) of $3,679 and the 11% forensic evidence recovery rate, reported by the Home Office. (2005), would suggest that the total costs of processing DNA evidence within property crime scenes is $889,964,816. It is reasonable to conclude that what Roman et al. (2009) state in their analysis into property crime scene high volume processing is entirely accurate; "*It is probably fair to characterize spending $3,679 to arrest a burglary suspect who would otherwise never have been caught, and who averages three prior felony convictions, as a small cost*" (p. 365).

As depicted in Figure 4.3, the costs of evidence processing are significantly lower than the costs that victims incur. The reality of the costs of crime are often lost to visual depictions, but consider the victim whose house is burglarized and who then feels apprehensive in their home, which should confer comfort and security. The loss of a few thousand dollars pales in comparison to the loss of security and the unfortunate reality that in approximately 88% of the cases, there will not be a successful resolution to the case. The formatting of the chart was specifically selected to highlight the uncomfortable reality that the cost of processing forensic evidence within property crime scenes is arguably not that expensive. As Ashikhmin et al. (n.d.) noted in their report, the pilot program produced a cost saving of more than $5 million in police costs and $36.8 million in property loss resulting from the expansion in processing of forensic evidence within property crime scenes. To further demonstrate a point, the costs incurred as a result of the activities of an average burglar with an offending history of ~100 incidents per year

(Visher, 1986), would result in a financial impact of $638,445. The fact that most juveniles can go undetected for several years before a criminal justice intervention demonstrates the potential financial impact a single offender has on the system. In addition, as noted in the section above, many of these offenders do not specialize, so their offending will transition from property and personal, violent and nonviolent, which significantly increases their financial cost to the system.

Improving evidence processing within property crime scenes clearly improves clearance rates and is financially sustainable in that it has the potential to intervene early in offending and improve clearance rates within unsolved cases. As the cost of processing samples decreases, through the inclusion of robotic platforms and improved detection and information sharing, and assuming a similar processing cost of $1,000 as noted for sexual assault kits, the cost of evidence processing while maintaining the 11% forensic recovery rates would cost $241,904,000 per year. While this is a considerable amount of resource expenditure, it pales in comparison to the $14,210,745,750 that burglary costs to society.

DNA Concerns and Legal Challenges

Originally, there existed considerable challenges, but as discussed in Chapter 3, the current legal climate supports the collection of DNA at property crime scenes. However, it should be carefully remembered that victim consent should be sought. From an offender's perspective, there is no expectation of privacy concerning samples recovered from a crime scene. That is to say that if they drink from a glass at the home, flick a cigarette to the ground, or spit on the sidewalk, they have provided that to the public and have no expectation of privacy. However, the expansion of forensic evidence processing and the associated challenges have an impact at a legal, ethical, and practical level.

STATUTES OF LIMITATIONS AND PROPERTY CRIME

Despite federal authorization and funding, and states supporting the collection of forensic evidence and database expansions, statutes of limitations have not kept up with expanded forensic protocol (Lynch et al., 2008). Specific to property crime scene statutes of limitations, the statute may expire in 5 years or, as Lynch et al. (2008) note, in some states the statute may extend until 10 years if the offender(s) is unknown or it may be as little as 3 years. The reliance upon and use of property crime scene processing exists to improve clearance rates but also to improve hits for prior unsolved or "cold cases." As discussed prior, it is common for evidence without a suspect to sit for more than 180 days before it is processed. In addition, as later detailed within the IPA interview of the rural Alabama agency, this was common practice for cases of this type.

To overcome these limitations, agencies and prosecutors have returned to a legal loophole known historically as a "John Doe" warrant or more commonly today as a CODIS warrant. While unconventional, the application of this type of warrant freezes the case in time. In essence, the DNA of the individual is charged with perpetrating the crime. Subsequently, when a match occurs, the clock restarts. California became the first state in 2000 to employ the tactic within a sexual assault case (Lynch et al., 2008). While little research exists to analyze the utilization of these warrants, anecdotal information suggests utilization of this practice when the state legislature has not modified statutes of limitations to account for DNA forensics.

Daubert Standard

Of importance within this standard is when the DNA is not accepted as admissible evidence. The court has upheld a unanimous viewpoint that DNA forensics is a valid and reliable scientific technique, supported by its conclusive strength and universal acceptance as a scientific principle. However, where the standard becomes a challenge is the expansion of the police role to collect scientific evidence. While Roman et al. (2008) highlighted that officers were equally capable of collecting forensic evidence from crime scenes, as compared to civilian forensic technicians, what remains unclear is how the court or that of the jury will view the officer as a suitable "expert."

The Daubert Standard reflects the evaluation of expert witness testimony. When evaluating testimony the court looks to two prongs of admissibility:

1. Relevancy prong: The expert's evidence must fit the facts of the case.
2. Reliability prong: The expert must have derived his or her conclusions from the scientific method.

While officers have become quite proficient at collecting fingerprints, studies have not been able to answer whether the decision of the court or jury is influenced by whether the officer or the forensic expert collects the evidence (when contamination is incredibly easy) or by situations where an officer undertakes the in-house lab facility analysis. Easily met is the relevancy prong, but the ability for an officer to meet the reliability prong concerning forensic evidence may pose a challenge.

The means to overtake this challenge have been ongoing but what remains unclear is how much of the knowledge and training disseminates to agencies and officers. As described earlier, there is a federal training curriculum on property crime scene evidence processing, which most certainly could be expanded and modified to meet basic forensic evidence collection certification criteria. However, as detailed in the Conclusion, the movement to collapse the responsibility of investigation and evidence collection to a single person may prove a complicated venture.

Ethical Dilemmas

While there are clear benefits to the agency, there are most certainly aspects within the expansion of DNA evidence that prove worrying at an ethical level. Arguably the most outspoken on the expansion of DNA evidence is the ACLU (2009) issuing multiple statements concerning the expansion, retention, and potential issues involved within forensic evidence. The ACLU argues that continued expansion is just one step closer to a national DNA database of all citizens. The organization has been very outspoken in ensuring that DNA evidence from rape cases is processed efficiently, but are highly critical of expansions within the arrestee levels. Certainly, it could be argued that the expansion of DNA collection to the arrestee level is cause for alarm. As Ford (2009) reports in an examination into police practice, a perception has to come to exist offering that police within the United Kingdom arrest and release individuals with the sole intention of collecting DNA for future comparisons. While no research has examined this practice within the United States, the potential for this practice is concerning to groups like the ACLU.

To connect this to crime scene processing, the success of scene processing is dependent on the amount and type of individuals within the system. While match rates will decrease as the system further builds the offender pool, the focus on arrestee leveling processing will aid in improving scene match rates (Goulka et al., 2010). Agencies that are efficient at offender and arrestee level processing and those more forensically active (submitting more scene profiles) will see a larger return on their investment (Walsh et al., 2002).

Joining the ACLU (2009) perspective, Simoncelli (2006) offers that the expansion of DNA databases (and by proxy evidence collection practices) is a reckless venture and one that ought to be resisted on matters of principle, legality, and practicality (p. 390). While writing from the perspective of DNA sampling from all persons (National DNA Registry), Simoncelli (2006) notes a diminishing return for the police service. She focuses on two primary points: social and financial costs. From a practical perspective, Simoncelli (2006) notes that the current DNA database process has disproportionately highlighted increasing the number of persons in the database, which arguably has created an imbalanced database. To increase the number of "hits" within the system, it is important to increase the inclusion of scene samples (Goulka et al., 2010). A second point offered by Simoncelli (2005) is that the recovery of property crime scene DNA is an exhausting and painstaking process. Noting statements from the Chief of Investigation of the Denver Police Department, the author claims that only 8% of burglaries can be investigated using DNA gathered from the crime scene (p. 392). However, as discussed earlier in this book, this claim would prove false based on the results of the DNA Field Experiment. In fact, one finding of the research was that, when properly trained, the quality of scene samples was nearly identical between civilian forensic technicians and sworn personnel. This was also noted by Bond et al. (2008) in their analysis of the value of DNA material recovered from crime scenes. When officers are properly trained, the collection of evidence is neither exhausting nor a painstaking process.

Despite research later refuting many of the points of critique offered by Simoncelli (2006) within her analysis specific to the police service, the author does offer one specific point that lends itself well to this research. Currently, the collection practices have come to highlight offender and arrestee DNA sampling, which has overburdened crime laboratories. While it is vital to match offenders to current samples, it is of equal importance to ensure that scene samples are processed to link offenders to their prior crimes (Goulka et al., 2010).

In times of financial constraints and with an ever-present focus on the status of the backlog, some states have made what could be considered dramatic changes in their policies to streamline costs. Arguably, a controversial adaptation to reduce overall costs is the decision to transition the financial burden of processing from the state to that of the offender or potentially even the victim.

SHIFTING THE BURDEN

Survey research conducted by the Interstate Commission for Adult Offender Supervision (2005) noted several state requirements that placed the financial burden on those convicted of crime. For example, the obligation within Arkansas, Pennsylvania, and South Carolina requires offenders to pay a $250 DNA sample fee (Interstate Commission for Adult Offender Supervision, 2005). The highest fee imposed on an offender was in Hawaii at $500 (Interstate Commission for Adult Offender Supervision, 2005). Additional research undertaken by the North Carolina Office of State Budget and Management (2006) discovered that several states utilize fees and surcharges to offset the costs for DNA processing. As noted in the ICAOS (2005) research, the most common fee assessed for convicted offenders was $250. However, Kansas, Idaho, and Hawaii all included fees of $400 or above and Arizona, Florida, and North Dakota levied fees for the actual cost of the forensic testing (Office of State Budget and Management, 2006). As states face financial burdens and continued pressure to expand processing across the arrestee and crime scene levels, it is important to note that in many of these instances, those most likely to be arrested are also those most likely to be unable to pay, returning the financial burden to the state. In the pursuit of expanded forensic practice, it would seem logical to transfer the burden to those convicted of crimes. However, it seems illogical to extend burden on those arrested for an offense.

At a practical level there is a real cost associated with the expansion of forensics and while there has existed a movement to transition the burden to offenders and arrestees, it should be noted that it is feasible to assume that victims may share in the burden. It was not long ago that stories emerged of rape victims being billed to cover the costs, or partial costs, of their sexual assault kits. If property crime scene processing becomes routine and the success rates increase, it is possible that the cost of testing could be transferred in whole or part to victims or, slightly more damaging, to a new insurance industry that is dedicated to testing, which is an entirely different argument and an equally important cause for concern.

CONCLUSION

By combining the forensic science literature and that of the criminal justice system with that of the relationship between technology, policing, and the investigative process, this book provides a framework to examine how the expansion of forensic evidence processing within property crime scenes is both beneficial and warranted, while understanding the potential for misuse. Horvath and Meesig (1996) offered that, "*the police criminal investigation process has remained relatively unaffected by the significant changes that have occurred in policing, the crime problem and technology in the past thirty years*" (p. 108). However, the most recent literature, including comparative research, suggests there has been a significant change in the investigative process. Agencies continue to look for ways to modernize. While such modernization may only exist as symbolic capital (Manning, 1992), there exists a clear movement to incorporate forensic practice into the investigative process at a standard operating procedure level.

In addition, while the movement to expand such processing may only reflect the politicalization of the technology, its politicalization may in fact ensure its success. The benefits to an organization (and that of a politician in support of such expansion) are clear. An agency can expect to see better clearance rates and improvements within their "cold hit" programs, and there is a very minor deterrence application ($< \sim 1-2\%$). In addition, the media is increasingly highlighting the importance of using DNA to identify the most heinous criminals from seemingly unfamiliar sources (property crime scenes) (see Smith Alling Lane's collation of news stories, www.dnaresource.com, for example).

Furthermore, there exists a clear practical benefit, supported by the underlying forensic science literature. To expand into property crime scenes is to improve policing. There exists a considerable scene processing backlog and cases where evidence remains uncollected and unanalyzed. While this book's literature review has provided the source of these backlogs and the evolution within technology to overcome these issues, there still exists an "unknown" within the literature. Research has demonstrated the cost benefits, agency benefits, and political benefits (and dangers). However, to date, no scholar has examined the current state of property crime scene processing and the factors associated with the decision to collect and process this evidence.

In the following chapter, I will explain the methodology utilized to answer these two specific questions to better understand the state of forensic crime scene processing and the decision-making process. It is the intent of the survey method used to highlight the experiences of officers. As Lipsky (1980) states, officers are your policy implementers. It seems appropriate to speak with officers, survey officers, and involve officers in the discussion and identify the factors that influence *their* decision to collect and process evidence. If only at a practical level, this book will be able to highlight *if* there has been a dissemination of knowledge concerning the benefits of DNA forensic evidence to the officers on the streets. In what has been millions of dollars spent to study the practice, it would prove advantageous to understand if any diffusion has occurred. Likewise, it would be valuable to understand the influence of additional *external* stakeholders within the investigative process. The following chapter highlights the methodology undertaken to provide a "holistic" view of evidence processing within property crime scenes to complete an analysis that peers into the "black box" of police agency and crime laboratory evidence processing (i.e., decision-making).

CHAPTER 5

Collecting Genetic Forensic Evidence

Gary Jenkins
Chief of Police, Pullman Police Department, Pullman, WA

> *I think we can move forward when we get the portable DNA machines, which will be great when we look at the work going on down at [Removed] and to have this will make it. The main issue is the time lag, YEA we got a suspect after a year identified, it does not really help us then...*
>
> **Forensic Technician**

Genetic evidence is also referred to as biological evidence, items that contain biological material. Biological material includes tissue, bones, teeth, blood, semen, or other bodily fluids, and items containing such material. The proper collection, handling, and storage of biological evidence is critical. Contamination or degradation of the material can render it useless for evidence and identification purposes. Anyone handling genetic evidence should follow well-defined best practices. Even those not directly handling genetic evidence must have situational awareness to avoid evidence contamination. The crime scene, or any area where biological evidence is located, must be protected from people and elements that could cause contamination of the evidence.

The manner in which biological evidence is packaged and stored is critically important. In most cases, DNA is best preserved in an air-dried, water-free environment. Water can cause degradation of DNA as well as facilitate the growth of yeast, mold, and bacteria. Best practices of biological material much of the time calls for storage in containers and packaging that are not air-tight so the items can dry and not be susceptible to degradation. This does not apply to all DNA related evidence; blood and urine samples collected in vials from persons are obvious exceptions. Once packaged and submitted by the collecting personnel, evidence should be stored in a secure location accessible only to personnel authorized to handle evidence after submission. Any transfer of custody and opening or breaking the evidence seal must be properly documented to maintain a proper "chain of custody" required for all potential evidence. Chain of custody refers to the documentation of custody, control, transfer, analysis, and disposition of evidence.

The environmental conditions during storage are also important considerations that affect the ability to prevent degradation and to safeguard the integrity of the evidence. Storage conditions must protect biological materials from sunlight, excessive heat, and moisture. No samples should be allowed to remain in direct sunlight or a hot environment, such as the trunk of a car in warm weather (which can easily occur immediately after collection at a crime scene). Also, depending on the specific type of material, storage may require temperature-controlled areas, refrigerators, and freezers. A temperature-controlled area is defined as one where the temperature is maintained thermostatically between 15.5°C and 24°C (60°F to 75°F) with less than 60% humidity.

I will provide a description of collection and storage methods for a few of the most common items of genetic evidence collected by law enforcement. While the specific collection details may vary from agency to agency, and some of the procedural details I describe here are specific to my agency, agencies should follow recognized best practices to ensure evidence integrity.

BUCCAL SWABS

Buccal swabs are collected from persons for DNA profile comparison. The sample could be from a potential suspect or it could be an elimination sample from a victim, a police officer who may have contributed DNA to the scene, a witness at the scene, etc. This is also the collection method utilized to comply with state mandated collection. The equipment needed includes two cotton-tipped applicators (our agency uses approximately 6-inch applicators), two drying and storage boxes, a pair of nitrile or latex gloves, and a surgical-type mask. Agencies may also receive collection kits directly from their state and/or crime lab for the purpose of collecting state-mandated buccal swabs. The person collecting the sample (who will be referred to as "officer" from here on out) wears the mask and gloves to avoid contaminating the sample with his or her own DNA. The officer opens the sealed, sterile cotton-tipped applicator two-pack at the stick end. The subject is directed to remove the applicator from the package and swab the inside of his/her cheek for 15 seconds. The subject is then directed to place the used applicator in the drying/storage box. The other applicator is placed unused in a separate drying/storage box as the control sample. Both drying/storage boxes are marked with the subject's name, case number, and "subject sample" or "control" as appropriate. The sample and control applicators in their respective boxes are placed in paper bags, sealed with evidence tape, and assigned separate evidence barcode numbers as the officer logs them into the evidence tracking system. The officer submits the evidence to the property officer via locking evidence lockers. Items are stored in a temperature-controlled environment in the evidence storage area of the property room until such time as they are sent to the lab or authorized for disposal.

SEXUAL ASSAULT EXAMINATION KIT (SAEK)

SAEKs are used to collect biological evidence from sexual assault victims, and may also be used to collect evidence from sexual assault suspects. The SAEK is approved by the crime lab that will be conducting the tests and potentially providing testimony in court. Collection of evidence for a SAEK is always done by medical personnel per established guidelines using instructions that accompany the kit. Upon completion of the examination, the kit and any other evidence, such as clothing that was worn during or immediately after a sexual assault, is transferred to the custody of a police officer. The officer returns the kit to the police department for further processing. The kit and any other evidence is sealed with evidence tape and assigned separate evidence barcode numbers as the officer logs them into the evidence tracking system. The officer submits the evidence to the property officer via locking evidence lockers. Items are stored in a temperature-controlled environment in the evidence storage area of the property room until such time as they are sent to the lab or authorized for disposal.

BLOOD SWABS

This procedure is valid for wet or dry blood, and for other wet or dry liquids. The equipment needed includes cotton-tipped applicators (our agency uses approximately 6-inch applicators), drying and storage box(es), a pair of nitrile or latex gloves for each sample to be collected, surgical-type mask, sealed container of distilled water, disposable coveralls, and head and foot covers as appropriate. The officer dons the coveralls and head and foot covers to prevent contamination of the intended samples. The sealed, sterile cotton-tipped applicator two-pack is opened at the stick end. The cotton tip of the applicator is prepared by wetting the cotton tip of the applicator with distilled water without touching the swab to the water container. This should be done by simply pouring a drop of water on the tip of the applicator. The tip of the applicator is applied to the blood to be collected and rolled to saturate the tip. The applicator is placed in a swab-drying box, and the box is closed and marked with the appropriate identifiers. The second swab from the previously opened package is used as a control. It is wetted in the same manner as the first swab then rubbed on a location in the vicinity of the blood that has not been contaminated by blood. The second swab is then packaged in a separate container and identified appropriately. If an uncontaminated area of the surface bearing the evidence sample cannot be located, the control swab should be left unaltered and packaged as previously stated.

The location of each sample collected should be documented in detail. Each blood spot sample requires use of a fresh swab and fresh gloves. All samples should be immediately secured in a temperature-controlled environment. The evidence should be transported to the police department as soon as practical. The items will be placed in a locking evidence locker to air dry for several days prior to being sealed by the collecting officer. The swabs are placed in separate paper bags and the bags are sealed with evidence tape and assigned separate evidence barcode numbers as the officer logs them into the evidence tracking system. The officer submits the evidence to the property officer via the locking evidence lockers. Items are stored in the temperature-controlled environment of the general evidence storage area of the property room until such time as they are sent to the lab or authorized for disposal.

WEARER SAMPLES (ITEMS WORN BY A PERSON)

Wearer samples consist of items that have been worn by someone whose DNA profiling is desired, i.e., clothing, jewelry, etc. The equipment needed includes a pair of nitrile or latex gloves for each item to be collected, surgical-type mask, disposable coveralls, head and foot covers as appropriate, and new, appropriately sized paper or cardboard containers. The officer dons the coveralls and head and foot covers to prevent contamination of the intended samples. Using the listed equipment, the collecting officer packages each item of evidence separately. The collecting officer should handle only one exposed item of evidence at a time and should change gloves after handling each item before handling another item to avoid cross contamination. Items of evidence should not be allowed to touch one another to avoid cross contamination. All samples should be immediately secured in a temperature-controlled environment. The evidence should be transported to the police department as soon as practical. The items should be placed in a locked evidence locker to air dry, if necessary, for several days prior to being sealed by the collecting officer. Again, separation of items being dried should be done in a manner as to prevent cross contamination or contamination from a previously processed item of DNA evidence. When dry, the items are placed in separate paper bags and the bags are sealed with evidence tape and assigned separate evidence barcode numbers as the officer logs them into the evidence tracking system. If the specific location of DNA on a particular piece of clothing is critical to prosecution of the case, the item should be folded with clean "butcher" paper separating the folds to avoid cross contamination to various areas of the item. The officer submits the evidence to the property officer via the locking evidence lockers. Items are stored in the temperature-controlled environment of the general evidence storage area of the property room until such time as they are sent to the lab or authorized for disposal.

TOUCH SAMPLES (ITEMS TOUCHED BY A PERSON)

Examples of "touch" samples include firearms evidence (bullets, magazines, cartridge cases, and firearms), swabs collected from firearms evidence, and samples collected from public or high-use surfaces. Touch DNA samples are collected in the same manner as blood or clothing samples depending on the item touched and the circumstances.

CONCLUSION

As stated above, the protocols described here reflect those of a single agency. Protocols will differ from agency to agency. For example, property officers or crime scene technicians may perform follow-up procedures on wet items after they have dried, rather than the initial collecting police officer. However, the basic handling procedures to prevent contamination and preserve the integrity of the evidence should be universally followed. Biological evidence is considered a biohazard and must be disposed of accordingly. Our agency contracts with a medical waste management company for disposal of biohazards.

Each crime lab will differ in their criteria for acceptance of evidence for DNA profiling. The state crime lab that conducts tests for my current agency will not routinely accept touch samples. The lab's position is that touch samples rarely provide interpretable or CODIS-eligible profiles. The lab does make exceptions with proper justification, such as cases involving violent crimes. The crime lab does also allow requests for expedited testing. When officers submit evidence and immediate analysis is required, the officer will submit a special lab request form to provide justification to the lab. This would be applicable, for example, if a suspect is in custody and the evidence is critical to determine identity.

Each agency and crime lab has its own requirements and protocols for getting evidence to and from the lab. The district or prosecuting attorney should have a hand in reviewing those protocols to ensure that they meet the legal requirements required in criminal proceedings. Agencies must properly account for evidence from collection through final disposition. The importance of maintaining a "chain of custody" cannot be overstated.

A document offering recommended best practices for the collection, examination, tracking, packaging, storing, and disposition of biological evidence at a national level is *The Biological Evidence Preservation Handbook: Best Practices for Evidence Handlers*, a publication of the Office of Law Enforcement Standards, the National Institute of Standards and Technology, and the National Institute of Justice, April 2013 (available at http://dx.doi.org/10.6028/NIST.IR.7928).

CHAPTER 6

Research Methodology

Is this helping you at all?

Focus Group

It seems customary to preface this section by acknowledging that some may skip this chapter, though I would urge any reader, specifically one who has made it this far into the work to understand the methods undertaken, to see the interrelationship between theory, research, and practice. In many regards, the methods section is one of the more important chapters of this work, as the discussion on the relative strengths and weaknesses of each of the selected methods is discussed. Far too often in books, the research methods are written in an abstract manner, often relegated to a few endnotes. While some works are seemingly able to undertake this strategy, this work includes interviews, a focus group, and a national survey; three methods that alone could be relegated to a brief section or across several end notes. However, as each method is built upon the inherent weaknesses of the others and enhanced each other method's strength, it is imperative that the research methods be fully detailed, so that the data collection techniques can be replicated by other academics or by practitioners in the field looking to better understand and improve their own forensic practices.

In order to reveal the status of forensic crime scene processing, specific to property crime scene evidence, and the factors that influence an officer's decision to collect and process evidence, the research incorporated three sources of data collection. The methods incorporate a quantitative component, including a national survey of police officers, and a qualitative component, including personal interviews with police officers and external stakeholders within the investigative process. These data sources were designed to answer two primary questions: (1) How routine is property crime scene forensics within the United States and (2) What external, organizational, and internal factors influence an officer's decision to process forensic evidence discovered at a property crime scene?

Developing a suitable sampling frame using officers proved rather challenging considering the reduction in financial assistance provided to researchers. However, with the generous assistance of the Southern Police Institute and Alabama Association of Chiefs of Police (AACOP), a suitable frame was identified and with a reduced sample size, it became increasingly important to include additional research methodologies. To answer the two primary research questions, triangulation was incorporated via survey research, open-ended questions, and interviews. This mixed methodology approach relies upon both quantitative and qualitative data sources to explore the status of property crime scene evidence processing and the associated decision-making factors. While the quantitative component would provide the "hard data" concerning the rates of property crime scene processing, it was not suitable alone to peer into the "black box" that is officer decision-making (Strom and Hickman, 2010). For this reason, interviews proved invaluable sources to understand these multifaceted influences.

Prior to the research being undertaken, an expedited approval was sought from the Washington State University Institutional Review Board. Consent was obtained from each participant within the study across the survey research and personal interviews. While consent was obtained, it is important to highlight that no personal or agency specific identifiers were included within the survey to ensure confidentiality and anonymity. When names are used, they have been altered, as forensic evidence collection has become a considerable topic of interest within the media and to understand the state of forensics and more importantly the decision-making process, it was important to provide anonymity within the research project.

DESIGN OVERVIEW

Traditionally, research within the investigative processes specific to forensic evidence has come to rely upon describing the state of processing, the creation of backlogs, the forensic laboratories, or undertaking an analysis into high-level crime incidents (i.e., sexual assault and homicide). However, even within the current research, few studies seek to involve officers and their experience and perceptions to highlight factors that influence their decision to process forensic evidence. Recognizing this limitation, it became apparent that there exists a wealth of information to inform the inclusion of forensic science within the investigative process. However, specific to property crime incidents, there were few studies that sought to involve officers as their primary sample to elicit their perspective on forensics within property crime scenes.

The Theory behind a Mixed-Method Design

As defined by Creswell (2009), "Mixed methods research is a research design (or methodology) in which the researcher collects, analyzes, and mixes (integrates or connects) both quantitative and qualitative data in a single study or a multiphase program of inquiry." As a methodology, mixed-method designs are not a new paradigm. Discussions on the approach can be noted as far back as the late 1950s, when Campbell and Fiske (1959) demonstrated the use of multiple research methods to validate findings. Later coined *triangulation* (Webb et al., 1966), the method is designed to minimize error to strengthen the confidence of the findings. Through incorporation of multiple research methods to study a single problem, a mixed-method design produces complementary strengths with non-overlapping weaknesses (Johnson et al., 2007), which enables a researcher to minimize error by collecting data from the same source but through different methodological designs. Denzin (1978) referred to this as a *between-methods* triangulation relying upon the inherent value of both the quantitative and the qualitative, while accounting for the weaknesses within each. As Creswell (2009) notes within his discussion of mixed methods as the "gold standard" of research designs, its explanatory power relies upon the understanding that neither a quantitative or a qualitative approach can solely understand a problem or explain a phenomenon. Johnson et al. (2007) view mixed-method research as a powerful third paradigm that "often will provide the most informative, complete, balanced, and useful research results" (p. 129). When undertaken and feasible, this research paradigm provides superior research findings and outcomes (Johnson et al., 2007, p. 129).

To identify accurately the status of property crime scene forensics and the factors that influence an officer's decision to process such evidence, it became clear that while quantitative data would prove invaluable to assess the "rates," understanding the factors associated with decision-making would require speaking with officers and allowing officers to express those factors through a dialogue with the interviewer. What follows is a detailed overview of the sampling frames, sample size, methods selected, and the modes of data collection.

Sampling Frame

The sampling frame consists of officers who registered for courses at the Southern Police Institute (SPI) and those of their respective agencies. Under ideal circumstances, a true national random sample would have been preferred. However, the fiscal reality of such a design was unattainable. The decision to utilize the SPI as a sample frame originated from experience working for the prior director of the institute,

Dr. William Walsh and current director Dr. Tad Hughes (chair of my graduate committee). During my tenure with the institute as a researcher, I was able to interact with officers completing the training curriculum and noted that they were diverse in location, and SPI has records dating back to the start of the training program.

The original database contained over 10,000 email addresses. While it was extremely exciting to have the potential to undertake one of the first large-scale police surveys using email requests and an internet survey modality, there was no feasible way to ascertain which email addresses were still valid. Unlike traditional mail surveys, it is not practical to determine if an address is still valid beyond "failed to deliver" notifications, which only reflect if the email address has been turned off at the server level. It is entirely likely that an email address could deliver the survey but the respondent could no longer have access to the email address (i.e., departed the agency).

To overcome this limitation, it was decided to select a period comprising the last 5 years and to select only those who enrolled at the institute. This strategy reflected the belief that those most recent emails and those who enrolled and therefore received email communications from SPI would be the most likely to still be valid. This consolidation brought the original list of potential respondents with email addresses down to 4,677, reflecting those who both enrolled at the institute and possessed a complete email address. Duplicates were removed from the sample, leaving 4,354 potential respondents.

Following the distribution of the first wave of participation requests, it was discovered that nearly 1,400 emails were undeliverable, indicating addresses that were no longer active. This was concerning, as only those emails received in the last 5 years were selected and only from those who enrolled in and completed SPI courses. The implications of this were profound in that over 25% of the potential respondents were no longer active at their respective agencies. Moreover, nearly 60 of the emails were auto-returned indicating the respondent was "deployed" and was not at the agency, suggesting a new point of contact. In these cases, those individuals were removed from the total sample. Following the first wave and subsequent removal of invalid e-mail addresses on the second and third waves of participation requests, the final sample contained 2,893, indicating a final sample of 66% of the original sample. There were 460 completed surveys returned, producing a response rate of 16%.

Delivery Mode

The decision to utilize the internet as the primary delivery mode reflected the fiscal reality of what a mail distribution mode would cost. While not the primary choice of survey distribution, the internet has proven to yield adequate response rates (Dillman et al., 2009). The internet survey delivery system Remark was utilized for the research project.

To improve response rate and reduce the four sources of survey error (sampling, coverage, measurement, and nonresponse), Dillman's (2000) Tailored Design Method (TDM) was incorporated into the the survey when applicable. The TDM method suggests a three-email contact strategy involving initial email invitation and two follow-up emails. The SPI sample frame incorporated the TDM approach.

Quantitative Method: Survey Research

The survey instrument incorporated a mixed-method approach utilizing closed-ended and open-ended question formats, cognitive recall, and appreciative inquiry to facilitate obtaining accurate information (Dillman et al., 2009; Dillman, 2000). Portions of the survey were modified from the PERF DNA Survey (Griswold, 2011). A central theme in this research and the guiding research question is the internal and external factors that influence an officer's decision to process forensic evidence within property crime scenes. To understand the factors, it was highly important that respondents be motivated to participate. To improve response rates and minimize response error, the questions were designed to reduce any potentially biased statements and anonymity was maintained to minimize issues of social desirability (Dillman et al., 2009). What follows is a detailed explanation of the survey mode.

The questionnaire format included four category items comprising 37 questions: agency information, lab information, officer perspective, and general information. The determination of the category items, partially based upon the PERF DNA Survey and valuable input from police colleagues, supported the development of the survey instrument. A pilot test of the survey was carried out on a series of police officers, former and current chiefs of police, and two committee members who all provided valuable contributions and helped identify unfamiliar answer choices and assisted in the creation of additional questions, including officer familiarity with CODIS warrants. Below is a summary of the survey categories and question content.

Agency Information (12 Closed-Ended Questions)

The determination to lead the survey with agency information would seek to determine the experience the agency has with forensics. Questions within this subsection highlight the familiarity of the agency with DNA forensics, its utilization of the forensic analysis specific to property crime scenes, current forensic policy, and sources of any potential backlogs. Prior research would suggest that agencies with more familiarity with forensic analysis and more integration of the practice into the agency would be more likely to expand evidence collection into property crime scenes.

Lab Information (3 Closed-Ended Questions)

While brief, the purpose of this subsection was to determine who performs DNA analysis for the agency, the accessibility of the facility, and the quality of the interaction and communication between the agency and the forensic lab. As a primary stakeholder, it became important to understand the relationship between officers and the facilities that they utilized as prior research had indicated the lab as a source of influence.

Officer Perspective (10 Closed-Ended Questions and 1 Open-Ended Question)

The questions within this subsection specifically focus upon the officer's experience and that of the factors that influence their decisions. Themes within the subsection include: current utilization of forensic evidence, the officer's perspectives on the expansion of forensic collection, benefits of forensic analysis specific to property crime scenes, an analysis into challenges of forensic analysis at a practical level (training, crime scene contamination, identification of evidence, etc.), influence of stakeholders, factors associated with the decision to collect evidence (modified from Strom and Hickman, 2010), and lastly the familiarity the officer has with the *DNA Field Experiment: Cost-Effectiveness Analysis of the Use of DNA in the Investigation of High-Volume Crime*. Each question was designed specifically to understand decision-making while accounting for financial constraints. This section measures cultural, organizational, institutional, and personal factors associated with the officer's decision to collect and process forensic evidence. The open-ended question attempts to identify incidents where the collection of property crime scene evidence could have prevented a subsequent violent crime. This was a later addition to the survey, originating from an interview with an officer who discussed how a case had influenced him to be more active in collecting forensic evidence at these crime scenes. The use of the open-ended question at the end of the subsection includes elements of appreciative inquiry to improve response rates. While open-ended questions yield lower response rates then closed-ended questions (Dillman et al., 2009), framing the question by recognizing the knowledge only the respondent has and its importance is highly likely to increase participation (Whitney and Trosten-Bloom, 2003).

General Information (11 Closed-Ended Questions)
This subsection contains general questions concerning the respondent's demographics (age, gender, education level, and years of service) and that of the agency, including agency type, size, state, and specific questions on the make-up and social class of the community that agency serves.

Statistical Analysis

The intended purpose of the study is to be descriptive in nature. While the survey results could certainly be used to predict police officers' evidence collection intentions, this would put the "cart before the horse." Currently, few research projects have sought to focus specifically on the factors that influence an officer's decision to process DNA forensic evidence. While historical research provides some factors, few studies within DNA forensic evidence have sought to collect and collate those influences. After careful discussion with several committee members, the decision was made that the study should be used to inform policy makers, to move forward the discussion within the expansion of forensic analysis, and to identify additional factors through the mixed-method design. If an entire set of influences were identified, and it is the intention of this book to illuminate many of those influences, the research results would assist future studies. Therefore, the focal emphasis on the statistical analysis is to *describe* the state of forensic analysis within property crime scenes and *identify* the factors that influence an officer's decision to collect evidence.

Quantitative Method: Interviews

This data source consists of interviews with police officers, police executives, forensic experts, and prosecutors. The interviews use an open-ended, semi-structured conversation technique, allowing the participant's first-hand knowledge to become a focal point of the conversation. The sampling strategy utilized within this data source comprised purposive sampling and snowball sampling. In combination, I was able to develop an interview sample comprising all stakeholders within the investigative process from across the United States.

Interpretative Phenomenological Analysis

The guiding philosophy within the qualitative component was to understand the perception of officers and additional stakeholders within the investigative process. Moreover, it was important to examine the relationship between high-volume forensics and its influence within the investigative process. The decision to utilize interpretative phenomenological analysis (IPA) as the guiding qualitative method was to tap into the participants' knowledge, to highlight their perceptions, cognition, experiences, and most importantly the personal accounts (Smith and Osborn, 2003). IPA acknowledges that experience is a combination of cognition and perception and to understand a phenomenon it is vital to allow the participants' experience to frame the study. Within IPA, there is no theory to frame the interviews nor is there a predetermined hypothesis (Smith and Osborn, 2003). Through the interviews, a set of themes will emerge. These themes allow for a pragmatic approach to understanding the phenomenon. As Smith and Osborn (2003) state, the power of IPA is reflected in the ability for the researcher and reader to take into account their own experiences (personal and professional), the findings of the research, and the current literature to better understand the phenomenon. As the intent of this research was to offer a pragmatic examination of the state of forensic analysis for an intended audience of practitioners and policy makers, IPA provided a unique methodical approach. While the utilization of this method within criminal justice has been limited, it is increasingly used where ethnographic research is not suitable and a more rigorous and in-depth analysis is preferred. Smith and Marshall (2007) undertook the method when examining barriers to effective treatment for street-level prostitutes. Most recently, McLean and Marshall (2010) examined police officers' perspectives of mental health issues and services.

As the sample frame utilized purposive sampling, IPA affords a researcher to undertake an in-depth examination while maintaining a practical application. That is to say, IPA does not require a large sample size nor does it establish a minimum sample size. IPA is bound to the participants and most importantly to those who agree to be included and therefore attempts to acquire the entire range of experience the participant holds (Smith and Osborn, 2003). In this regard, IPA sacrifices breadth for depth (Smith and Osborn, 2003). However, the thematic expression of what the qualitative study reveals via IPA can produce a detailed analysis, rich with exploratory and explanatory power. At a practical level, IPA includes a specific methodology for interviews that includes guidelines, methods, and techniques to assure that any findings may be supported through the interview process.

Interview Sample and Summary of Interview Process

Recruitment of participants occurred through two primary paths: participant requests within the AACOP newsletter and snowball sampling originating from current contacts. While IPA does not require a minimum sample size, the reasonableness associated with attempting a large sample can overwhelm a researcher who is new to the method (Smith and Osborn, 2003). I made the decision that the sample size would reflect the current recommendation by Smith and Osborn (2003) for early practitioners within IPA, a sample size of three for each stakeholder. As prior research noted that officer decision-making is not reserved to the agency, additional stakeholders were included within the interviews. The final interview sample included the following: Police Officers ($n = 3$), Police Executives ($n = 3$), Prosecutors ($n = 3$), Forensic Experts ($n = 3$). In concert, the perspectives of those within the investigative process reflect a moderate sample size for IPA ($n = 12$) (Smith and Osborn, 2003).

As discussed prior, forensic analysis is currently a "hot media topic," so to improve reliability and facilitate more meaningful dialogue with participants, I assigned each participant a pseudonym. Pseudonyms were assigned according to the position of the individual. For example, Forensic Expert #1 became Frank, Police Officer #1 became Powell, and this continued for each participant within the project. Table 6.1 provides the background information of each participant.

While there is no set collection method, the recommended approach is a semi-structured interview with one or two broad questions to develop a two-way dialogue and establish an early rapport with the participant (Smith and Osborn, 2003). It is important to note that the interview is not an interrogation, but the purpose is to maximize the opportunity for the participant to express his or her expertise

Table 6.1 Participant Overview

Participant Name	Role	Gender	Agency Type	Years of Service	Higher Education
Powell	Police officer (detective)	Male	Large urban	20+	Graduate
Patton	Police officer	Male	Medium suburban	10+	Graduate
Paul	Police officer (detective)	Male	Large urban	20+	Graduate
Larry	Police executive	Male	Small rural	20+	Graduate
Lars	Police executive	Male	Medium suburban	20+	Graduate
Lee	Police executive	Male	Large urban	20+	Graduate
Frank	Forensic expert	Male	Large urban	20+	Professional
Fenton	Forensic expert	Male	Small rural	2	Graduate
Fred	Forensic expert	Male	Large urban	16	Graduate
Patricia	Prosecutor	Female	Large urban	20	Professional
Patty	Prosecutor	Female	Large urban	21	Professional
Parker	Prosecutor	Female	Medium suburban	10	Professional

(Smith and Osborn, 2003). In developing the questions, it is important that they be neutral, avoiding jargon or assumptions of technical proficiency, and developed to facilitate an in-depth examination of the participant's experience (Smith and Osborn, 2003). While open-ended questions are preferred, the use of closed questions is acceptable if the intent and context are to engage the participant to continue with the dialogue (Smith and Osborn, 2003). What follows are the questions used for each of the participants. All interviews began with a statement of confidentiality and anonymity and a general question concerning a participant's background.

Police Officer

- Can you walk me through a typical property crime scene call?
- Under what circumstances would you make the determination to collect DNA evidence?
- What do you think of the recent developments to expand evidence processing within property crime scenes?
- As a police officer, where do you believe you are most influenced to process forensics evidence at a property crime scene?

Police Executive

- What is your outlook on forensic analysis within property crime scenes?
- What do you think of the current focus to expand property crime scene forensic testing?
- How can we improve forensic analysis within property crime scenes at the agency level?
- What do you think of the recommendation that officers collect forensic evidence?
- (*If needed*) Do you believe your officers are prepared to collect evidence or should they be responsible for evidence collection?

Prosecutor

- How influential is your department in having forensic analysis completed (*Follow-up: Property Crime Scenes*)?
- How do you believe the expansion of forensic analysis into property crime will affect your department?
- What do you foresee as potential benefits or consequences in such an expansion?

Forensic Experts

- What changes do you believe are necessary to expand forensic analysis into property crime scenes as a routine investigative practice?

On average, each interview ranged between 45 minutes to an hour, with the longest interview exceeding 2 hours with a Police Executive whose agency was very familiar with DNA forensics and wanted to share their innovations and their challenges. All interviews occurred over the phone or via Skype at a time requested by the participant.

Analysis of the Interviews

The interview process included a transcription of each session completed during the interview, as it was not feasible or authorized by participants to have a digital recording of the interview. Under ideal circumstances, it is preferred within IPA to have a recording to which you can listen and identify themes (Smith and Osborn, 2003). However, in speaking with several participants during selection, many requested not to be recorded. The most common response was that some of what they would discuss could be viewed negatively if identified back to their agency. For example, Lee discussed an innovation within the agency that rewarded officers for collecting forensic evidence at a scene, which was an innovation even the higher command staff was unaware of and if it became public knowledge, they would face considerable scrutiny.

As their expertise was invaluable to the study, and because it was a condition of their inclusion into the research, the decision was made not to record the interviews, which proved to be a challenging venture. Following the first interview, it became apparent that a noise-canceling headset would be vital to the success of the interviews, or at the least muting and unmuting the phone to reduce the background noise of the keyboard. During the first interview transcription, the participant would pause and ask if I was able to get that, or would seek confirmation, if only to see if I was following along. I suspect this was a result of the clicking sound of the keyboard, which was distracting them. Following the first interview, I transitioned to a Bluetooth headset, with noise canceling technology, which seemed to eliminate the issue during subsequent interviews.

Expressing Themes

Smith and Osborn (2003) provide a framework for IPA, which involves reading the transcript closely and multiple times to become familiar with the participant's account. Through multiple readings, additional themes may become identified, which may be identified by the structure of the participants' answers (how they answered the question) or the use of code switching within the dialog they used. For example, during one interview, a forensic expert and former police officer would transition between speaking as a scientist (objective), to recounting cases and the importance of expanding forensic evidence into property crime scenes because of the cases he worked and seeing victimization firsthand. With each read, I became more familiar with the experiences of the participants and how they viewed the expansion of forensic evidence and the factors that influence their collection practices.

Following transcription of the interviews and collation within AnSWR, thematic analysis occurred, which was then input into Microsoft Excel. The resulting analysis produced long lists of themes, from which I was able to cluster many of the themes to create superordinate themes. Of importance in the thematic expression is that the first stage of analysis involves creating concise phrases from the text and the secondary analysis produces abstraction of the phrases, which can be expressed as themes. Take the following analysis of "Frank," the forensic expert.

> **Interviewer:** What do you think of the current state of forensics?
> **Frank:** What we have right now is just not working, we are inundated with evidence and bogged down in testing marijuana (pause) . . . they keep sending us evidence, want us to travel 1–2 days to testify, and then expect us to be on call to collect evidence. Then we are blamed when a mistake happens. We need a smarter process in place.

In the analysis, I noted frustration, lack of control over time management, frustration with the internal (organizational goals and values) and external (political, police agency, and prosecutorial) pressures on prioritization, and directed anger. In concert with the additional analysis, I was able to express two major themes reflecting the current literature: Overburdened Crime Labs and Ineffective Forensic Process. Of importance is that within the analysis, the entire text becomes data, but it is not expected that each sentence will generate a theme. The clusters that form and the themes that emerge are interpretative in relation to the researcher, which requires that the researcher continue to return to the transcript to ensure that what becomes expressed reflects the true intentions of the participant. Once the phrases are clustered and the themes identified, it becomes possible to create superordinate themes. These reflect as top-level themes or "global themes."

In what is likely more familiar to a criminal justice reader is the analytical process of thematic networks. Attride-Stirling (2001) offers a set of analytical tools to aid qualitative researchers, which enables a researcher to create web-like illustrations, expressing the findings of the researcher by leveraging the themes discovered during the interviews. As Attride-Stirling (2001) notes, the development of the thematic network begins by identifying basic themes, moves to organizing themes, and then becomes a global theme. Important within the model is that many global themes may result (p. 389). Of importance within the structure depicted is that the basic themes may connect with additional organizing themes, which are then expressed into global themes. By using this approach, the researcher is able to provide a very detailed and visual depiction of the interviews.

LIMITATIONS OF DESIGN STUDY

As of 2008, there were 18,000 state and local police agencies. The final sample (removing incomplete surveys) yielded 441 surveys. At the 95%

confident level, this research produces a margin of error of approximately 4.6%. The use of the mixed-method design provides ample explanatory power to reduce the weakness within this quantitative component. Ideally, a true national random sample would have been preferred, distributed via mail, and incorporating TDM (Dillman et al., 2009). However, that design was unattainable and the intended design does incorporate a mixed-method approach to address the obvious weaknesses within the quantitative and qualitative measurements.

In addition, some critics could offer that there is an official source of data on the status of property crime scene processing within the CODIS funding program. Any agency that receives federal funding is required to provide statistics concerning DNA collection, including the number of items pertaining to property crime scenes. While this would provide strong support for the status of evidence collection, it would have reduced generalizability in that only agencies that receive funding are required to submit reports. Likewise, data collection of this type would also miss those agencies that collect but do not process evidence, "simulating evidence collection."[1]

The use of IPA, while important, is a potential source of concern. It was not possible to record interviews, and while transcription did occur, it very often involved shorthand to keep pace with the participants. Thematic expression could be limited because of the nuances missed within the speech patterns and specific use of certain words. For example, during one interview, a police officer would use the word complainant, if then only to correct the term with citizen (never using the word victim). In reviewing the transcription of the interview, I would have missed this had I not noticed it during the interview and specifically highlighted it as an important element. The purpose of any research is to be valid and reliable, and specific to the qualitative component, it should establish trustworthiness, resulting in credibility, transferability, dependability, and confirmability (Lincoln and Guba, 1985).

The recommendation to ensure credibility is to allow participants to review the transcripts or notes of the researcher for verification (Lincoln and Guba, 1985). While this is a suitable method to increase credibility of the findings, I found it limiting in that aspects of social

[1]The practice of simulating evidence collection is discussed in Chapter 8 within the findings section.

desirability could certainly influence participants' analysis of the dictations that had occurred. That is to say, in reading their interview they may deem a line of answers as possibly being something they ought not to have said. As an alternative, during the interviews, I would notice key statements that reflected the literature or emerging themes and would state them to the participant for confirmation. Initially, this was challenging. However, as the interviews progressed and I became more familiar with the interview process and themes expressed, it became easier to verify that the participants expressed those specific themes.

Transferability relates to the generalizability of the participant's selection; in other words, will the sample transfer to other similar populations? As this research utilized purposive sampling, a component of transferability (Lincoln and Guba, 1985), the sample includes officers from across the United States, reflecting different agency sizes, a wide range of experience, and educational backgrounds. The one limiting factor within transferability is the limited participation by females within the research. Ideally, it would have been preferred to have two females and two males participate within the interviews across each stakeholder category to ascertain if gender influences an officer's decision to collect evidence within the scenes.

Dependability and conformability are interrelated concepts, wherein dependability examines the process of inquiry and confirmability examines the validity of the findings (Lincoln and Guba, 1985). While mutually exclusive, these concepts are interrelated and can be confirmed with a rigorous assessment process (Schwardt et al., 2007). To that end, it was important to use a debriefer. A committee member was selected as the debriefer, because of her familiarity with the IPA process. Following interviews, a discussion would occur concerning how the themes were identified and the process of expression was validated. Furthermore, the interviews were conducted before the results of the national survey were analyzed. This was a purposeful decision to remove any potential for interpretations to be influenced by the results of the survey.

Despite incorporating three methods of analysis, it is important to highlight that there are limitations and potential sources of error. It is the intent of the mixed-method design to overcome these potential weaknesses and enhance the reliability and validity of the study through convergence of the data. Further validation would be reinforced through the officer survey and the detailed IPA interviews. In this manner, there is always a cross validation of the findings. If the survey research denotes little influence by the prosecutor's office concerning forensic analysis, and all participants reflect this, it can be said that the prosecutor has limited influence on an officer's decision to collect evidence. Likewise, when there is a divergence within one or all of the modes, it is important to understand how the divergence could occur.

CONCLUSION

This chapter discusses the methods undertaken, the rationale, and the potential limitations of the study design. In writing this chapter, I became quickly aware that no study is perfect. It is not feasible to design a perfect study, as there are always going to be sources of error or perceived weaknesses. The goal of research is to select the design best suited to answer the question. As I reflect on the study design, I recognize the inherent power of the mixed-method paradigm. The use of this method has great explanatory and exploratory power, but does require considerable knowledge and expertise to bridge the methods into a powerful research design and to interpret the findings across three modes. The decision to incorporate these two overlapping methods will offer insight into the current state of forensic evidence processing pertaining to property crime scenes and the factors that influence officer decision-making. Additionally, this research offers policy makers a straightforward approach in which to design and implement changes to improve their forensic practices.

CHAPTER 7

Research Findings

> *We used to have a 24-hour crime scene tech – those positions went away – now normal duty hours and on call – if they do not believe they [the expert officer] can process it they ask the tech. One of the major issues for us is the budget, we have two budgets criminal investigative division and patrol division – CSI comes from CID – so what happens is that there may not be any more overtime budget for the month, which can limit sending out a tech even when they are needed. [Me: Does it really get that bad?] Got so bad, we had an officer who had to use a box of Qtips, unopened, to collect blood because no one was available.*
>
> **Police Executive**

The purpose of this chapter is to report the results of the national survey and stakeholder interviews. This chapter is subdivided into three areas. The first section provides the detailed analysis of the stakeholder interviews, analyzed with interpretative phenomenological analysis. This information is presented first to establish the factors that influence an officer's decision to process or ability of a stakeholder to influence evidence collection within property crime scenes and provide context for the national survey results, which are presented later. Moreover, this process will greatly assist the reader in better understanding the presentation of the thematic tables with specific context originating from the interview synopsis. The second section describes the results of the national survey. Section three collates the findings of the qualitative interviews and quantitative survey results into a mixed-method presentation of the findings to indicate areas of interaction and disconnect in what was reported. The relative strength of those factors emerging are then said to be highly influential when reported across both methods or exploratory when expressed within only one method.

STAKEHOLDER INTERVIEW RESULTS

As described within the methods section, the 15 interviews were conducted across the investigative stakeholder continuum, comprising patrol officers and detectives, police executives, forensic experts and technicians, and prosecutors. The analysis of the results utilized interpretative phenomenological analysis (IPA). As the direct benefits of IPA were explained in the preceding chapters, it is important to denote that the following analysis does not contain the complete transcripts as compiled. The raw interview material contains information that would allow identification of the individual, and presentation of information in this manner is not a suitable vehicle to inform the decision-making process and subsequent influence on police officers. I write each interview in such a way as to help the reader to understand the organizing and global themes. The utilization of block quotes stresses important themes and a guiding narrative complements the expression of the global and organizing themes.

To assist in the presentation of the organizing and global themes, section one is subdivided into four areas reflecting each of the investigative stakeholders: police officer, police executive, forensic expert, and prosecutor. Each subsection then contains the interview synopsis with direct quotes from the interviews and ends with a thematic table containing the influences as expressed by each stakeholder. It is important to again note that each person interviewed is given a pseudonym and any specific information that could reveal the person's identity has been removed. This decision proved incredibly important, as discussed later in the interviews, as an incentive program discussed below would subject the officer and agency to considerable scrutiny and criticism in how they have introduced innovations to improve forensic evidence collection. Moreover, it was discovered that some agencies, even with clear and viable forensic evidence, were greatly inhibited from collecting evidence at property crime scenes. What follows are the interview summaries, thematic tables, and expression of unique themes.

Police Officer Interviews

The officers interviewed reflected a broad range of agency types and years of service. The minimum education for any of the officers was an undergraduate degree and the highest reflected a graduate degree (Masters of Science or Masters of Art). All officers interviewed were male and held positions as patrol officers or detectives within each organization. Table 7.1 provides the participants' information.

Powell: Detective

Powell possesses a considerable degree of familiarity with genetic evidence. He has been an officer in a large urban agency for the past

Table 7.1 Police Officer Participant Information

Participant Name	Role	Gender	Agency Type	Years of Service	Higher Education
Powell	Police officer (detective)	Male	Large urban	20+	Graduate
Patton	Police officer	Male	Medium suburban	10+	Graduate
Paul	Police officer (detective)	Male	Large urban	20+	Graduate

20 years, and currently is a detective within the special investigations division. Powell had responded to an open interview request with a high degree of eagerness to participate. From our first interaction, it was clear that Powell would provide a wealth of insight into the topic reflected in his candidness on his organization and most importantly their forensic policy. The agency that Powell works for has an engrained standard operating procedure that requires the collection of forensic evidence when present at a scene. I was immediately intrigued by what prompted this policy and the excerpt below provides a backdrop to their high utilization of genetic evidence in property crime cases.

> *The policy began with an incident involving one of our officers, while off-duty and on the way to an ATM, he was robbed at gun point and taken to their car. As they shoved him into the car, he was able to get his weapon and shoot one of the individuals, both escaped. Blood was collected at the scene, it was processed, but there was no hit. Years later, we continued to check for a hit and we received a hit in the system two states over. The individual was arrested on a marijuana charge and apparently they require that DNA is collected. He was extradited, charged with robbery and attempted murder, and from that moment on we have been collecting and processing forensic evidence and adjusted our policy.*

As Powell described the incident, there was a clear sense of how the incident had influenced the other officers. However, incorporating what is a complete forensic collection protocol within the agency's standard operating procedure (SOP) certainly must have faced some resistance. As budgets are certainly on the minds of the administrators, I had asked if there was any resistance within the organization, and Powell stated, "*Money is always tight, but this was one of our own; the entire organization was behind the transition.*"

After explaining the policy, I had inquired about the process. Powell explains the process for a typical property crime call.

> *Because evidence collection is routine, the responding officer will make a decision if there is suitable evidence and if there is, he will call out an evidence technician, which can be either an on-duty officer or a civilian, we use both. If the evidence is viable, it is collected and processed.*

With a SOP-centered collection practice, Powell does not believe that victims or the prosecutor have any influence on the decision to collect evidence. Rather, they look internally and expect processing to occur in cases. The following excerpt reflects this sentiment.

> *If the officer is not calling out an ET for evidence collection often, I want to know why. Maybe he is not trained how to identify evidence or properly assess the quality of a sample, but if there is evidence the expectation is a full forensic response.*

With clearly high utilization of forensic collection and processing within property crime scenes, I inquired about the costs of processing. Powell jokingly responded that "*there is always a cost; you just have to ask yourself if it is worth it.*" To Powell, the agency had very poor hit rates or success rates with DNA evidence within property crime scenes, but that was unimportant. According to Powell, "*you play the odds; we collect now, in hopes that it helps us later.*"

With marked use of the practice, the funding to support it, and the institutional buy-in within the organization, it became clear that the next level of discussion would need to highlight the forensic lab. With marked utilization and routine practice, Powell had noted, "*It is not uncommon to shut down a house*" for processing. The process could take 30 minutes to a few hours, wherein the evidence technician would process the entire scene looking for viable samples, collecting those samples, and then processing those samples. Of importance within how Powell describes the agency's collection practice and his perception of the benefits, is the reality that the agency has the benefit of having an in-house facility that is capable of processing a multitude of forensic evidence, including traditional physical forensic evidence and computer forensic evidence.

Despite the clear utilization of this evidence type and the routine collection practice, there had to be a limiting factor, some factor that inhibited the decision to collect evidence at these scenes. It seems within the agency, training and the reality of patrol work become the primary inhibitors. The following excerpt provides some insight into this issue.

> *We have the resources to process scenes, what we have to continue to improve is recognizing evidence.... I just had an officer responding to a robbery at a convenience store that did not collect the big gulp cup that the person threw as they ran. We continue to see these things happen when the responding officer either overlooks evidence or as it commonly happens is trying to get to the next call in the queue.*

At this level, training to identify viable evidence is incredibly important. Despite the agency possessing considerable resources (funding, in-house lab, available evidence technicians) one of the limitations is clearly training as Powell states, "*If they cannot identify it, it does us no good to have this policy.*" This is an important point because the decision to collect then becomes considerably reliant on not the resources of the agency but rather the ability for an officer to recognize what is viable evidence quickly, and to then call out the evidence technician for collection. Additionally, Powell had noted that there is pressure on the responding officer to take the report, do a quick assessment, and then move on to the next call in the queue. Most important is that this pressure originated not from administrators, but within the patrol officers. Powell expressed this rather succinctly, "*Someone else is covering your calls when you are stuck at the scene waiting on the ET* [Evidence Technician]."

As I concluded the interview with Powell, I had inquired on the challenges that agencies and cities will face as forensics aligns towards high volume processing within police agencies beyond violent crime. Powell offered this final point, "*It* [the expansion of forensics into property crime scenes] *is great for the agency but the outcome for the system not certain, I look at it this way, why limit police effectiveness, to reduce strain on the system.*"

Summarizing the interview with Powell, the wealth of insight and reality that the agency has a SOP-centered collection practice is phenomenal. However, despite all of the resources, there are intrinsic influences affecting the officer's decision to collect. The reality of police work and pressures to "share the load" of calls does influence an officer. Additionally, officers who lack training on identification may miss important evidence and the expectation of full forensics means that if an officer is not using the evidence technician at calls, the question becomes, "*why*." It became equally feasible that officers would collect evidence aware that its viability would be quite low to ensure that they were actively pursuing forensic evidence. This is a point of contention acknowledged by the forensic experts.

Patton: Patrol Officer

Patton is the former Chief of Police of a midsize agency, and current part-time patrol officer with a tri-county consolidated agency. Patton had transitioned into the part-time position as he pursued his PhD. The current department that Patton works for is comprised of three overlapping city agencies that consolidated resources to reduce costs, which includes an interoperability agreement allowing officers to effect arrests in any of the three jurisdictions. As a result, there are approximately 10 officers on at a time. While consolidation was not uncommon to hear about, I was interested specifically in how consolidation could influence forensic practice; the following excerpt provides details in this area.

> *The consolidation was a bit of a mess, there was a lot of inconsistencies, policy that had to change as we were basically becoming a single department, when it comes to our forensic policy, the standards had to become uniform across agencies, meaning our training, procedures, and policy all had to become singular. You can't have one officer doing one thing and another doing something else, agreeing on policy was important and that had some influence on our current [forensic] practice.*

With the consolidation, the agency lost access to a dedicated crime scene person. Moreover, through consolidation the agencies lost considerable resource allocations, which required going to the state for evidence collection. Patton expressed some frustration at this level.

> *The state would take hours to come out to collect evidence, even fingerprints, and it was ridiculous. You could have an officer on the scene for hours waiting for a person to come out, so I trained a person to collect evidence and it saved officer time to tie them up on the scene. [Me: You trained them?] Yea, I am trained through the state on forensic evidence collection and back when I was a Chief, I would send my officers out to classes through the state MTU [multiple training units].*

As Patton explained, it became too frustrating for everyone involved to rely upon the state; they had lost resources, were covering what are three overlapping jurisdictions, and were entirely reliant on the state for collection and processing of evidence. This was further complicated by the reality that often a state technician would be sent not from the local district but from the closest district with an available technician. This could result in extended delays and was even more frustrating because as Patton describes, "*We have a good working relationship with our district facility, they get back to us on our evidence but we do have to wait, which is just what happens with the amount of evidence they see daily, it is not uncommon to wait a few months for evidence to be processed.*"

As was common in the interviews, the reality of a backlog was ever present. However, as Patton noted, the backlog had little influence over whether they collected evidence at a property crime scene. Once the officers were trained and certified on basic evidence collection, they were able to process basic scenes like burglaries and car thefts, but in cases where it was a violent crime or a large scene with multiple samples, policy dictated that they would call the state facility for processing. As Patton explains, "*We have to be cautious because of the defense, we are qualified to collect evidence but I am not certain we are qualified enough to meet the standards the defense would likely argue in a high profile case.*"

As the interview continued, the conversation turned to victims and their influence on the officer's decision to collect evidence, specifically those victims of property crime scenes. According to Patton, the victim became their primary influence. The following excerpt depicts just how influential victims can be on the process.

> *The CSI effect has seen a tendency for . . . callers (Patton then changed the word to* complainants, *then changed the word again to* citizens*) to want to collect evidence. In the 90s we would look around for obvious evidence. . . . and tell them "if we hear anything we will contact you" – noting what was done at the point. CSI came around and they [victims] believed we could do anything, solve anything, catch everyone, and it came expected to do the basics. Let me back up, we had to do the rudimentary to appease the citizen (. . .* complainant*). I did basic evidence collection and then I took a class on fingerprinting. When we went through the class, the instructor said, "If all else throw some dust around, to dust a little bit, for some PR. It is about pacifying them, they expect for evidence to be processed at the scene. Smaller communities almost need that community satisfaction component. Larger agencies do not need them. The gap is so small between the access to city government, so at a small agency we have to process and make sure the citizens are satisfied. WE [emphasis intended] have no buffer."*

The influence of victims on the process was something other stakeholders had expressed. However, Patton presented it from a uniquely different perspective, in that for most of the officers, the collection of evidence or in many cases, the simulation of evidence collected became necessary to appease victims. However, Patton offered additional points on genetic evidence and the decision to collect evidence as noted in the following excerpt.

> *There is really no meaningful benefit thus far. Let me qualify that, we are not seeing any better hit rates, but it is the threat that comes with the physical proof, and is the best way to get them to crack. We use the threat of the evidence as a tool, we say "How long do you think it will take for the crime lab to link this to you?" and in our state lying in the course of any offense class is another felony and we get to charge them the cost of crime lab work. It also helps that these guys have no idea what we can do with technology, I shouldn't tell you this but we had an officer a while back put a man's hand on the top of the photocopy, told the man it was a lie detector, and he confessed. The belief is that the crime lab can do almost anything – CSI perpetuates this myth that the science can do anything. The gap between what the average citizen has and the actual practitioners is immense, forensics is almost like magic. When you tell someone that it is only a matter of time before forensics can solve this, it is the magic that it will link them and it is expensive so we tell them that we will charge them for the forensics or they can confess now and I can stop the paperwork, and they will confess because they will pay the bill to process the forensics.*

In summarizing my interview with Patton, I was reminded of the practical reality of what forensics provides. While it can be incredibly important at a national level (CODIS), pragmatically it is but a tool and officers will adapt to the tool and leverage the asymmetric knowledge difference. As officers became trained, they were more likely to collect evidence. Moreover, their decision to collect evidence at a property crime scene would reflect any pressure from victims or the perceived expectation to collect evidence. In the end, the agency had increased its collection and processing of forensic evidence within property crime scenes. However, there was no perceived benefit to the expansion, as of yet, beyond community satisfaction and ability to leverage forensic evidence knowledge to assist in a confession.

Paul: Detective

Paul has a combined experience of over 30 years, is currently a detective in a large, metropolitan agency, and is nearing retirement. We sat down early one morning to discuss the state of forensics within his agency and the associated influences on an officer's decision to collect evidence. It was apparent immediately that Paul possessed considerable experience and familiarity with genetic evidence as he immediately identified the current limitations preventing his agency from pursuing property crime evidence processing.

> *Being honest, a large issue for us is prioritization, we devote forensic resources to serious personal crime, and then there is the issue that we have no one to go out and collect and process – budget is an issue, there's no money to investigate the case or send out an evidence tech. In some instances, we take property calls over the phone.*

As Paul continued to describe the state of forensics within the agency and the state, he had noted how recently two regional crime labs had closed, which had a significant impact on staffing and as a result, his agency had to fall back on the county for collection and processing. While this meant there was a closer facility to work with, it also incurred higher backlogs as a result of lack of proper staffing, equipment, and in many cases training. While this was not a new addition to the research, it proved to open up another line of discussion that had not been discussed prior in any interview; not every county has a lab, so a single county lab can serve multiple agencies, which creates considerable problems as the following excerpt expresses.

> *We have very fragmented police departments across the state, everyone treats forensics different. A statewide policy is lacking, we need one. The larger cities have the resources, the labs, and when you look at what the smaller agencies have it is like two worlds, if you are not in a large city agency, it seems impossible, when you really think about the pay, there is a real disparity in pay and expectations [Me: In what regard?] Grant money is available but the training is highly apprenticeship based and there is a backlog on evidence technicians becoming qualified. Our evidence technicians are civilians but then you get into the politics of it all, we wanted to hire a tech early this year, the money is there for officers, tougher to get money for non-sworn, we ended up with a few new officers and no tech.*

As I expressed the themes of the interview on subsequent reads of the transcript, there was an unfortunate reality; the political payout was greater for hiring more officers versus more evidence technicians. In talking with Paul, he offered that much of it came down to what they reflected, "*When you have an officer on the street, it says something to the community.*" Moreover, as Paul described, evidence technicians are viewed as costly.

This relationship between access to a technician and use of that technician was a point that Paul discussed often in the interview. However, this created an additional complication as Paul discusses:

> *You have probably heard a dozen times about the CSI effect, but you know, it has an influence on our decisions. When you have a violent crime, if there is evidence, you are going to take it, and there is really no influence on if we do or do not collect, but when you are dealing with property crime, we do a lot for PR, and it sits in the evidence room. Victims have influence. [Me: Are there any characteristics about the victims that have a larger influence?] Political affluency certainly has some influence. . . .and of course, the higher the financial loss, the more likely we are to call out a technician.*

I continued to return to the characteristics of the victim, but as Paul frequently noted, there is always going to be an influence based on where the victim lives. In his perspective, the type of community certainly has an influence and if victims of higher status make processing of forensic evidence more likely, it is equally possible, but he would not state, that the lower the status of the victim, the less likely it is that an officer would call out for collection. The goal according to Paul is for the agency to be as effective as possible. In the end Paul offered that, "*Crime is crime, a criminal is a criminal regardless of the type of crime committed, ultimately the goal is to treat evidence equally, but you are going to have to change not just the agency or even the officer, but the community must change as well in how it views crimes.*"

To Paul the expansion and increasing use of technology is going to prove incredibly important but in his closing point, Paul wanted to express how we must be cautious in how we apply technology to problems, and wanted to ensure that I was able to maintain this focus in my conclusion. I end here with the last excerpt from Paul.

> *Technology is going to be the best thing but also a hindrance, we will need better trained officers, but then we have to think about the costs to hire, retain those officers. Something we rarely think about is how it changes the type of officer we have. I also think about can we [older officers] keep up. Even then, if we can hire officers able to use the technology, I am worried if we can retain them.*

Thematic Expression

The process that informs an officer to collect genetic evidence at a property crime scene is shaped by the interaction between external factors, organizational factors, and personal factors. These factors independently and in concert are able to influence an officer's decision to collect evidence. As to be expected, agency policy, which was a factor of the organization's size, budget, and call volume (interrelated) primarily influenced officer decision making. While much of the themes contained in the table reflect those common within decision making across any matter, there are several unique themes (points of influence). The unique organizing themes emerging from the interviews highlighted the influence of victims, perception of worth, and age of officer.

The ability for a victim to influence the decision to collect was both a product of the CSI effect influencing the victim and the expectation that if evidence was not collected it could result in a complaint. This resulted in discussions on "simulated evidence collection," a term coined reflecting the decision to swab, powder, or collect nonviable samples to demonstrate that the victim received the full resources of the agency. In some cases, evidence could be collected with no intent of formally processing the evidence. Subsequently, it became important to discuss the socio-economic status of the victim, as it is entirely feasible that more affluent victims can increase processing, while those of lower socio-economic status receive less forensic attention, although this was not stated outright in interviews. This is a point of discussion within the following chapter as a future research topic.

Concerning perception of worth, as a second unique theme, it is important to highlight the cases showing how processing of property crime scene evidence was beneficial. However, it was the case of the off-duty police officer that stood out as a very important theme and source of future research. Here the entire policy of the organization was reformed around a specific incident where a fellow officer was victimized. To see an agency embrace full forensics for all crime types was remarkable. However, the fact that the agency possessed an internal lab certainly facilitated the adaption.

The interplay between older and younger officers proved to be a unique organizing theme within the research. While age has typically been expressed as a factor within decision making, the unique relationship here factors in the ability for younger officers to be influenced by more seasoned officers to process less evidence because of the reality of the call queue. Within the interviews, it became very clear that while perceptions of worth are influential, the reality of police work, signified by the ever present call queue, can influence an officer to move on to another call or a task deemed more worthy of time.

The expression of the global themes, organizing themes, and organizing concepts are depicted in Table 7.2.

While it was not the intention of the research to rank the factors, rather the purpose here was to identify relevant sources of influence, and it seems appropriate to indicate the organizing theme most expressed within interviews, that is, the policy of the organization. As to be expected, agencies that possessed a standard operating procedure for the treatment of genetic evidence at property crime scenes made the decision-making process that much easier and removed additional influences. If evidence was present, it would be collected, which was made significantly easier by the availability and response time of technicians. However, once the policy of the organization became that of officer discretion, the interplay between the external, organizational, and personal factors became of vital importance. Unique influences expressed within the police officer interviews were the influence of victims to collect, have collected, or to simulate evidence collection or collection without the intent to process to appease the victim or to meet the expectations that forensics has occurred.

Police Executive Interviews

The interview participants for the police executives all possessed graduate degrees, had over 20 years of police service, and ranged from a Patrol Sergeant to a Chief of Police. Of importance to highlight here is that agency size reflected each agency type, which proved incredibly beneficial. All participants were male. Table 7.3 provides the participants' information.

Larry: Chief of Police

Larry is the chief of police for a small, rural police agency servicing a population of about 4,500. The agency employs three full-time and four part-time officers and according to Larry is "*extremely focused on DNA evidence*." The interview with Larry was rather brief in comparison to the other executives or even that of the officers, which is important to highlight not in the brevity of the content but rather the emphasis on a very specific influence that the Chief was extremely keen to discuss.

Table 7.2 Police Officer Thematic Expression

Global Theme	Organizing Theme(s)	Organizing Concepts
External factors	*Victim influence*	Smaller agency more influence, larger agency less influence
		Victim affluence (status)
		Buffer between victim and officer
		Simulated evidence collection or collection but no expectation to process
	Lab facility	External lab
		Working relationships
		Evidence prioritization
	Evidence technicians	Availability of technicians
		Response time of technicians
	Prosecutor	Influence noted more frequently in larger agencies
	Crime scene characteristics	Easily recognized and viable evidence for collection
		High value of items stolen
		Unique scene (similar MO to other scenes)
Organizational factors	*Policy*	Standard operating procedure (agency wide – collect if present)
		Officer discretion
		Informal policy (incentivized evidence collection)
		Formal policy (check with patrol sergeant)
	Organizational commitment	Command staff acceptance and support tragedy (personal experience or reflection)
	Overlaps with personal factors	Institutional buy-in
		Future focused
		Perception of worth – property crime
	Nature of police work	Call volume (relates to availability of evidence technicians & dedication to time on task)
		Incident reported over the phone
		Incident evaluation (enough to pursue, suspect, specific items taken that are easily tracked, witness, resources to spare)
	Lab facility	Internal lab
		Working relationship
		Evidence prioritization
Personal factors	*Training*	Academy training
		Agency training
		State training
		DNA
		Gov training

(*Continued*)

Table 7.2 (Continued)

Global Theme	Organizing Theme(s)	Organizing Concepts
Personal factors	*Nature of police work*	Perception of worth
		Perception of victim
		Reality of call queue backlog and sharing the load
	Incentives	Intrinsic reward (i.e., crime fighter)
		Extrinsic reward (i.e., time reduction)
	Officer characteristics	Age – younger officers
		Older – less likely to collect
		Perception of worth of property crime
		Personal stories of success

Table 7.3 Police Executive Participant Information

Participant Name	Role	Gender	Agency Type	Years of Service	Higher Education
Larry	Police executive	Male	Small rural	20+	Graduate
Lars	Police executive	Male	Medium suburban	20+	Graduate
Lee	Police executive	Male	Large urban	20+	Graduate

The interview with Larry originated from an open request for interview participants and his email reflected his great desire to share his agency's protocol in its comprehensive use of genetic evidence. As Larry describes, "*My agency is very active with DNA evidence both within property crimes and in personal crimes, if we see it we collect it.*" Recognizing that Larry comes from what can only be described as a very small and rural agency was fascinating. From a financial perspective it became important to understand how it was that the agency was able to maintain a rather standard operating procedure for dealing with forensic evidence. As Larry explains, "*The costs are there, really you can never really get away from the costs but I believe it is important and if there is evidence, our task is to collect it.*" As the conversation continued, Larry transitioned into discussing the relationship between his agency and the lab, "*We have been fortunate to have a great working relationship with our lab, they do blood work for us but latent prints [tactile DNA] are not focused on, which has a lot to do with the fact that we had three crime labs close recently.*"

As Larry further explains, there have been considerable financial constraints within the state, which has resulted in a decrease in lab facilities and total services provided by the state. In fact, as Larry describes, "*We can send out evidence and it could take 18 months, with no suspect identified, maybe 180 days with a suspect. If it is high priority, say a sexual assault, we could get results in 90–120 days if we have a suspect in custody, if not it really depends on the lab.*" As the conversation continued, Larry expressed how the lab backlog is truly not an influence on his decision or that of his officers to collect evidence at a property crime scene (or any scene for that matter).

> *There is always going to be a backlog at the lab, we still collect it, send it out, we just end up playing the waiting game, which is more of a frustration for the county attorney than us. It's [DNA forensic evidence and property crime] going to pay off in the end.*

It was refreshing to hear Larry have this positive outlook on the practice, but it remained unclear what exactly contributed to the agency having a standard approach to genetic evidence collection. It is at this point that Larry expressed exactly what contributed to the practice.

> *If I had to pick the strongest influence, I would say it was the CSI effect [Me: Why is that?] . . . There is not much to do in the area, so we have a lot of people that watch those crime dramas, there is this expectation that DNA is everywhere. They want it collected, they even expect that it is discussed in court. One of the first questions a Grand Jury will ask is on DNA. They want to see it. What really started us collecting it at property scenes was that the public wanted it, the lab makes it a low priority, but we still collect it.*

As we continued to discuss the influence of the victim, it became clear and Larry affirmed that a large part of their policy is influenced by the reality that there is a direct line of communication from the victim to him. There is no buffer zone to insulate the agency from the complaints, the suggestions, or the requests of victims. When Larry or his officers respond to a scene, if they identify forensic evidence or even if the victim makes note of an item that is not theirs, they will collect it, even if it is not viable for processing.

As one of three police officer executives interviewed, Larry highlights specifically how financial constraints, while a limitation, are countered by the belief in the inherent benefit of the evidence and the pressure they receive from victims. As I concluded the interview, I began to wonder if the CSI effect is dualistic in that the community has a misconception on the reality of forensic evidence but it is quite possible that the effect is in fact influencing officers and executives to collect information, because that is what a "*Modern Agency*" would do. The use of the term modern agency originated here, as often in the interview Larry would acknowledge how modern the agency was despite their location and size. I note this here not as a criticism or as a negative commentary, quite the contrary, as the policy of the agency and their focus on genetic evidence collection and processing sets it apart from other similar sized agencies. The primary influence at this level is a Chief (executive command staff) introducing and applying forensic policy with the goal of improving community satisfaction, the image of the agency, and in the long run improved information sharing leading to higher clearance rates.

Lars: Sergeant

Lars is a sergeant within a small, suburban police agency with approximately 25 officers and possesses over 20 years of experience. Lars is a trained evidence technician and unlike other police executives or police officers firmly believes that the primary influence is not the agency, the officer, or the prosecutor, but rather the lab.

> *Training is adequately done for DNA and our first responders will do a preliminary assessment and they make the call if it should be collected, they may check with me or another sergeant but once the call is made, they can collect it. Now the issue is that we rarely collect evidence, even if blood is available it is still rare because the demand on the crime lab limits us greatly. We cannot push it [property crime scene evidence] because of personal crime priority, you know burglary evidence is just not a priority. In fact, we have two public labs, county and state, the level of priority is property crime dead last on the list.*

Demand on the lab facilities was an issue often brought up throughout the interviews. However, as Lars expressed, he believed that the agency was capable of expanding their collection into all scenes as expressed in the following excerpt.

> *We could have a policy to collect it [DNA], we have no technical limitations, no major expense issues, no real resistance, we just have to fix the demand [on the lab].*

As Lars continued to explain, there was no real involvement of the prosecutor and the lab technicians from the county or state were always willing to come out and collect evidence when the officers were unable to handle or were not comfortable processing a scene, typically large scenes with multiple evidence types. The officers were adequately trained, and while there was minor pressure from victims, the agency rarely would simulate evidence collection. If they collected evidence, it was processed.

The relationship between collection and processing became a central focus of the interview following this point. According to Lars, the linking of collection to processing at a policy level was certainly a strong influence on the decision to collect. When forensic evidence was collected within the agency, it had to be processed, which meant that an officer would either collect or have collected the crime scene evidence and would have it submitted for processing, but because of the prioritization it would receive the lowest priority and in some cases could be relegated to obscurity. As Lars describes, the turnaround on property crime evidence could take months and the belief was that to inundate the lab with property crime requests could potentially cause the lab to treat other evidence types submitted by the agency as secondary. In essence, the lab could prioritize requests from the agency as nonpriority because it was deemed that the agency was submitting property crime scene evidence. The perception of use was also a theme expressed within several other interviews, wherein there was an influence to not collect or send for processing evidence within property crime scenes so as not to appear to be "*overusing the service.*"

Lee: Patrol Sergeant

Lee is currently a patrol sergeant within a medium sized agency representing a population of 275,000, with a current staffing allocation of approximately 400 officers. Lee has been in this position for approximately 10 years but possesses nearly 30 years of police experience from prior military and federal law enforcement positions. In describing the agency, Lee had acknowledged one current factor that influences their forensic collection practice and that is the four generations of officers within the agency, ranging from 1 to 35 years of service. The agency has been fortunate to have a wealth of experience, which has proved beneficial, but it has also proven detrimental to pursuing a more active forensic collection practice, as described in the following excerpt.

> *If I were to describe our collection policy, I would say it is basic, we do not have a formal policy on property crime scenes. I have yet to see any specific property crime scene training. We have teams and each team has an expert officer that is assigned and trained to collect evidence but they do not handle*

> *the larger scenes (homicides, sexual assaults that are large, major accidents). Minor scenes are what they primarily handle.*

In a follow-up to the point on training, I had inquired why officers were not sent out to training. Lee explained that the agency was already understaffed by approximately 50 officers and currently to send one officer away for training would see them fall below minimum patrol staffing. Additionally, the agency has witnessed a reduction in technicians or as Lee notes, "*We are keeping officers but releasing technicians.*" The decision to create an expert officer who was trained in forensic evidence collection was a direct result of the removal of several forensic technician positions. This officer works with the crime scene technician to help evaluate the scene and may collect evidence at the scene, but it is the primary responsibility of the crime scene technician. However, the availability of this person has become significantly reduced over the years as the following excerpt describes.

> *We used to have a 24-hour crime scene tech ... those positions went away ... now normal duty hours and on call ... if they do not believe they [the expert officer] can process it they ask the tech. One of the major issues for us is the budget. We have two budgets, criminal investigative division and patrol division – CSI comes from CID – so what happens is that there may not be any more overtime budget for the month, which can limit sending out a tech even when they are needed. [Me: Does it really get that bad?] Got so bad, we had an officer who had to use a box of Qtips, unopened, to collect blood because no one was available.*

The financial reality was very apparent, as expressed in all of the interviews, but what Lee then explained was significantly more insightful on how property crimes are viewed within the agency. The conversation had initiated with the perspective of victims and the recognition that victims often ask for forensic testing, but because of the process used for incident handling within the cases, the victim is unlikely to have any real influence over the decision.

> *For property crime scenes we use a point system to determine what is a workable case, if the case does not have enough points, a letter is sent to the victim saying at this point the case is unworkable.*

I was unable to ascertain the exact way the points are allocated but as Lee explained, like most agencies, the perception of worth for dedicating resources, including officer time, is very minimal for property crime scenes, "*they are viewed as the lowest of the scale, no one cares to process the evidence*." Moreover, CODIS warrants were almost never issued on property crime scene cases, not because the process required considerable resource investment but rather the belief is that there are already considerable warrants out and adding to them for DNA recovered at a scene would only exacerbate the issue. For reference, the agency has approximately 20,000 warrants on backlog.

As the interview neared its end, the conversation had turned to his officers and their treatment of forensic evidence; it is here that I learned of an innovation that had originated years prior, an innovation to incentivize officers for their collection and processing of forensic evidence and subsequent "hits" within CODIS or Automated Fingerprint Identification System (AFIS). The following excerpt describes the innovation and subsequent organizational issue.

> *What I am about to tell you is not official policy, in fact I am quite certain that if it got out we would face some considerable blowback for it. It started with taking prints; they are such a pain to take. No one was collecting evidence, it was business as usual, so we created an incentive. What happens is an officer gets 3 hours off if they get an AFIS hit, meaning they get to go home early and there is no limit. We did this to get officers to take prints. Works for CODIS as well. Been working for 3–4 years, but it is causing an issue with the resources to process, [we] had to hire a person to just process prints and our CODIS backlog grows.*

It was fascinating to hear of an innovation to reward officers, which certainly would influence an officer's decision to collect or have collected evidence. It also reminded me of how important anonymity was to the research and the fact that Lee had revealed an informal policy that if known to the upper command staff, would pose a considerable risk to those who created the policy. Moreover, the potential community backlash in incentivizing what the community believes as "standard" was a real risk. However, with the development of the policy, there was an unfortunate organizational rift that formed between the younger officers and older officers.

> *The incentive program works, but we had this issue arise. New officers are processing everything, but the older officers complain because they end up handling the cases. An average scene can take several hours for larger scenes and a burglary can take 30 minutes to 2 hours to take photographs, look for fingerprints, speak to victims, canvas neighborhood and as the older officers see, they are out handling the calls in queue that the younger officers are unable to take because they are sitting at a scene. Then there is the issue that the older officers do not see the benefit of processing.*

Despite the agency's informal incentive program, there was a disconnect between the newer officers and the older officers, which would explain how despite the incentive program the agency did not possess an active forensic program within these crime scenes. The reality of the call queue, coupled with the resentment of the older officers, was likely limiting expansion of the practice. However, Lee provided an additional explanation for why the incentive was vital to the agency.

> *We are a COMPSTAT agency, we use it, we have the meetings, we go over the rates, the hard data, which is what the higher-ups believe in but it limits forensics. We created the incentive because when we went to COMPSTAT, [evidence] collection went down, you get so focused on performance that forensic is an afterthought.*

In summarizing and expressing the themes within the interview, the new additions were innovations and policing model. I had not considered the influence of COMPSTAT on forensic practice. While Bayley and Dixon (2010) had briefly mentioned the influence of forensics on community oriented policing, the influence of COMPSTAT on the decision to process forensic evidence at a property crime scene must be considered and therein originated a new organizing theme.

Thematic Expression

The thematic expression of the police executive interviews exposed several familiar organizing themes across the primary global themes of external, organizational, and personal factors (Table 7.4). Of importantance was the transition from street level bureaucrat to administrator, beholden to the bureaucracy of resource management, policy formation, contract negotiations, and community expectations. As expected the reality of the budget had a significant influence on the discussion on policy formation or whether officers collected forensic evidence within property crime scenes. Budgetary issues were universally noted throughout the interviews. However, the budget was but one influence.

The unique themes expressed within the interviews reflected the interplay between the community expectations of what a modern agency should undertake, grounded within the CSI effect and the influence of the CSI effect on the organization, and administrators who seek forensic collection to demonstrate modernity within the agency. Consider the small, rural chief of police who, despite a limited budget, had facilitated a broad collection policy for forensic evidence,

Table 7.4 Police Executive Thematic Expression

Global Theme	Organizing Theme(s)	Organizing Concepts
External factors	*Victim influence*	Limited buffer – direct line to command staff – from minimal to significant influence
	Community influence	Public expects forensic analysis
		CSI effect
		Crime prioritization within the community
	Lab facility	External lab (cost of using the facility, expedited costs for rush processing)
		Evidence backlog
		State or county labs
		Evidence prioritization
	Evidence technicians	Availability of technicians
	Prosecutor	Limited influence on command staff
Organizational factors	*Policy*	Available funds for policy (standard operating procedure, informal policy)
		Collect and process policy
	Budget	Funding for property crime scene testing, training, technicians
		Funds to send out technicians to scenes (overtime, on-call)
		Hiring officers vs. hiring technicians
	Organizational commitment	Modernity of the agency
		Enticing officers (older and younger to process)
		Future focused – it will pay off in the future
		Willingness to send officers to training
	Nature of police work	Call volume (relates to availability of evidence technicians, dedication to time on task, and available funding)
	Lab facility	State or county labs
		Evidence prioritization
		Working relationship
Personal factors	*Training*	Forensic evidence training
	Nature of being an administrator	Fear of losing access if perceived to "overuse" the lab facility
	Job performance	Clearance rates – priority of calls
		Influence of police model (COP vs. COMPSTAT)
	Incentives	Using technology to fullest
		Modern agency
	Officer characteristics	Personal stories of success

regardless of crime type. A second unique theme that emerged was the perception that increased use could result in seeing differential treatment of future forensic samples at the lab facility. This was expressed often within discussions concerning the lab backlog and crime prioritization within the lab, compounded by agency policy. A third unique theme that emerged reflected the organizations' policing model. This was expressed across all interviews as the influence of community-oriented policing and COMPSTAT on the decision to collect forensic material. While COP seems to influence small organizations, lacking the buffer between the community and the command staff, COMPSTAT was suggested to undermine forensic expansion and routine collection. For example, in the COMPSTAT agency, the lower level command staff created an innovative incentive program to increase the collection of forensic evidence and overcome a lack of evidence collection, even within cases that contained forensic material.

Forensic Expert Interviews

The inclusion of forensic experts within the interview sample was incredibly beneficial to further understand how the decision to collect evidence is significantly influenced by working relationships and the pragmatic expression of the multiple roles forensic experts undertake. The education experience ranged from graduate to professional degrees with one expert holding a medical degree. Years of service spanned from 2 to over 20 years within small rural and large urban agency types. All forensic experts were male. Table 7.5 provides the participants' information.

Frank: Forensic Expert (DDS)

Frank presented as a unique interviewee with a background encompassing positions such as a patrol officer, police investigator, forensic odontologist, oral and maxillofacial surgeon, expert witness, and a practicing defense attorney with a combined experience of over 20 years within a very large urban city. Deciding on how to best use his

Table 7.5 Forensic Expert Participant Information

Participant Name	Role	Gender	Agency Type	Years of Service	Higher Education
Frank	Forensic expert	Male	Large urban	20 +	Professional
Fenton	Forensic expert	Male	Small rural	2	Graduate
Fred	Forensic expert	Male	Large urban	16	Graduate

interview within the book was complicated. Frank holds a DDS, JD, MS, and considerable professional certifications. I decided not to place Frank into a category; rather I used the interview and the themes expressed to place him in his own specific category.

After introductions and explaining the intent of the research, I inquired about the overall perception of genetic evidence. Frank immediately and without hesitation started expressing the frustration within the lab, noted in the excerpt below.

> *The issue we face is the lack of spending by the state; there are not enough forensic experts. Think about all they have to do, they are required to travel, what can be one or two days, to be in the courtroom to testify, they are in the lab, in the field, and are often on-call to do all of these. We cannot put an officer on the stand [Me: Why?] . . . the officer will not meet the threshold for the Daubert Standard, so we need the evidence technician in court, but the same technician in the court room is often the same that is going to be called for assistance at a scene, in court or on the way back from court, testing and court testifying is too burdensome to do both.*

From the excerpt, it is clear how the multitude of positions that Frank has held reflect here. The reality of overburdened lab technicians and laboratory facilities is very clear within the literature, but what Frank expresses here is not so much the burden concerning the amount of evidence, rather the multitude of roles that the forensic technician is expected to fulfill. Recognizing the increased expectations, I inquired about how this may influence decisions by the officer to call an evidence technician.

> *Of course it influences the officer, you are working with these people, you rely on them to help you do your job. If they are overworked, even stressed, you may not call them out to a scene where evidence is likely present but where it is most likely not needed.*

Often the reality of working relationships can go undiscussed at this level; here Frank offers that the decision to call an evidence tech can reflect in their working relationships with the technicians. Additionally, the ability for officers to recognize potential sources of evidence becomes important.

> *I had a case I was working, a local robbery, patrol had worked the scene, and I was called out, in talking with the clerk he notes that the person had walked in with a Subway cup and left it on the counter, the officer did not think to collect it.*

Following this example, I had transitioned the dialog into specifically property crime scene calls. When speaking on the use of evidence within property crime scenes, Frank notes how there is a clear lack of awareness as to the benefits, which can have disastrous results.

> *There is little to no dissemination of the benefits to collecting evidence at these scenes, we get officers at the scenes who contaminate evidence or just do not even notice there is evidence. Early in my career I encountered a car burglary where the only thing missing from the car was the registration, apparently the person used it to follow her to her home, DNA was at the car, we had blood from a cut forearm, it was not collected, never processed, about a month later the girl was raped at her home.*

Frank went on to offer additional examples where evidence was not collected but none of these offered the unfortunate reality that can result from a lack of processing, the rapist was never identified. As Frank would describe, property crimes are treated as unworthy of resources; they receive less time, less dedication, and as is commonly occurring, are "*handled over the phone*." As the interview progressed, it became clear how police and defense attorney experiences such as his reflect in how genetic evidence becomes used.

> *DNA is important, but it is meant to only help us, we know how to investigate these cases but if we come to overuse it, horrible things can happen. Let me offer you an example I offer to students when I teach. A few years back I had this case where a young man met this girl at the bar, and they went out to her car, they had aggressive sex, so much so that she had torn skin off his back, and he said that was enough and got out and left. Later that night she is found dead in the parking lot, head smashed in with a rock. You cannot pull prints of the rock, so we have evidence of sexual trauma, DNA belonging to the guy, and witnesses that see them leave and hear them having sex in the parking lot. Detectives go out, meet the guy, he admits having sex but come to find out she had a boyfriend, who had watched her outside the bar, got into an argument, smashed in her head, and the only way this comes out was because someone noticed him at the scene. They had a suspect, evidence tying him to the scene, and clear indication of some type of violence. The coroner report noted she had vaginal tearing. Had they stopped investigating, it is entirely possible that the prosecutor would have pursued the case.*

As this excerpt illustrates and nearly every other interview noted, forensic evidence is but another tool to assist the investigation, but it is not the "*be all and end all*." The institutional knowledge that the police and forensic technicians possess is vital to the successful resolution of cases. I heard about cases like this often in the interviews, but what later became important in the interview was that there was a clear sense of emotional investment in the cases. It is at this point that Frank expressed what was an entirely new set of themes, as highlighted in the following excerpt.

> *The issue I see now is that the experts are becoming tools for the prosecution, technicians and experts are becoming emotionally involved and this is when mistakes happen, they see their importance in solving cases and see themselves as not objective, neutral scientists but rather as crime scene investigators solving crime.*

In the interviews with the forensic technicians, this became very noticeable in how they view their role; they are not disconnected but rather become emotionally invested and seek confirmation, acceptance, and even admiration for their role in solving crime. To their credit, everyone seeks acknowledgement of their successes regardless of how minor their role. However, what is meant to be an objective, scientific tool here becomes enmeshed within the investigative process.

In summarizing the interview with Frank and expressing the themes within the interview, it is clear how his insight into forensics and associated issues proved invaluable. The expansion of genetic collection and processing will undoubtedly add to the burden of the forensic technicians, which will influence the working relationships between officers and technicians. Currently, the perception of technicians as "crime solvers" may be providing the incentive to overcome their increasing burden. Frank offers that forensic technicians must step back from this perspective and become once again disconnected. This is an aspect that additional research must focus on.

Fenton: Forensic Technician

Fenton is a young forensic technician, who recently passed his forensic boards, with about 2 years of professional experience. He works on-call for a small agency, part-time, as their lead forensic technician. His agency reflects a small rural agency, with about 35 officers, a very small executive staff, and about 24 patrol officers. The physical location of the agency places it in close proximity to the county courthouse, local jail, a public and private prison, and holding center for immigration detainees. With this close proximity and creation of specialized task forces, between two to three patrol officers are shared with other agencies as members of multi-agency taskforces, and several patrols officers are assigned very specific tasks, taking them out of active patrol. On average, the agency has about 15 active patrol officers working cases.

Despite the close proximity, partnerships, and specialized task forces, the agency has yet to receive any funding specific to their genetic testing. As Fenton describes, he has made requests for additional funds to improve his department but he is unable to get through his primary barrier, the Chief of Police. As Fenton notes, "*The Chief is a great guy, he supports me and the officers, but he is old school, he does not see the benefit in DNA.*" Like most forensic technicians and even officers interviewed, the influence of the command staff is very noticeable in determining whether they collect and process genetic evidence.

To better understand the complexity of the relationship between the Chief and Fenton, it is important to understand the context of the crime in the community. The crime in the area is primarily property crime as homicides are incredibly rare in the area as are sexual assaults. The primary call type is property crime scenes, which from 2009 to 2010 nearly quadrupled because of new home constructions that remained unfinished, vacant, and in many suburbs, complete construction materials and tools remained available for would be thieves. Additionally, it is important to describe the climate of the area: it is hot, windy, and can often be very humid. According to Fenton, "*there is a belief that if there is a visible print, you can pull it, but you know more often than not, I am rarely able to pull a print because of the climate.*" Over the last year, Fenton has had success in collecting genetic evidence, but the Chief is still reluctant to allow Fenton to send out genetic evidence for processing, despite his successes.

One success story involved a series of break-ins at a new construction site, seven burglaries in total with the same method of operation. The on-scene officer noted that commercial tools had smudges on them and called Fenton out to process the scene. When he arrived at the scene, he attempted to pull the print for processing, but because of the placement on the tool, it was impossible to pull a viable print so instead Fenton made the decision to swab it for tactile DNA. According to Fenton, he figured, "*what the hell, take a chance.*" When he went back into his office, he completed the paperwork, submitted it for analysis, and several months later he received word that a match had been found in CODIS. I had asked him how the Chief felt about the decision, "*Well he did not say much, and I did not think he would because here we had seven burglaries and no leads. However, once we got the hit from the system (CODIS), he told me good work and I provided the information to the detectives.*"

Despite demonstrating success with collecting and processing genetic evidence recovered at property crime scenes, the Chief was still reluctant to expand the processing. The influence of the Chief and the unwritten policy of the agency for handling evidence ensured that Fenton would collect fingerprints when able and would limit his collection of genetic evidence, unless absolutely necessary. As Fenton explained had he been able to pull a fingerprint off the tool, he knows he would not have attempted the DNA swab. The following excerpt denotes the frustration Fenton experiences.

> *We do not pay for evidence processing, I can send off as much as I want to the lab, we pay for my kits but evidence costs us nothing and yet the Chief still is resistant to allowing me to submit evidence for processing.*

At a thematic level, this was very interesting but more importantly at a practical level, I wanted to know exactly what could be influencing the resistance to processing. While there is clear influence from the command staff, I wanted to know what influenced the command staff. It was extremely rare to hear from any interviewees that their cost of processing was already covered by the state and therefore I used this opportunity to uncover more. Fenton provides some additional insight into this issue as expressed in the following excerpt.

> *I can send evidence to one of the four major crime labs. We no longer are charged but the Chief is apprehensive to send a lot to them for fear we will lose the access. The state got funding, so no one pays, but when I talk to the techs at the lab, they always tell you about the agencies that overused the service because they had money.*

In this regard, Fenton had highlighted a common theme in that perceptions matter and the fear of losing access to the service, be it through overuse, reduction in funding, or simply being charged for the actual service, influences the decision to both collect and process evidence. To highlight the level of frustration at the lab, Fenton provided the following example.

> *One of the lab technicians that I have worked with on a few cases told me how agencies [large agencies primarily] would inundate them with requests*

simply because they had the money. In some cases, they did not even need evidence [processed]. He tells me about this case where the person is on camera, identified by several witnesses, and the agency still sent in DNA to be processed.

At this level, there is clear indication that the command staff may be partially influenced by the fear of losing access to services if they are perceived to be overusing the service. Moreover, there exists a dualistic dilemma wherein the expectation at the prosecutorial level is for full processing while the agency seeks to minimize the use of the process unless vital to the case. The following excerpt from Fenton notes these additional influences.

The county attorney has a large say in what I do at a scene, let me qualify that, the county attorney often wants me to return to a scene to process it for additional evidence when sometimes there was no DNA at the scene to begin with.

Despite my additional questions attempting to elicit the influence of the prosecutor, Fenton provided nearly identical statements. It was clear that while the prosecutor influenced the decision to collect, it was inasmuch the decision to obtain more evidence, not necessarily the decision to collect evidence. In this regard, the prosecutor became a positive influence to expand evidence collection and processing of forensic evidence while the agency reflected a desistance mechanism to reduce collection of genetic evidence. However, this was reflected in the treatment of forensic evidence by the prosecutor. As the interview continued, I had inquired if there were any additional factors and it is here that an additional factor emerged, the victim.

Victim influence on the decision to collect genetic evidence was not a new theme within the research. However, Fenton would describe the influence and the unintended consequence of the practice. The following excerpt summarizes the influence and the potential consequence well.

When you are called to a scene, victims want DNA processed. They want me or the officer to tell them or better yet explain to them why it is not there if I leave with no swabs. I had this case, attempted criminal damage case, some kids set nails under tires at three houses, we had a dust storm, so hand prints are all over, I take some swabs, try to pull prints, nothing really usable, have this homeowner come over and notes there is a condom that he says is not his in his front yard, wants it collected, so I go over and collect it. I know it's not going to be of any use, but you take it for a little PR [public relations].

As we discussed this influence, I had been reminded of the literature on evidence room backlogs and I had asked Fenton about his evidence room. It appeared to me that simulated evidence collection could in fact be a source of some of the high backlogs discovered. Fenton provided some additional insight in that it was certainly feasible to have large backlogs of evidence because he has been known to collect evidence when it was not needed to simply appease a victim; according to Fenton, this directly related to the "*small town atmosphere*" of the agency.

Throughout the interview, Fenton had offered many unique points, but what intrigued me most was his enthusiasm to expand or more importantly, to convince the Chief that expanded use of genetic evidence is warranted and beneficial to the agency. In closing the interview, I had asked what about the practice influenced this perception of the benefits. It is here that Fenton offered what was entirely unique across all of the interviews. He was familiar with the national study and had recently completed the free, online training that was made available at DNA.gov. Prior to the training he was not convinced that it was going to be beneficial, but in closing Fenton offered the following, which summarizes well how influential training can be to disseminate benefits, "*In this job, you have to stay current and for professional development, I had found the* Free Training on DNA in Property Crime Scenes. *After I had gone through it, I could see where I was potentially missing evidence and after the last module, I knew that expanding my collection was going to help us, I believe it works.*"

Fred: Director of Forensic Training Center

Fred has 16 years of crime scene investigation experience and several additional years within police investigations. His selection as a forensic expert reflected his current role as the director of a training facility for forensics. Fred provides training, education, and collection assistance to state and local agencies and specializes in homicides and sexual assaults and evidence detection. Frank describes his career as "*I've kinda done it all.*"

> *I started in the military, like a lot of the officers, and worked a lot of different cases, nothing with evidence at first, but we had the opportunity for training, I then got out and started working with the state [crime] lab, I started with a specialized forensics taskforce on officer involved shootings, then got into computer forensic, homicide, and rape task forces. As time went on, I really*

had done it all in forensics and decided that I wanted to see an improvement in forensic training, which brought me to the training facility ... Things have moved so fast, now it is not just about collecting or lab work, we now include training on how to present forensics in the court.

In his capacity as director and his prior experience within the police service and evidence collection, Fred possesses amazing insight into the overall factors that influence decision making and as the interview proceeded, he wasted no time highlighting the current reality and challenges.

The challenge here for us is not expanding but the priority. Prioritization is an issue, property crime is low. Violent crime continues to receive the highest priority, but it all gets done. You just end up waiting months. [Me: How long on average?] It depends on how many items, the prosecutor for the case, the viability of the evidence, or even what we rarely talk about is the pressure on the directors. [Me: In what way?] They get pressured on rape kits to get them tested quick and then you have a DA who may be calling daily or even hourly to get updates ... On average you can expect a few months or longer ... with property crime cases you are waiting the longest [Fred returned to his point on the lab later in the interview, it was moved to here to further express the frustration at the lab level] Labs are still inundated with older samples to get processed and into CODIS; prioritization comes from all levels, current cases, backlogged cases, offender samples, and now arrestee samples.

As the conversation continued, Fred had taken time to explain how training is first-and-foremost an issue within decision making.

New detectives want to collect everything, so they collect everything at the scene, the obvious is easy but you never know what may contain evidence so they collect everything that is relevant; out of the ordinary, items moved, things open, cigarette butts all over or they may even take a random sample of them, when it gets to the lab, they are going to test those in the best condition, those that logically hold the best useable evidence, the condition of the item. When we are dealing with an item alleged to be contaminated it may have evidentiary value – connect the suspect to the crime scene – not for the court – but for the investigation.

Specific to this excerpt, Fred had spent time discussing how new detectives and patrol officers who have received training on forensics become those most likely to collect or request processing of a crime scene for forensic evidence. Moreover, Fred had noted that there seems to be a decrease in utilization as officers become more aware of "*how investigations work*," which is to say that overtime officers must balance their time on task against the benefits of collecting or requesting for scene processing. At first, they receive considerable evidence from these officers and as Fred explains, "*Everything tends to be sent in and we have to sift through it.*"

As we continued discussing the lab and the pressures, Fred expressed how influential the district attorney can be in the process or rather how the disconnect between the lab, the officer, and the prosecutor can become so vast.

> *One issue is the field people [local officers, detectives] want in to work or are beginning to work a case and then the CSI techs [from the state] come in and often need to take it over if the DA requests. He may want new techs to reduce any legal challenges (high profile cases).*

As the conversation continued, Fred had explained how the prosecutor had a clear influence on the lab, which he expressed with a great deal of specificity in that the evidence technician becomes overworked and the burden placed on the lab great.

> *You hear all the time now, about how there is no money, but funding is always an issue, we can adapt to the new work flow, but there needs to be better resources for court testimony, you are seeing more negative lab testimony, which is double the workload, called to testify on evidence and called to testify why evidence was not there, this happens all the time and you still have no real willingness to hire more [evidence technicians].*

Fred had offered major themes, which supported what other forensic experts and officers had noted, but most important from this interview were the suggestions offered on how to improve genetic evidence collection within property crime scenes. According to Fred, what is limiting expansion is not necessarily funding, which is always an issue he offered; rather the complication is better education, or more succinctly, education that reaches all levels of the organization to inform them of the benefits, and then better training, certification, and a unified policy on the treatment of forensic evidence within these cases. As Fred explained, "*Currently everyone goes about it their own way; we need a unified system, if anything to reduce challenges by the defense.*"

Thematic Expression

The forensic evidence technicians (ET) proved an invaluable and incredibly insightful addition to the research. They represented both sworn and non-sworn personnel, held a range of a few years to decades of experience, and possessed graduate, terminal, and professional degrees. Often the role of the ET is examined within the context of simply collecting evidence, which initiates via officer request, prosecutor request, or formal policy. However, as expressed within the interviews, the ET is influenced across several factors in deciding whether to collect evidence, which is not limited to an officer's decision to call for scene processing.

The unique themes expressed within the interviews highlight the overburdened crime technicians, victim influence, ineffective forensic process, image of technician, and command staff. While some of these are expressed as unique themes across the other interviews, their potential to influence evidence collection is firmly present as an organizing theme.

A consistent theme within all of the interviews is the reality that the workload on an ET is considerable. The multiple roles they are responsible for within the criminal justice process is astonishing. Their involvement does not end with collection. All of the participants discussed their frustration or that of other ETs or lab technicians who can become responsible for evidence collection, evidence transportation, processing, training, and court testifying. While none of the participants had carried out all of these roles, they all discussed how these multiple roles, coupled with the limited availability of ETs, made these positions incredibly stressful. This was compounded by the recognition that the other stakeholders were not familiar with the "multiple hats" the ETs wear. Prosecutors would expect collection, or inundate a lab with processing when evidence is present, but would also call out an ET to conduct negative evidence testimony when no suitable evidence was discovered. This was equally time consuming because it would require the ET to document the scene and explain how they arrived at the conclusion that no viable evidence was discovered.

Apart from the numerous roles and responsibilities, an additional unique theme expressed related to ineffective forensic policy, wherein collection (packaging, paperwork) and submission of marijuana for testing not only created a backlog in the forensic labs for processing but also would occupy the time of the ET preventing them from spending resources on additional tasks. The recent increase in types of synthetic cannabinoids has resulted in new policy requiring submission of the evidence for analysis (influenced by the prosecutor) because officer field kits are no longer capable of identifying them. This requires allocation of precious resources to determine that the evidence is a synthetic narcotic.

Despite being a unique organizing theme within the police officer interviews, it is still important to highlight the expression of victims as an influence as a unique theme. The reality is that both sworn and nonsworn ETs become influenced by victims to collect evidence at their scene, which can result in "simulated evidence collection." In some cases, evidence may be collected with no intent of formally processing the evidence. Important here is the recognition that victims are capable of influencing the officer to call out an ET for scene processing (or policy may dictate they are called), and the victim then is able to influence the ET to collect evidence, even if no viable sample is present.

The unique organizing theme reflecting the image of the technician is problematic. Either expressed as "emotion" within the cases worked or "winning" over officers by solving a case, it became apparent that such influences on the ET are the pragmatic reality that is their emersion within the investigative process as "crime fighters," "crime solvers," or "officers in lab coats." This becomes important because forensics is meant to epitomize democratic policing, where it is a disconnected, neutral, objective scientific tool and the technicians should reflect these qualities. This presents as both a unique theme and as a policy issue in that the expansion of forensics and further alignment of forensics within agencies may prove problematic for issues of accountability, oversight, and potential for misconduct.

The last unique theme expressed is that of the command staff, which certainly appears to be a common theme within decision making, but becomes unique within the context of evidence submission and budgets. As expressed in the interviews, there appears to be an influence where command staff are inhibited by the belief that if they submit evidence from lower prioritized crime scenes, they may lose access to the reduced costs for processing or receive reduced priority for their submissions for being deemed to "overuse" the service. This was echoed across several interviews and is unique in that some agencies that did not pay for processing were not collecting forensic evidence, even when present, because of the perception of worth and the reality that the labs are overburdened. Table 7.6 presents the full thematic expression.

Table 7.6 Forensic Expert Thematic Expression

Global Theme	Organizing Theme(s)	Organizing Concepts
External factors	Overburdened crime labs	Internal and external pressures on prioritization
		Submission of evidence with no probative value
		Processing time of evidence
		Forensic evidence backlog
		Non-uniform state policy for forensic evidence
	Overburdened crime technicians	Multiple responsibility (responsible for evidence collection, testing, training, and court testifying)
		Daubert standard
	Prosecutor	Negative evidence testimony
		Full processing expectations
		Disconnect between prosecutor and lab
	Victim influence	Expectation is to collect
		Public relations
		Simulated evidence collection
	Perception of forensics	Recognize value of DNA – specific to high level crime not property crime
	Scene contamination	Untrained officers
	State resource allocation	Agencies first then labs
	Environment	Forensic evidence degradation
	Collection request	Officer decision
Organizational factors	Command staff	Resistance to forensic processing
		Perception of worth, value of forensic evidence
		Fear of losing access to services
	Ineffective forensic process	Synthetic cannabinoids, marijuana testing
	Resource allocation	Overtime, on-call, available technicians
	Training	Officer detection of viable evidence
		Quality control
		Certifications
	Working relationship	Relationship between sworn and non-sworn
		Win over officers – show worth of technician
	Policy	Informal policy
Personal factors	Image of technician	Officer in a lab coat
		Crime fighter
		Crime solver
	Working relationships	Relationship with officers
		Relationship with lab testing technicians

Table 7.7 Prosecutor Participant Overview

Participant Name	Role	Gender	Agency Type	Years of Service	Higher Education
Patricia	Prosecutor	Female	Large urban	20	Professional
Patty	Prosecutor	Female	Large urban	21	Professional
Parker	Prosecutor	Female	Medium suburban	10	Professional

Prosecutor Interviews

Three prosecutors were interviewed reflecting large urban and medium suburban agencies. Each prosecutor possessed considerable years of service and familiarity with genetic evidence. Table 7.7 provides the participants' information.

Patricia: Former Prosecutor

Patricia presented an interesting interview participant; she had been a prosecutor in a very large, urban city for the past 20 years. This was until 1 year ago when she decided that she would transition into defense work, much to the criticism of some of her colleagues. She was knowledgeable, skilled, and highly adept at presenting forensic evidence within the courtroom and working with laboratories and agencies in trying cases. Patricia valued the investigative benefit and prosecutorial strength that genetic evidence provided. With one opening question, a few follow-up questions, and the occasional statements, Patricia led me through her influence on the investigative decision-making process in what was nearly an hour and a half. The insight she offered and the influence of her department on the investigative process mirrored much of the other prosecutors. Her unique transition into defense work provided meaningful points of reflection on just how the criminal justice process would have to adapt to account for expanded processing of this evidence type.

I began with the primary guiding question on how influential her department was on the processing of forensic evidence. Patricia quickly and without hesitation offered, "*Very.*" As Patricia went on to describe, her decision to charge a case reflected the severity of the offense, the weight of the evidence, and the resources at her disposal. Concerning DNA evidence, Patricia made a very interesting analysis in that, "*what we [prosecutors] ask ourselves is if the DNA is worth it, it is a fantastic tool but it takes months and months to get processed and even then what you may send out may not come back completely processed.*" This was a similar point of contention that Patty noted, in that there was conflict between the office and the forensic laboratory. There was disconnection between what the prosecutor believed needed to be processed and what the laboratory technician deemed viable. This disconnect also extended into the officers' decision to collect evidence. In reality, there was clear prioritization of cases and evidence and if there were little evidence within a burglary, the prosecutor would be unlikely to pursue the case. Likewise, if there was evidence linking the person to the scene (i.e., eyewitness, caught with the stolen property, or etc.) and there was genetic evidence at the scene, the officer would be more likely to collect the evidence to ensure that the prosecutor would not return the case file for additional preparation. Consider the following points expressed by Patricia.

> *There is a sense of superiority within the office, we have the final decision. Officers most certainly would be influenced because they [officers] are preparing cases for us and therefore our priorities and expectations influence how they prepare the file.*

Additionally, as Patricia highlighted, often you may have a case where evidence is not processed but where the strength of the evidence was so overwhelming, there was no need to spend the resources to have it processed. However, when the grand jury convened, there was almost a "*group think belief where DNA is absolute.*" According to Patricia, to not present forensic evidence to the grand jury or even to a trial jury was to open up a line of questioning by the defense as to why it was not processed. This is known as "*negative evidence testimony,*" wherein the prosecutor would need to put an expert on the stand to present "*why DNA evidence was not found at the scene or would not be at the scene.*"

Lastly, Patricia offered that like any investigative tool at the disposal of an agency, resources are always going to be important. The decision to collect genetic evidence at a crime scene would be influenced by the office. However, what most has to change to accommodate the increased use is putting money into the prosecutor's office. As Patricia offered while the agency has the ability to influence an officer's decision, a change in the agencies practices would require the office to adapt. With stronger evidence linking a person to an incident,

Patricia noted that the office would certainly see "*more plea bargains*" and "*more cases.*" It is here that Patricia offered the most interesting insight; she noted that the expansion of forensic evidence analysis within property crimes scenes would be a catalyst for change within the office. The agency already was familiar with using diversionary programs, but for cases of felony burglary, the only penalty was incarceration. With increased collection and processing by the police, the leadership within the prosecutor's office would have to "*acknowledge and implement restorative and rehabilitative alternative programs.*"

In summarizing my interview with Patricia, I was reminded how connected each of the institutions are within our system. A change in police practice will influence the courts, and that of corrections. It was clear that Patricia had direct and indirect influence over an officer's decision to collect and process DNA. However, if the police agency made dramatic changes in their collection and processing of forensic evidence there would most certainly be challenges for the office to overcome. This was echoed in the last point offered by Patricia.

> *The more tools, the more effective, the better at it and the quicker we get at using this evidence type, the more we are able to obtain justice. The office will just have to adapt and how we adapt will matter for the community.*

Patty: Prosecutor

Patty epitomized the perception of a prosecutor. She was direct, inquisitive (always asking for additional clarification or additional research to support a line of questions), and possessed 21 years of prosecutorial experience working within a large, urban, and by her accounts a "*highly focused*" office. The office has been highly cited for its streamlined approach to felony prosecutions, resulting from the creation of a specialized unit that evaluates felony violent and property crime scene cases. It is here that the office becomes as noted by Patty, "*very influential in the forensic process.*"

As Patty explains, when the unit evaluates cases brought to them by the officer, they will evaluate the evidence and "if the case does not have enough evidence or DNA was not collected, they [evaluating prosecutor] may send it back for more evidence." The felony review stage and subsequent approval of the case for trial by the Assistant District Attorney has created a system where the prosecutor has the final say over whether an officer collects evidence. By the account of Patty, "They [Police] want charges; we [Prosecutor] want to win." For the police to get their charges in felony cases, they will, as noted by Patty, "Do as we request." If the police do not, the case does not move any further. Furthermore, because of the highly streamlined approach, DNA is used only when it is advantageous to the prosecutor's office. As Patty depicted, "if there is overwhelming evidence, we do not need to test the forensics." I had asked Patty if this limited the use of CODIS and linking of unsolved cases to suspects. Her perspective was that "current resources allow for us to focus on the cases we have, not the cases that are potentially out there."

Unlike the other prosecutors, Patty had direct involvement with the collection and processing of forensic evidence. Patty does send evidence directly to the lab to be processed. It is at this point that it became very clear that there was considerable contention and even resentment reflecting the conflict between the prosecutor and the forensic lab. The following excerpt from the interview clearly depicts this conflict.

> *I may want 50 items tested, just had 100 valid requests in a case where a kid killed his father, the crime lab wants to tell me we do not need to test this, or this is not important [the lab technician]. They [lab technical] will selectively decide what is important and not important to test. I had recently sent in 42 items of evidence and they had the audacity to send me back 8. I do not tell them how to process evidence, but here they are in essence trying to tell me how to argue a case, they believe they can tell me what is important and not.*

While there is clear conflict between the prosecutor and the laboratory, Patty acknowledges there are issues that force prioritization within the lab. As Patty notes, "*The crime lab is overburdened and more DNA is being required, there are mandates to increase processing, but no additional funding.*"

The point of being overburdened is a clear reality across all levels. There exists legislative policy that has mandated that facilities process certain evidence within a particular time. However, often neglected is the reality that a quick turnaround on processing does not mean the case makes it to trial faster. Consider the following example offered by Patty, "*Right now, sex assault kits are required to be processed in 30 days. Rape charges may take a year to charge and then often we are dealing with consent not identification.*" There is internal and external pressure on labs to process the kits so that other evidence types become secondary.

> *Properly crime scenes are a low priority, and the burden on the lab simply creates additional problems, I even had a homicide last year that took a year and a half to get all [the evidence] tested.*

To return to the influence on the officer to collect evidence, Patty highlights the reality that juries expect the evidence to be presented.

> *We now put on negative evidence testimony, putting on a fingerprint expert or forensic expert to explain why forensic was not available – to counter the expectation that it is always there, we have to demystify forensics to overcome their burden of doubt.*

In this line of discussion, it became clear how frustrated she has become with the expectation that society has placed on forensics. She offered a very humorous closing argument that she delivered, explaining to the jury how "*It (DNA) is not like Pig Pen from Charlie Brown.*"

Like Patricia, Patty expressed the reality that with an increasing use of DNA (if only collection), there would be a transition within the office. As she expressed "*More evidence can only help us, it provides good evidentiary value, but it may force us to adapt our approach to adjudication.*" However, Patty was quick to follow up that because of the "*fiscal and backlog reality, it is not feasible to collect all evidence, even if there is [genetic] forensic evidence at a scene.*" If the police agency is able to improve their collection of genetic evidence, Patty firmly believes that we will see clearly more plea bargains. Patty offers this basic statement on the expansion, "*More evidence, more pleas – less evidence, more likely to go to trial.*" It is important to frame this statement by noting that the conversation had transitioned into a dialog concerning felony cases with evidence linking the person to the scene.

Lastly, Patty provided an example in the inherent dangers in the overuse of genetic evidence. Patty provided me the following case to illustrate her point.

> *I recently worked a case involving a young mother murdered, brutally, shot four times, and her throat slit. Swabs worked up another male profile [DNA]. We knew about the guy as she has recently gone out on a date that*

Saturday, she died on Monday. As the man explained he did know her and he did have sex with her on the night of their date. They had had anal sex on their first date and she ended up dead on Monday. At the jury trial, I had to explain why his DNA was there and how this was not a rape murder, but a murder only committed by another man.

As I listened to Patty offer this example, I was reminded of the other perspectives across the stakeholder continuum that genetic evidence is but a linking item to establish a connection to a scene. Here Patty had a case where the defense had offered that there was DNA from another man found inside the victim and that there was clear indication of trauma and she was brutally murdered. The clear weight of genetic evidence and the perception of the jury have, as noted by Patty, "*significantly influenced how we try cases.*"

In summarizing my interview with Patty, she clearly details her influence on the decision of officers to collect evidence at a scene, reflected in her expectations and evidentiary threshold for pursuing a case. However, her expectations are influenced by her interaction and thus working relationship with the laboratory and the technicians working the cases. With a streamlined approach to evidence collection, Patty becomes the gatekeeper to the processing of forensic genetic evidence across all felony cases. Therefore, I gathered from this interview how the experience, familiarity, and perception of the evaluating prosecutor might influence the officer's decision to collect evidence.

Parker: Prosecutor

Parker was an enthusiastic and eager participant wanting to share with me her experience, knowledge, and outlook from the initial conversation we had. She possessed nearly 10 years of experience, representing a medium suburban area within what she would consider a "*small agency, with little money.*" Parker has considerable knowledge presenting genetic evidence within the courtroom but expressed that concerning property crime scenes, "*We were lucky to see fingerprints taken, property crime is simply so low we rarely see it presented.*" However, as Parker walked me through her experience and the associated challenges and opportunities that have emerged, she shared an important insight that all three prosecutors have come to share during the interviews – that of the view of the jury, which is detailed by the following excerpt.

The jury is media driven, they think we can do everything, duplicate what is done on CSI, in the courtroom, but it falls flat.

The impact of the CSI effect on the courtroom is well documented as discussed within the literature review. However, the CSI effect did little to change how evidence was collected. The influence of the prosecutor on officer decision making as expressed by Parker was present but not overly influential because the goal was to win, as the following excerpt expresses.

> *Being honest, I have little influence on the officers' decision making, but that does not mean there is no influence in general, it depends on the level of the prosecutor, new prosecutors get what they get, so they need to work with officers to win their cases. Because of the time it would take to get DNA tested, we would ask, do we need it to win? If it is too costly, or will take too long, we may not take it to trial.*

The practical reality of a prosecutor's experience has an influence on officer decision making. Parker was relatively new within the office, so her ability to request additional forensic collection or processing was dependent on what she considered "*Being nice*" or fostering a good working relationship with the lab. As the interview continued, Parker began to discuss how the backlog is a barrier but prosecutors have been working around it for years.

> *The backlog is the main issue, it is problematic, we have to wait, and wait, and wait months and months, a few times a year. It slows us up so we go into court a year later. Lots of time, we get the case, it just got submitted and then it gets to the lab, so we have to wait for it to process, luckily as a prosecutor I have some pull to get the DNA pulled and get it out of the hopper so I could get it tested because I needed it. To work up a case to see it settled. So they [forensic technician at the lab] wait until you call, the DNA could stay in the hopper and it could take 3–6 months. I call the lab, tell the technician that I am about to present a case, and more often they pull it out and get it tested over the next few days. The working relationship is key, you need them as a friend, on your side, because they are so vital, they hold your ability to go to court.*

As Parker denotes here, the backlog is always an issue, it has been for years, but through fostering a good working relationship with the lab and lab technicians, the backlog may possibly be sidestepped to see evidence processed when the prosecutor is ready to go to court.

As the interview continued, I had inquired about any recent challenges that she has experienced and immediately Parker expressed issues involving negative evidence testimony. According to Parker, "*Negative evidence testimony will likely increase, because the defense attorney will mention why it [forensic evidence] was not collected, so you have to rebut it, because we tried and there wasn't.*" With a jury expecting to see evidence collected, when it is not, it is only natural for the defense to present a challenge to the case. As Parker jokingly stated, "*you cannot blame them, I'd do the same. . . . Defense attorneys are aware of our backlog and continually try to poke holes in the cases, why was it [forensic evidence] collected and not processed.*" In this regard, it can be expanded to include the issues within simulated evidence collection, which only open up more criticism.

Lastly, I had inquired about the future of forensics, specific to how a routine genetic treatment towards property crime scenes would influence her office. Parker very eloquently and almost immediately stated the following, "*The burden is not on the court, because you have the plea, it takes minutes, the trial can take a day or even days. No reason to take the case to trial, just settle left and right, there is no reason for a diversionary program, just plea it out.*" Unlike the prior prosecutors, who expressed potential issues or an opportunity to force a change within the office, Parker clearly saw no need for the court to change, rather routine analysis only makes more efficient the use of pleas. Routine treatment as Parker expressed epitomizes the court system; it would make it significantly easier to close cases.

Thematic Expression

Until recently, the involvement or subsequent influence of the prosecutor and that of their office was anecdotal concerning forensic evidence collection. As expressed within the three interviews, the influence of the prosecutor within collection can be said to be moderately influential. The unique organizing themes emerging within the IPA interviews include jury perception and CSI effect, crime prioritization, and career success.

As expressed by each of the prosecutors within the interviews, juries have come to expect forensics within the courtroom. This expectation has fostered a need to either have available expert witnesses to testify on recovered evidence or calling forth a forensic technician or officer to explain why no suitable evidence was recoverable. The CSI effect has permeated all aspects of the criminal justice system, most specifically the agency, officers, and the courtroom.

The influence of the prosecutor can be said to be moderately influential as the familiarity that the prosecutor has with genetic evidence and the associated costs of processing does influence how they evaluate cases, as noted by both Patricia and Patty. However, the ability for the prosecutor to stipulate that genetic evidence be collected within property crime scenes is minimal. As discussed by each prosecutor, they have little influence beyond calling for additional processing, or ensuring that an attempt was made to collect evidence, when they evaluate a case file. They do so based on the propensity or likelihood that the defense may challenge that evidence was not recovered, playing to the CSI mentality, or if this evidence can ensure a conviction. As Parker noted, if the prosecutor does not prepare an expert witness list including forensic experts, it is likely that the defense will simply raise the question within the court.

Expanding on the influence that the prosecutor has on officer decision making, the prioritization of cases causes prosecutors to devalue property crime scene cases except those deemed high profile or those where the use of forensic evidence may link a suspect to several scenes increasing the notoriety. In this regard, the influence of the prosecutor can facilitate in both collection and processing. As expressed within the interviews, the influence of the prosecutor at the collection level is minimal, but the influence of the prosecutor in what is processed can be significant. As noted by Patty, she controls what is processed or more succinctly, she submits for analysis forensic evidence. Those prosecutor officers that control processing can certainly exert considerable influence on an agency. If a prosecutor does not value property crime scene cases and will not authorize processing within those cases, unless there is a specific threshold, it is certainly feasible that it can inhibit collection at the agency level as Patty suggests.

Career success was a final unique organizing theme. While a reader is likely to claim that career success is a general theme in all work environments, it is very important within the work of the prosecutor and their influence on officer decision making. Each interview participant noted very specifically that their goal is to "win." Each selected for prosecution cases based on their ability to win those cases. As genetic evidence becomes more routinely analyzed (collected and processed), prosecutors will witness more efficient prosecutions and more effective outcomes, for example, the average sentence for a residential burglar noted in the Denver study increased 10-fold (Ashikhmin et al., ND), and as an outcome will likely come to influence agencies to

Table 7.8 Prosecutor Thematic Expression

Global Theme	Organizing Theme(s)	Organizing Concepts
External factors	Jury perception	Negative evidence testimony
		CSI effect
	Crime labs	Overburdened crime labs, turnaround time on evidence, disconnect between the office and the lab
	Forensic funding for evidence testing	Funds for backlog testing, limited funds for evidence testing, synthetic cannabinoids
	Daubert standard	Evidence technicians, collection, testing, testifying
	Police agency policy	Formal policy, officer discretion
	State policy	Mandate to increase processing
	CSI effect	Weight of genetic evidence
Organizational factors	Crime prioritization	Personal vs. property
	Felony review stage	Specialized evaluation teams to evaluate cases for prosecution
	Budget	Evidence testing, expert testimony, prioritization of cases
	Case loads	Plea bargains, diversionary programs
Personal factors	Reputation	Winnable cases, cases of value (community and individual perception)
	Perception of property crimes	Value in testing evidence
	Career success	Take cases based on those with the most return, focus on the now not the later
	Experience	Value of forensics, necessity of forensics, familiarity with success of property crime scene evidence

become better trained in forensic evidence collection. At the prosecutor level, DNA evidence in property crime scene cases may be prioritized lower based on the crime type, but having nearly guaranteed conviction rates when forensic evidence is present and selected for prosecution, longer sentences, and in many cases, linking the suspect to multiple crime scenes is a tremendous motivation to officers. Table 7.8 contains the thematic expression of the prosecutor interviews.

NATIONAL SURVEY RESULTS

This section provides the results of the national survey of police officers across the United States. Presentation of the results is provided in descriptive format to provide an unfiltered portrayal of the factors that influence officer decision making in concert with agency policy and contextual points within the treatment of genetic evidence from property crime scenes.

Survey Response Rates

After removal of invalid email addresses and redeployed officers, the final sample included 2,893 potential respondents; of those potential respondents, 460 surveys were completed, and removal of surveys with >75% missing values resulted in a final sample of 441. The response rate for this survey was 15% with an error level of 4.3% at a 95% confidence interval. The survey took approximately 20 minutes to complete as indicated within the Remark system, when controlling for obvious outliers (one respondent is indicated as having taken 2,680–2,700 minutes to complete the survey). Table 7.9 provides an analysis of the response rates across each participant notification wave that occurred.

As Table 7.9 indicates, each subsequent participation request improved the response rate on average 3.6%, which while not a large improvement, did provide moderate gains within the sample improving the overall sample by nearly half (an increase of 210 participants). A standard nonresponse analysis was then conducted, identifying all those respondents who failed to complete more than 75% of the survey (reflecting missing information within the agency or officer sections of the survey). Subsequently, the sample was reduced by 19 respondents, which resulted in a final sample of 441, reflecting a 15% response rate.

Of the 441 officers who responded to the survey, 87.3% (n = 384) were male and the average age was 44 with a minimum age of 25 and a maximum age of 66. The majority of respondents were White and non-Hispanic or Latino – 86.4% (n = 381) of the sample reflects white or Caucasian (non-Hispanic or Latino). Representation of other races were significantly lower reflecting at 2.9% (n = 13) for both black and American Indian officers. Asian and Native Hawaiian or Pacific Islander officers represented five officers comprised under 2% of the total sample. 5.7% (n = 25) of officers declined to provide the racial demographic characteristics.

Table 7.9 Survey Response Rates

Participation Requests	N	Response Rate	% Change
Initial participation request	25	0.086	
First reminder	364	125	+ 3.9%
Second reminder	460	0.159	+ 3.4%

Concerning education levels, 43.4% (n = 190) of officers held a bachelor's degree, though it should be noted that 17.4% (n = 76) possessed some college experience but did not possess a graduate degree. Just over 18% (n = 80) of the officers possessed a graduate degree. The range of education levels is as expected. The complete frequencies and percentages for the respondent data are displayed in Table 7.10.

Concerning the agency variables, the majority of officers worked within municipal police departments – 66.4% (n = 293), while 26.1% (n = 115) of officers were associated with a sheriff's department, 5.9% (n = 26) from a state agency, and 1.6% (n = 7) worked within either a tribal or federal agency. The majority of officers responding to the survey (56.3%; n = 247) worked within agencies with more than 100 officers; 19.6% (n = 86) worked within agencies with staffing levels of between 50 and 99 officers; 14.6% (n = 64) between 25 and 49 officers; and 9.6% (n = 42) in agencies with less than 25 officers.

Allowing for the margin of error (4.3%), on average the majority of officers served communities reflecting middle- to working-class neighborhoods: 32.1% (n = 140) of officers served predominately middle-class neighborhoods; and 30.7% (n = 134) serving working-class neighborhoods. Only 3.7% (n = 16) of officers served predominately upper-class neighborhoods. Nearly 10% of officers indicated that they work within what they would classify as poor neighborhoods. Additional analysis of the "other" answer category (n = 42) revealed that officers worked across a variation of "working and poor" (n = 2), "working and middle" (n = 1), and "lower to upper with a large gap" (n = 1). The primary answer provided within the "other" category reflected "all classes equally represented" (62%).

The racial demographics for the primary service populations were nearly equally divided with 43.7% (n = 191) of officers servicing primarily Caucasian areas and 46.2% (n = 202) servicing what they considered to be highly diverse; 8.2% (n = 36) of officers indicated that they work within largely minority neighborhoods and only four officers indicated they worked within a largely immigrant community. A complete analysis of this information is displayed in Table 7.11.

Vital to the decision to collect genetic evidence is the relevant experience officers possess and the quality of the training they have received. Concerning experience, 38.6% (n = 157) of officers indicated

Table 7.10 Frequencies and Percentages for Sociodemographic Variables

Variable	N	Percent
Gender		
Male	384	87.3
Female	56	12.7
Total	440	100.0
Age		
20–30	11	2.5
31–40	127	29.4
41–50	221	51.2
51–60	65	15.0
61–70	8	1.9
Total	432	100.0
Race*		
White or Caucasian	381	86.4
American Indian or Alaska Native	13	2.9
Black or African American	13	2.9
Asian	5	1.1
Native Hawaiian or Pacific Islanders	3	.7
Other	8	1.8
I do not wish to provide this information	25	5.7
Ethnicity		
Hispanic/Latino or Hispanic/Latina		
Yes	22	5.0
No	394	89.3
I do not wish to provide this information	25	5.7
Education level		
Some school no diploma	1	0.02
High school diploma or GED	8	1.8
Some college no degree	76	17.4
Vocational school graduate	8	1.8
Associate's degree	70	16.0
Bachelor's degree	190	43.4
Master's degree	80	18.3
Doctoral Degree	4	0.9
Professional degree (JD)	1	0.2
Total	438	100.0

**Respondents were able to indicate multiple responses for the racial demographic question and as such, the total is higher than the total sample of 441.*

Table 7.11 Frequencies and Percentages for Agency Variables

Variable	N	Percent
Agency type		
Municipal police	293	66.4
Sheriff's department	115	26.1
State agency	26	5.9
Other (tribal, federal)		1.6
Total	441	100.0
Agency size		
< 25 Officers	42	9.6
25–49 Officers	64	14.6
50–99 Officers	86	19.6
100+ Officers	247	56.3
Total	439	100.0
Community characteristics		
Social class		
Upper	16	3.7
Upper middle	61	14.0
Middle	140	32.1
Working	134	30.7
Poor	43	9.9
Other	42	9.6
Total	436	100.0
Community makeup		
Primarily Caucasian	191	43.7
Largely immigrant	4	0.9
Largely minority	36	8.2
Diverse	202	46.2
Other	4	0.9
Total	437	100.0

that they possessed between 6 and 10 years of experience working with genetic evidence; slightly fewer officers (25.6%; n = 104) reported between 1 and 5 years of experience; 15.5% (n = 63) had between 11 and 15 years of experience; 5.7% (n = 23) had 16–20 years of experience; and just 2.2% (n = 9) had 21–25 years of experience. It is important to note that 12.5% (n = 51) of the officers surveyed possessed no experience of working with genetic evidence. The average number of

Table 7.12 Frequencies and Percentages for Officer Training and Genetic Evidence Collection Experience

Variable	N	Percent
Genetic evidence experience		
No experience	51	12.5
1–5 years of experience	104	25.6
6–10 years of experience	157	38.6
11–15 years of experience	63	15.5
16–20 years of experience	23	5.7
21–25 years of experience	9	2.2
Total	407	100.0
Quality of training received		
Excellent	34	7.7
Very good	92	20.9
Good	139	31.6
Fair	103	23.4
Poor	49	11.1
Did not receive training	23	5.2
Total	440	100.0

years of experience officers possessed with this evidence type was 7.88 with a minimum of no experience and a maximum of 25. The standard deviation was 5.5.

The officers' evaluation of the training they received specific to this evidence type indicated that 31.6% (n = 139) would rate their training as good, 23.4% (n = 103) as fair, 20.9% (n = 92) as very good, 11.1% (n = 49) as poor, and 7.7% (n = 34) as excellent (Table 7.12). The majority of officers positively evaluated their training, which as Patton commented on during the IPA interview, "*it's OK.*" It is important to note that 5.2% (n = 23) of the officers indicated that they received no training. This is even more important when placed within the context of the 51 officers who possessed no experience of working with genetic evidence.

Geographic Profile and Geomapping of the Survey Participants

The geographic profile of the sample indicates that there is a broad representation of officers from throughout the United States, including a participant representing the US Department of the Interior

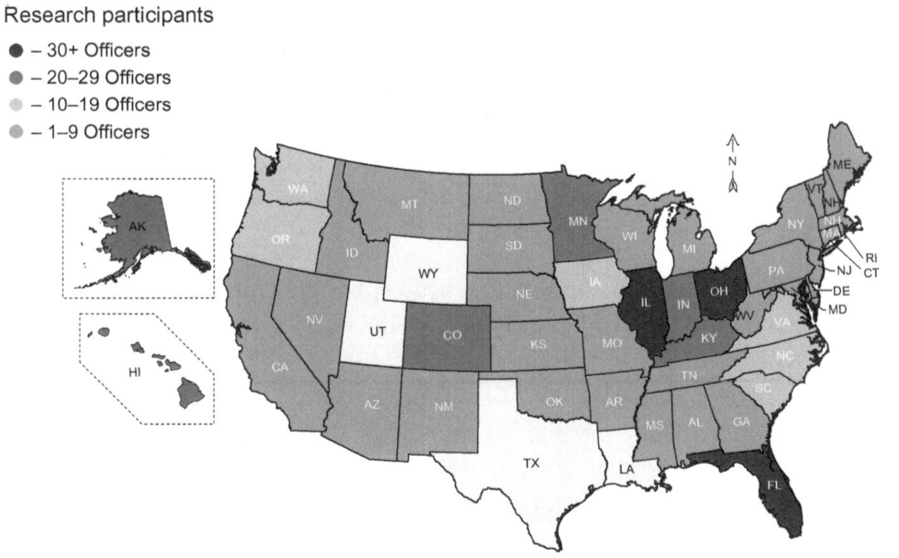

Figure 7.1 GeoMapping of research participants.

BIA/OJS – Crow Agency, located in Montana. The states with the most participants included Florida (80), Illinois (44), and Ohio (32). The least represented states included North Dakota (1) and Hawaii (1). Two respondents did not indicate their state, resulting in a geographic profile of 439 respondents. In completing the geographic profile, it was unexpected to see both Texas and New York not represented in the survey as their police populations are considerable. Figure 7.1 shows the geomapping of the final sample.

Survey Results Question Analysis

The following section provides a more detailed analysis of the research findings, giving the descriptive results of each survey question, presented as asked on the survey and divided into each primary field (Agency Information, Lab Information, and Officer Perspective). It is the intent of this approach to provide readers with the results of the national survey in the most easy to digest manner. The last section of this chapter contains the mixed-method analysis of the results with specific analysis of the associated factors that influence an officer's decision to collect or call for collection of evidence within property crime scenes.

Agency Information

The majority of officers indicated that their agency had more than 5 years of experience of routinely collecting genetic evidence for all crime types: 45.9% (n = 202) had over 10 years of experience; 39.8% (n = 175) possessed more than 5 years, but less than 10 years of experience; 11.1% (n = 49) had 2 to 5 years of experience; and 3.2% (n = 14) had 2 years or less of experience.

Specific to genetic evidence within property crime scenes, 29.3% (n = 129) of officers indicated it is collected "*a few times during the year.*" Accounting for the margin of error (4.3%), nearly equal numbers of officers, 25.9% (n = 114), indicated that genetic evidence was collected "*more than once a week.*" This demonstrates that in many cases, there is no consistency in the treatment of evidence from these crime scenes. The IPA interviews revealed that treatment of this evidence type is highly dependent on numerous factors and no standardized approach seems to exist across the United States; 18.8% (n = 83) of officers noted that evidence is routinely collected "*two to three times a month,*" 12.7% (n = 56) "*about once a month,*" 8.4% (n = 37) "*about once a week,*" and 5% (n = 22) indicated that they do not routinely collect evidence. However, collection is common in that 65.8% of officers indicated collection of such evidence once a month and nearly a quarter of officers indicated collection more than once a week.

While collection of this evidence type is important, it holds little investigative benefit unless processed for comparison. Concerning agencies that routinely collect and process genetic evidence within property crime scenes, there was again a nearly even split with 31.4% (n = 139) indicating that it is "*seldom*" analyzed and 31.4% (n = 137) expressing that it is "*frequently*" analyzed. At the other extreme, 18.3% (n = 80) of officers responded that this evidence type is "*almost always*" and "*hardly ever*" analyzed. Of importance here is that only 1.1% (n = 5) of responses were missing for this item. There was a 50/50 split in whether the property crime scene genetic evidence collected was processed.

When asked to rate their satisfaction with the treatment of genetic evidence within property crime scenes, 33.9% (n = 149) indicated that they were "*somewhat satisfied,*" 33% (n = 145) indicated that they were "*very satisfied,*" and 22.3% (n = 98) were neutral in their evaluation. Few officers indicated that they were "*somewhat dissatisfied,*" or "*very dissatisfied,*" with 8.2% (n = 36) and 2.7% (N = 12), respectively.

When asked to evaluate the current policy, 62.9% (n = 275) of officers indicated that primarily their agency is neither expanding nor reducing policy within this crime type. That said, 32% (n = 140) of officers indicated that their agency is expanding policy to see better genetic evidence treatment within property crimes scenes, and a very small percentage (5%; n = 22) expressed that their agency is reducing genetic collection and processing. Tables 7.13 and 7.14 contain the complete frequencies and percentages for this subsection of the survey.

Table 7.13 Frequencies and Percentages for Agency Genetic Forensic Treatment

Variable	N	Percent
Period of routine genetic evidence analysis		
Less than 2 years	14	3.2
2 to 5 years	49	11.1
More than 5 years, but less than 10 years	175	39.8
10 or more years	202	45.9
Total	440	100.0
Routine property crime scene collection – last year		
Not at all	22	5.0
A few times during the year	129	29.3
About once a month	56	12.7
Two to three times a month	83	18.8
About once a week	37	8.4
More than once a week	114	25.9
Total	441	100.0
Collection and processing of genetic evidence		
Almost always	80	18.3
Frequently	137	31.4
Seldom	139	31.9
Hardly ever	80	18.3
Total	436	100.0
Satisfaction with agency treatment of genetic forensic practice		
Very dissatisfied	12	2.7
Somewhat dissatisfied	36	8.2
Neutral	98	22.3
Somewhat satisfied	149	33.9
Very satisfied	145	33.0
Total	440	100.0

Table 7.14 Frequencies and Percentages for Agency Genetic Forensic Treatment – Continued

Variable	N	Percent
Policy treatment of genetic forensic evidence		
The agency is expanding policy	140	32.0
The agency is reducing policy	22	5.0
The agency is neither expanding nor reducing policy	275	62.9
Total	437	100.0

Collection

It appears that there is already overlap in responsibility for evidence collection within the agency with 59.7% (n = 243) of patrol officers being responsible for collection, which exceeded the reported 52.1% (n = 190) of officers who indicated that civilian crime scene technicians were responsible for collection. The sworn officer crime scene technician is utilized in appropriately 64.2% (n = 237) of agencies. Most surprising is that 82.9% (n = 348) of officers indicated that investigators are responsible for evidence collection. While respondents were able to indicate across all roles within the organization, it was surprising to discover that investigators are responsible for evidence collection at this level.

When evaluating those who collect genetic evidence, the vast majority of officers indicated that collection would be rated at "*good*" or "*very good*," with 41.1% (n = 181) and 38.4% (n = 169), respectively; 18.2% (n = 80) would rate those responsible for evidence collection as "*fair*." Very few officers expressed ratings of "*poor*" or "*very poor*" with only 1.6% (n = 7) and 0.7% (n = 3) responding. The complete frequencies and percentages for this are given in Table 7.15.

Respondents were asked to indicate what guided their decision to collect genetic evidence within property crime scenes. Respondents were able to mark any selection within the list and the results determined that in 93.6% (n = 393) of cases, investigator discretion guides the officer's decision; 42.1% (n = 171) of officers were guided by formal agency policy, though 35 respondents did not answer the question. Informal agency policy provided guidance in 55% (n = 219) of cases, with a nonresponse rate of 49. Most surprising was the 62.2% (n = 245) of officers who indicated that they collected genetic evidence

Table 7.15 Frequencies and Percentages for Agency Genetic Forensic Responsibility

Variable	N	Percent
Responsible for evidence collection		
Patrol officers		
No	164	40.3
Yes	243	59.7
Total	407	100.0
Investigators		
No	72	17.1
Yes	348	82.9
Total	420	100.0
Sworn officer: crime scene technician		
No	132	35.8
Yes	237	64.2
Total	369	100.0
Civilian: crime scene technician		
No	175	47.9
Yes	190	52.1
Total	365	100.0
Evaluation of those who collect genetic evidence		
Very poor	3	0.7
Poor	7	1.6
Fair	80	18.2
Good	181	41.1
Very good	169	38.4
Total	440	100.0

at the request of or with guidance from the prosecutor. 28.2% (n = 55) of officers indicated that additional sources guided their decision to collect evidence, primarily reflecting command staff guidance, crime scene technician quality assessment, budgets, and the policy of the crime lab (n = 16), which also dictated if evidence would be processed by the facility. Moreover, several respondents noted that the state lab would only accept samples where there was a known suspect and would not accept genetic evidence for nonpersonal crimes. The complete frequencies and percentages for this are given in Table 7.16.

As discussed within the literature review, there has been considerable progression within policy to see the collection of offender genetic

Table 7.16 Frequencies and Percentages for Guidance on Evidence Collection

Variable	N	Percent
Guidance		
Agency policy (formal)	171	42.1
Agency policy (informal)	219	55.9
Request or guidance from prosecutor	245	62.2
Investigator discretion	393	93.6
Other	55	28.2

Table 7.17 Frequencies and Percentages for Offender Sample Collection

Variable	N	Percent	Total
State policy on offender samples			
All arrests	13	3.6	362
All felony arrests	170	42.3	402
Certain misdemeanor and/or felony arrests	171	45.8	373
All convictions	30	8.8	342
All felony convictions	257	67.5	381
For certain misdemeanor and/or felony convictions	213	59.3	359

samples, which has placed a burden on agencies and labs to meet the influx of additional samples. When asked about official state policy, 67.5% (n = 257) of officers indicated that they collect genetic samples from "*all offenders convicted of a felony*," 59.3% (n = 213) for "*certain misdemeanor and/or felony convictions*," and only 8.8% (n = 30) have a collection practice for "*all convictions*."

While the collection of genetic samples at the conviction level places minimal burden on the agency, the arrestee level collection policy does see an increased burden. According to respondents, over 45.8% (n = 171) of agencies collect genetic samples "*for certain misdemeanor and/or felony arrests*" and 42.3% (n = 170) collect for "*all felony arrests*." Very few agencies were required to collect arrestee genetic evidence for "*all arrests*" with only 3.6% (n = 13) reporting this requirement. The complete frequencies and percentages for this are shown in Table 7.17.

As discussed within the literature review in detail, the utilization of forensic evidence requires considerable resource expenditures, which exceed the pure costs of analysis. Managing genetic evidence is both challenging and complicated in that the utilization of this evidence type involves numerous stakeholders and there are considerable obstacles presented. Respondents indicated that the primary obstacles in managing cases within genetic evidence reflect "*Conflicting philosophies between agency and outside lab(s)*" and "*Lack of money to pay for analyses*" with 57.1% (n = 252) and 53.5% (n = 236) responding. This is a vital point in that as indicated within the IPA interviews, all participants noted how lab policy presented a challenge or as many detailed a "*barrier*" to property crime scene genetic evidence analysis. The indication was that lab policy would limit processing to only those crimes where identification of a suspect had occurred or may completely deny submission of property crime scene DNA evidence. It is of interest to note that the conflicting philosophies exceed the economic burden, with 53.5% (n = 236) of officers expressing that "lack of money to pay for analysis" was a primary obstacle. While the margin of could reflect lab policy (both formal and informal) and resource expenditures at nearly identical levels, this is a very important contributory finding in that lab policy, as an external stakeholder, presents a primary obstacle. 35.6% (n = 157) expressed that there was "*Not enough communication between forensic analysts and investigators*" and while communication is vital, this was not strictly reserved to personal communications. Moreover, 33.8% (n = 149) of officers expressed that the computer and technology systems were an obstacle within managing cases, and 30.6% (n = 135) of officers noted that a "*failure to withdraw evidence prior to analysis*" (when the case was solved) presented an obstacle. As noted in the IPA interviews and as expressed within the open-ended content analysis, this often presented a challenge in that an agency that had solved a case, believing the analysis was not needed, would still incur the budgetary loss.

Concerning internal obstacles, 20.6% (n = 91) of officers indicated that there were "*Conflicting philosophies regarding prioritization of cases*" within the agency, including 18.4% (n = 81) expressing that "*differing views within the agency on the usefulness of DNA evidence*" presented an obstacle. Moreover, 16.3% (n = 72) of officers indicated that "*lack of follow-up by investigators after DNA results are received*" presented an obstacle to successful utilization of this evidence type.

The content analysis of the "other" answer category indicates that predominately the lab backlog, facility policy on the prioritization of cases, and agency treatment are the primary obstacles. Officers expressed backlogs of 2–3 years and on average a year or longer to see a sample processed, often including violent crime samples. The following statements provided by officers more or less summarize all the responses.

> *Our state lab added additional personnel to help ease the backlog but then our corresponding increased use of DNA analysis has slowed the process back down. Five years ago, DNA was primarily used solely for major crimes of violence against people. Now we routinely collect and submit for cases involving property crimes (felony only).*
>
> *We are able to call the analysts directly. The Lab does not take any sample we'd like to submit. On major crimes cases, we are required to have a meeting to discuss the case and narrow down the evidence that can be submitted. We are only able to submit 9 evidence items (does not include victim, suspect or witness DNA standards) at a time.*

Additionally, a respondent indicated that in a burglary case where they had a suspect identified, the sample took a year to be analyzed. As discovered from the IPA interviews and expressed within the survey, there is considerable conflict between the agency and the laboratory, where lab policy has come to shape organizational practice within the treatment of genetic evidence. The complete frequencies and percentages for this subsection of the survey are given in Table 7.18.

Table 7.18 Frequencies and Percentages for Obstacles of Managing Cases with Genetic Evidence

Variable	N	Percent
Obstacles managing cases		
Conflicting philosophies regarding prioritization of cases	91	20.6
Conflicting philosophies between agency and outside lab(s)	252	57.1
Differing views within the agency on the usefulness of DNA evidence	81	18.4
Too many evidence samples collected for cases	123	27.9
Inappropriate communication between forensic analysts and investigators	67	15.2
Not enough communication between forensic analysts and investigators	157	35.6
Lack of follow-up by investigators after DNA results are received	72	16.3
Failure to withdraw DNA analysis request prior to analysis (case solved)	135	30.6
Lack of interoperability between agency and forensic lab systems	149	33.8
Lack of confidence in available labs	34	7.7
Lack of money to pay for analyses	236	53.5
Other (please explain):	30	6.8
Total	441	100.0

Table 7.19 Frequencies and Percentages for CODIS Warrants		
Variable	**N**	**Percent**
Utilization of CODIS Warrants or "*John Doe*" Warrants:		
Yes	72	16.3
No	366	83.6
Total	438	100.0

A final item within this subsection, reflected at a training level, concerned familiarity with utilizing a "*John Doe*" warrant or CODIS warrant. As discussed prior, a CODIS warrant freezes the case in time. In essence, the DNA of the individual is charged with perpetrating the crime and when a match occurs, the clock restarts. By submitting a CODIS warrant, officers are able to sidestep the statute of limitations for cases. As discovered, very few agencies utilize CODIS warrants within property crime scenes. In fact, 83.6% (n = 366) indicated that they were aware of no one in the organization filing this type of warrant within a property crime scene case (Table 7.19).

Lab Information

This section provides information on the utilization of the lab and the working relationship between the agency and facility. Respondents were asked to indicate who performed genetic analysis for their agency. Results indicated that agencies predominately utilize a state facility for their analysis across all crime samples (n = 295). Agencies fortunate to have in-house facilities accounted for nearly 20% of the sample (n = 84). While agencies did utilize the federal laboratory, no agency indicated utilizing the facility for property crime analysis. Agencies indicating the use of a private laboratory to process property crime evidence was rare at only 9% (n = 40).

When asked to evaluate the accessibility of the lab facility, 76% (n = 333) found the facility to be accessible, reflecting in the ability to talk to analysts directly or submit *any* sample to the facility. This question covers the submission of any sample, not just property crime scene evidence. Communication between the agency and the lab was generally indicated as satisfactory, with only 6% (n = 26) indicating that communication was "*very poor*" or "*poor*." The complete frequencies and percentages for this subsection of the survey are shown in Table 7.20.

Table 7.20 Frequencies and Percentages for Relationship with Lab Facility

Variable	N	Percent
Accessibility		
Very accessible	161	36.8
Somewhat accessible	172	39.3
Neutral	56	12.8
Somewhat inaccessible	35	8.0
Very inaccessible	14	3.2
Total	438	100.0
Communication		
Very good	128	29.2
Good	178	40.5
Fair	107	24.4
Poor	20	4.6
Very poor	6	1.4
Total	439	100.0

Officer Perspective

This section provides the results of the questions specific to the officer's perception on the treatment of genetic evidence from property crime scenes. The questions reflect their current collection practices, the effectiveness of genetic evidence in these cases, the expansion of the treatment, influences on the decision to collect, and familiarity with current research.

Specific to prior utilization of genetic evidence within property crime scenes, 48.7% (n = 214) of officers noted that they have called for collection and processing of genetic evidence in "*less than 10% of property crime cases.*" While an observer may deem this low, this is an important finding in that the current recovery rate of suitable genetic evidence is approximately 11% (as discussed prior). Also, 19.6% (n = 86) of officers have requested analysis in "*10 to 25% of property crime cases,*" and only 6.2% (n = 27) have called for analysis evidence in "*50% or more property crime cases.*" However, 18.5% (n = 81) of officers did indicate that they have not requested DNA evidence to be analyzed. The complete frequencies and percentages for this subsection of the survey are shown in Table 7.21.

When asked if officers believe genetic evidence assists in apprehending offenders in property crime scene cases, 80% indicated that it is

Table 7.21 Frequencies and Percentages for Collection and Processing Requests

Variable	N	Percent
Requests for collection and processing		
I have not requested DNA evidence collection and processing	81	18.5
Less than 10% of property crime cases	214	48.7
10 to 25% of property crime cases	86	19.6
More than 25%, but less than 50% of property crime cases	31	7.1
50% or more of property crime cases	27	6.2
Total	439	100.0

helpful. Moreover, 41.5% (n = 182) expressed that genetic evidence is helpful "*a great deal*" and 39.4% (n = 173) indicated it is helpful "*a fair amount.*" Additionally, 16.6% (n = 73) believed that genetic evidence was not very helpful within these cases and 2.5% (n = 11) expressed it was rarely if ever helpful.

Officers were then asked whether they favored or opposed expanding genetic evidence analysis within property crime scenes, first with no additional funding source and second with a specific funding allotment attached to the expansion. The results were 64.6% (n = 285) of officers "*strongly favor*" the expansion of genetic analysis within property crime scenes; moreover, 23.1% (n = 43) indicated that they "*somewhat favor*" expansion. Less than 2% (n = 11) "*somewhat oppose*" or "*strongly oppose*" expansion without a funding allocation. Equally important in this analysis is that every respondent answered the question. When an appropriate funding source was provided, 75.5% (n = 332) of officers "*strongly favor*" expansion, an increase of nearly 11%. In fact, 93% (n = 413) of officers indicated that they favor expansion of genetic analysis within property crime scenes.

Recognizing that officers favor expansion of genetic analysis, it becomes important to analyze their perception of expanding collection at the officer level, namely, 36.6% (n = 161) of officers were "*very much in favor*" of seeing responsibility for collection extended to the officer level. Additionally, 23.4% (n = 103) indicated that they are "*somewhat in favor*" of this responsibility being extended to them. However, 19.8% (n = 87) were "*neutral*" about extending the responsibility to officers. Moreover, 12.7% (n = 56) "*somewhat oppose*" and 7.5% (n = 33) "*very much oppose*" making officers responsible for

Table 7.22 Frequencies and Percentages for Expansion of Collection

Variable	N	Percent	% Change
Expansion of genetic evidence – no funding			
Strongly favor	285	64.6	
Somewhat favor	102	23.1	
Neither favor nor oppose	43	9.8	
Somewhat oppose	8	1.8	
Strongly oppose	3	0.7	
Total	441	100.0	
Expansion of genetic evidence – funding			
Strongly favor	332	75.5	*+ 10.9*
Somewhat favor	81	18.4	− 4.7
Neither favor nor oppose	24	5.5	− 4.3
Somewhat oppose	3	0.7	− 1.1
Strongly oppose	0	0.0	0.0
Total	440	100.0	
Officer responsible for evidence collection			
Very much in favor	161	36.6	
Somewhat in favor	103	23.4	
Neutral	87	19.8	
Somewhat oppose	56	12.7	
Very much oppose	33	7.5	
Total	440	100.0	

evidence collection. The complete frequencies and percentages for this subsection of the survey are given in Table 7.22.

The collection of genetic evidence presents several challenges. According to officers, the most pressing challenges reflect training, with 68.9% (n = 304) of officers expressing the need for "*better training within evidence collection techniques.*" This was closely followed by 56.2% (n = 248) of officers wanting "*better training within evidence submission and analysis process.*" As indicated in the prior analysis, those responsible for collection of evidence were predominately sworn personnel and the third highest rated challenge reflected "*difficulties in identifying possible biological evidence*" with 51.2% (n = 215) of officers expressing this challenge. The remaining challenges identified by respondents reflected evidence collection, scene contamination, and as detailed within the IPA interviews, storage space or more specifically insufficient storage space for genetic evidence.

Content analysis of the other category item suggests that the laboratory policy and resources within the laboratory presents a considerable challenge for agencies. The following statements reflect the range of challenges and reflect the core themes that inhibit expansion as noted within the IPA thematic analysis.

> *Crime scene contamination by first responding patrol officers and victim residents prior to trained investigators arriving at the scene. Lab technicians with my agency, as with most agencies will not respond to the scene of a simple burglary.*
>
> *Currently our state lab, due to overwhelming submissions, will not, in most cases analyze property crime DNA evidence. An extraordinary situation would have to exist for them to do so.*
>
> *DNA processing is available for all violent crimes but we do not normally process touch DNA on property crimes due to the labs policy. We do not do in-house DNA processing with the exception of sample collection.*
>
> *The primary problem becomes a backlog at the state lab for the processing of DNA evidence. Most property crimes involve what is termed here as "touch" DNA. Due to the high volume of DNA submissions, "Touch" DNA can only be submitted at the request of the Commonwealth Attorney by signed letter-head. This is not an overly oppressive problem except when the priorities of the case differ between the prosecutors and law enforcement.*

As the excerpts note, there is overlap within scene contamination but within the majority of statements provided by officers, the laboratory presents a considerable challenge, which is complicated by the additional local policies that have emerged concerning property crime scene evidence. For example, as described above by an officer, having a formal written request by the Commonwealth Attorney is bound to present a challenge and inhibit expansion. Likewise, several officers indicated that a challenge is the increased workload resulting from collecting the homeowners' and additional occupants' DNA for the process of elimination. The collection/analysis and elimination of DNA samples as several officers mentioned presents a challenge beyond the laboratory. In this situation, officers must first convince victims and additional occupants of the household to provide samples, which then must be submitted to the lab for elimination analysis. Training, scene contamination, increased collection, willingness of the victim to submit samples for analysis, and local policy all present challenges to an agency, which only become more complicated when the limited storage capacity is taken into consideration.

Table 7.23 Frequencies and Percentages for Challenges within Collection

Variable	N	Percent
Challenges within collecting genetic evidence for property scenes		
Difficulties in identifying possible biological evidence	215	51.2
Evidence collection techniques	121	27.4
Evidence contamination	175	39.7
Evidence packaging	81	18.4
Problems with the availability of proper collection kits/tools	127	28.8
Insufficient storage space for DNA evidence	150	34.0
Better training within evidence collection techniques	304	68.9
Better training within evidence submission and analysis process	248	56.2
Crime scene contamination	157	35.6
Other	38	8.6
All officers responded (n = 441).		

Currently, collection and analysis depend greatly on several factors and while no uniform collection policy seems to emerge within the research, the reality is that agencies are already experiencing insufficient storage space, with 34.0% (n = 150) indicating that any future expansion will need to take into account the vast increase in samples needing storage. The complete frequencies and percentages for this subsection of the survey are shown in Table 7.23.

Concerning stakeholder influence, 84% (n = 368) of officers indicated that investigators had the greatest influence on the decision to collect genetic evidence. Crime scene technicians expressed a strong influence with 73.5% (n = 302) of officers denoting that the evaluation of the technician would influence their decision to collect evidence from property crime scenes. Patrol officer influence can be viewed as moderately strong. Concerning those stakeholders with moderate influence, the command staff, i.e., the Captain and Police Chief, possess nearly identical levels of influence. Those with the least influence on officer decision making are the victim and victim advocate, whose role can be said to be very weak. As noted prior, the prosecutor's office does influence the collection of evidence with 62.2% of officers indicating that the office has guided agency policy, both formally and informally. The relative influence of the office as displayed here can be said to be moderate. The complete frequencies and percentages for this subsection of the survey are given in Table 7.24.

Table 7.24 Frequencies and Percentages for Stakeholder Influence on Decision to Collect

Variable		Influence			
Stakeholder	N	Strong	Moderate	Weak	None
Patrol officer	438	43.8	30.1	19.2	6.8
Investigator	438	84.0	12.8	2.5	0.7
Captain	417	34.8	24.7	17.5	23.0
Police chief	427	39.1	17.3	18.7	24.8
Crime scene technician	411	73.5	11.9	3.2	11.4
Prosecutor	434	42.2	29.3	15.0	13.6
Victim advocate	423	4.3	13.7	29.8	52.2
Victim	427	11.2	24.8	35.6	28.3

Table 7.25 Frequencies and Percentages for Influences on Decision to Collect

Variable	N	Percent	Total
Property loss is high (>$5,000)	342	78.6	435
Characteristics of the crime scene are similar to other cases	396	90.6	437
A suspect has been identified	345	79.9	432
Suspect has not been identified	314	73.5	427
Analysis requested by the prosecutor	352	82.8	425
Analysis requested by the victim	139	33.0	421
Other	30	16.9	178

When presented with a preset list of influences, 82.8% (n = 252) of officers expressed that they would collect evidence if requested by the prosecutor, while only 33% (n = 132) would collect evidence at the request of a victim (Table 7.25). Those primary influences reflected identification of the suspect, similar scene characteristics, and high property crime loss, with over 70% of officers indicating they would influence them to collect evidence. The content analysis of the other category once again denotes the relative influence of lab policy. For example, respondents acknowledged that evidence was being collected, but lab policy would most often limit processing by limiting submission. The following excerpts express the perceptions of respondents.

We recommend collection in all cases if applicable, although our state crime lab does not process DNA on misdemeanor cases.

We do collect them but we can't send all to lab for testing because of backload. They stay in property until a suspect is identified. If he/she doesn't confess, they sent for testing.

Until our state lab can do the analysis it does not matter what anybody else wants.

Our State lab will only process person crimes.

A theme emerging within the IPA interviews was that of a process aptly named "*simulated evidence collection*," a term coined reflecting the decision to swab, powder, or collect nonviable samples to demonstrate that the victim received the full resources of the agency. In some cases, evidence could be collected with no intent of formally processing the evidence. While the majority of officers (70.7%, n = 309) indicated that they were not familiar with an officer engaging in this practice, 29.3% (n = 128) admitted having engaged in the practice or knowledge of an officer who has done so at a scene (Table 7.26). This is a surprising result considering that prior research has revealed substantial backlogs within evidence rooms pertaining to untested samples.

The final question asked reflected officers' familiarity with the national DNA Field Experiment to highlight how knowledge transference takes place from the National Institute of Justice to agencies and officers (Table 7.27). While it was anticipated that few officers would be aware of the study, the study found that 92.4% (n = 403) of officers are not familiar with the national report. This is alarming considering the amount of resources dedicated to informing police officers of the

Table 7.26 Frequencies and Percentages for Simulated Evidence Collection

Variable	N	Percent
Simulated evidence collection		
Yes	128	29.3
No	309	70.7
Total	437	100.0

Table 7.27 Frequencies and Percentages for National Report Knowledge Dissemination

Variable	N	Percent
Familiarity with the "DNA Field Experiment"		
Yes	33	7.5
No	403	92.4
Total	436	100.0

results via reports and presentations, and the creation of a training curriculum specific to property crime scene DNA evidence.

MIXED-METHOD ANALYSIS

In concert, the national survey and IPA interviews have identified several unique factors which, when reported across both methods, offer improved reliability and validity. As noted within prior research, the discretion of the responding officer has the greatest influence over whether evidence is collected. However, concerning processing of this evidence, the relative influences of the laboratory facility, officer training, and prosecutor are contributory. The role of the laboratory was a common source of discussion across all interview participants. The ability for the lab to dictate submission policies placed considerable influence on officers when determining the relative worth of evidence. Moreover, when discussing the importance of genetic evidence within property crime scenes, police officers, command staff, and forensic technicians expressed the evidence type at varying levels of importance.

Over 80% of officers within the national survey indicated that they believed this evidence type to be "helpful" in solving property crime cases. Additionally, over 80% of officers favor expansion of genetic analysis within property crime scenes without changes to current funding practices. The number in favor exceeds 90% if funding is supplied. In both the survey and the interviews, the majority of officers favored being responsible for evidence collection. The national survey results indicated that over 50% would take on that role, with 20% being neutral on this issue. This was a surprising result until it was discovered that over 80% of investigators are currently responsible for evidence collection at some level.

While officers favored expanding into property crime scene collection and analysis, a universal challenge emerging within the research is the need for better training within evidence collection techniques. Recognizing the role officers have come to hold within evidence collection from low-level scenes, there is a clear need for better training. Few officers reported the quality of training as exceptional and this was compounded by the lack of familiarity with CODIS warrants and identification of evidence at property crime scenes.

The importance of improved training is incredibly poignant considering the levels as reported in the national survey with 82.9% of respondents indicating that investigators were responsible for evidence collection to some degree. As agencies consider grappling with reduced budgets and increased expectations and pressures to utilize forensics, the natural response has been to assign additional tasks to the officer level, which has included low-level genetic collection. This is complicated further by the revelation that over 90% of police officers have no familiarity with the national DNA Field Experiment or as discussed within the To see unfamiliarity levels, as reported within the national survey, at that level was unimaginable considering the funding expenditures that took place to disseminate the information to police practitioners.

As a unique theme, the influence of the community was identified often within the IPA interviews, leading to a phenomenon known as "simulated evidence collection." The results of the national survey indicated that victims have a weak influence on officer decision making, which when framed within the context of the IPA interviews suggests that the primary influence of the community is not on the actual victim but the perception the officer holds of displaying modernity. The victim may request that evidence be collected but the decision to collect is not facilitated by appeasement of the victim but rather the ability to display the skills necessary to undertake evidence collection by the officer or to call for an evidence technician to process the scene. It can be said that the CSI effect has influenced the very officers it portrays.

The influence of the prosecutor's office was highlighted across the entire stakeholder continuum both in the IPA interviews and the national survey. The majority of officers did indicate that the office influenced their decision to collect. However, it is important to note that there was no influence prior to their involvement, meaning the influence of the prosecutor was not indirect. Rather, the influence of the prosecutor was primarily displayed when they requested information be collected at a scene, often indicated by calling for additional processing before they would accept a case. Additionally, while the influence was deemed moderate, several officers expressed their frustration that they needed to seek the formal approval of the office to submit property crime genetic evidence. At this level, the prosecutor can be said to have a significant influence.

A final unique point offered within both the IPA interviews and the national survey is the influence of the laboratory. Across each method, the results identified clear examples of how lab policy and not agency policy would dictate what is collected and processed. Often officers expressed their frustration because the facility would not process samples unless there was a suspect or would not process property crime scene samples regardless of case characteristics. In fact, when asked what the primary obstacles were, respondents within the national survey indicated that the conflicting philosophies between agency and outside lab(s) presented the greatest challenge, exceeding that of lack of money. It is important to highlight that several IPA participants noted that they did not pay for processing and yet still had no influence on the processing of genetic evidence within these cases. While the explanations offered were understandable, the reality of the influence the laboratory holds over collection and processing is remarkable.

CHAPTER 8

Where Do We Go from Here?

> *We are a COMPSTAT agency, we use it, we have the meetings, we go over the rates, the hard data, which is what the higher-ups believe in but it limits forensics. We created the incentive because when we went to COMPSTAT, collection went down, you get so focused on performance that forensic is an afterthought.*
>
> **Police Executive**

While prior studies have introduced academics and practitioners to the current policy and utilization of forensic evidence, the external, organizational, and personal factors that influence an officer's decision to collect genetic evidence within property crime scenes were unexamined. Moreover, often missing was the involvement of those investigative stakeholders. Prior research had surveyed these stakeholders, but few have directly engaged them in the challenges, the issues, and the opportunities involved in the treatment of genetic evidence. By building on prior research, the intent of this book was to identify those factors influencing the collection of this evidence type to add to the discourse on the treatment genetic evidence receives across the crime continuum.

Despite a wealth of research on forensic analysis, the primary contribution of previous forensic literature has been to depict the state of forensic backlogs, source of backlogs, and to denote the investigative benefit of forensic practices (Strom and Hickman, 2010). The outcome, while incredibly significant to academics and practitioners, has been unable to peer into the "black box" of evidence processing, to offer exploratory and explanatory factors that influence an officer's decision across the investigative stakeholder continuum, reflecting the officers, the command staff, forensic technicians, and prosecutors.

This present study utilizing a mixed-method research design provides both a qualitative and quantitative exploration into factors influencing the decision to collect genetic evidence and those additional factors currently missing from the discourse on forensic evidence collection. The IPA (interpretative phenomenological analysis) interviews revealed a wealth of information, highlighting the experiences, perceptions, and the frustration of those within the investigative stakeholder continuum. Officers, detectives, command staff, civilian forensic technicians, and prosecutors are fully aware of the inherent benefits of expanding utilization of forensic evidence within these crime scenes, but the practical reality of the day-to-day operations of their respective agencies, offices, and tasks inhibits such expansion. As discovered, there are external, organizational, and individual factors that influence decision making, and specific to officer decision making within collection, the external factors are suggested to have the greatest influence at an exploratory level.

Officers indicated that collection of genetic evidence within property crimes scenes is routine. Moreover, they currently see themselves as being tasked with collecting forensic evidence, as not being resistant to tasks, and even support expanding collection because they see the worth of this evidence. However, the challenge is not convincing officers of the worth of this genetic evidence, but seeing evidence collected and *processed*, which is the primary inhibitor of collection practices. To collect evidence just to see it lie untouched in the evidence room is defeating the purpose of collecting it in the first place and potentially opens up a line of questions from the defense with regard to why evidence collection occurred but not processing. As expressed within the IPA interviews, at the command staff and prosecutorial level, the fiscal reality presents a challenge and while agencies are collecting evidence, that evidence is not being processed, which potentially creates a negative feedback loop ensuring that future evidence is less likely to be collected.

LOOKING FORWARD: CHALLENGING THE DOMINANT PARADIGM OF POLICE PRACTICE

There is no way to discount the ability for fiscal reality to inhibit expansion. Expanding forensic analysis into property crime scenes will be expensive. A crude mathematical analysis denotes that on average it will cost nearly 900 million dollars to expand into property crime scenes at the present processing costs. If analysis were capable of achieving the optimum level, identified by the $1,000 efficiency level as discussed within the literature review, the average cost nationally would be ~$240 million. While it is easy to highlight rough estimates of processing costs, administrators are often limited by fixed budgets. Expanding processing cannot be done swiftly and without proper planning. However, to use cost as a barrier to limit the expansion undermines the clear benefits that expansion affords an agency.

As discussed prior, the Denver study revealed a cost savings of more than $5 million in police costs and $36.8 million in property loss as a result of the expansion in processing of forensic evidence within property crime scenes (Ashikhmin et al., ND). While not all agencies were capable of achieving the same results, at a comparative level expansion within the treatment of genetic evidence clearly shows a cost—benefit ratio in support of expansion. The challenge that police administrators and the legislature must overcome is that the inherent benefits are not immediate, nor are they highly visible to the community. A prevented crime is a crime that garners little public attention unless linked to a specific intervention (i.e., an offender apprehended before committing an offense). Moreover, a formal criminal justice intervention into the offending cycle of a burglar receives the immediate benefits when prolific but to intervene and subsequently prevent *potentially* upwards of a hundred burglaries has little lasting impact on the community or even the officers who work the case as the benefits are not immediate. Scholars no doubt will seek to examine the deterrence capability of a fully integrated and uniform treatment of genetic evidence within this crime type. However, most pressing on the police administrator is recognizing that while the benefits to clearance rates and cold case resolutions will be immediate, the cost savings will not manifest directly in the budgets of the agency.

One of the best analogies offered is that the police are akin to an emergency room. A product of their environment and the tasks they engage in, the outcome is decision making focused on the immediate, not long-term, which is not a product or an indication of some short-sighted limitation but a result of the practical reality of the day-to-day operations of the agency. To ask police administrators to trust in research, to expand processing, and to treat all evidence types as equal is asking a lot from them. The benefits are clear but there are other problems that inhibit expansion, notably forensic labs across the nation. In the national study, nearly a quarter of officers indicated that collection of genetic evidence within property crime scenes occurred on average once a week or more; 63% indicated collection levels of once a month or more. Despite clear collection practices, even if an agency seeks to employ a full collection practice, lab policy and their philosophy on the processing of property crime scene evidence presents as a barrier to expansion.

LOOKING FORWARD: THE LAB AND THE LAB TECHNICIANS

As indicated in this research, lab policy inhibits processing of genetic evidence from property crime scenes. There are several specific examples from officers across the nation suggesting that lab facilities only process genetic evidence when a clear suspect is identified. With this simple policy, full treatment of forensic evidence is stalled. Fundamentally, a forensic identification system can exist to link offenders to scenes or scenes to individuals; the current treatment of genetic evidence has created a system that undermines itself by the very practices it employs. Moreover, the increased collection of offender, arrestee, and suspect genetic samples has inundated the lab with increased processing as well as an increased focus on testing synthetic cannabinoids, as indicated within the IPA interviews.

Further limiting forensics is the unfamiliarity of the command staff with the workload and requirements of their forensic technicians, be they local staff or on-call personnel. Forensic technicians have seen their workload and responsibilities greatly increased. In addition to being understaffed and often viewed as a burden on an agency (a feeling expressed in all interviews), forensic technicians enjoy the responsibility of having multiple responsibilities. As discussed by each of the forensic experts, a technician can be responsible for evidence collection, evidence packaging and transport, evidence processing, acting in the capacity as a supply repository for officers, conducting training, conducting interviews for public relations, testifying in court on evidence they collected, and testifying in court when requested to explain why evidence was not present at a scene or on a person (negative evidence testimony), and for many technicians, being on-call to assist other agencies. The multiple "hats" that a forensic technician wears within the organization is apparent in the seemingly increased role within collection that officers have as indicated in the research.

Unlike officers who can end a shift and the next set of calls will go to a new patrol officer or the detective who is unable to be assigned a new case because of his or her current caseload, the work of a forensic technician never ceases. To see the expansion of forensic evidence collection within these incidents is to make clear modifications within the treatment of forensic evidence, which transitions well into the policy recommendations section.

POLICY RECOMMENDATIONS

Practical benefits at the officer or agency level are not more arrests or better case clearance rates but less work on the part of the officer. There is clearly more work on the part of the administrator to keep staffing of forensic technicians at an appropriate level. Also, there is clearly more work on the part of the officer who may be required to collect evidence or wait for a forensic technician to arrive at the scene. However, as indicated within the present research, officers are supportive of expansion and believe agencies should expand.

Traditionally, research suggests that more funding must occur to see expansion and I find that recommendation to be irresponsible and short sighted. Currently, states spend annually over a billion dollars on forensic analysis. Providing more funding without specific recommendations on where that funding allocation occurs simply ensures that the current CODIS system will maintain its inefficiency.

Recommendation: Appropriate Collection and Retention of Offender Samples

The primary source of a conflicting philosophy is not solely the view that property crime scenes are "lesser than" others. Officers believe in expansion, as do the forensic experts involved. The overburdened crime labs and conflicting philosophy are the result of continued expansion of collection and retention policies that have witnessed collection move from the felony offender to the misdemeanor offender, to the arrestee, and now to the suspect level. It is at this level that often policy recommendations are made to allocate more funding to CODIS, which would not address the overwhelming issue that the expansion of individual DNA sample collection has stemmed from the utilization of CODIS and thus the processing of scene samples.

The continued expansion of individual genetic sample retention policies has fostered a conflict wherein scene samples see extremely long turnaround times in processing and denied processing (i.e., when lab policy dictates that a suspect must be identified for processing to occur), and the outlook is to connect the offender to prior violent crimes within the system. As detailed in previous chapters, there is considerable evidence suggesting that processing property crime scene evidence is advantageous to intervening in subsequent offending and clearing cold cases. If a person is in fact guilty of the crime for which they are convicted, then their genetic information will be entered into CODIS.

To improve both collection and processing of genetic evidence within property crime scenes, it is recommended that states modify their laws moving collection to the arrestee and suspect levels to prioritize crime scene samples. Those convicted of offenses will see their genetic profiles collected and retained within the CODIS system. The current movement to expand the collection and retention of genetic profiles has inundated labs with samples only further forcing them to prioritize cases at the detriment of scene samples. Moreover, a policy that allows for the collection of genetic profiles for comparison within CODIS is ripe for abuse. Over the last few years, police in the United Kingdom have been accused of arresting individuals simply to obtain the genetic profile (BBC News, 2009). Whether these allegations are true or false does not change the fact that there is potential for great abuse. It is imperative that agencies and legislatures collaborate to create strong accountability mechanisms.

In making this recommendation, it has not gone unnoticed that legislatures have used this topic as a political tool to garner votes. To them I offer that to re-appropriate funding for scene processing provides significantly better press releases and stump speeches. They could highlight cases involving the apprehension of a habitual offender versus the collection and retention of Johnny Criminal, whose encounter with the criminal justice system cost the state considerable funds and who is highly likely to recidivate (within the context of states that collect and retain at the misdemeanor offense level).

To revise the current collection and retention statutes is a necessary and controversial recommendation that seeks to better align evidence collection practices. The following recommendation details the rationale for transitioning evidence collection responsibilities to the patrol officer.

Recommendation: Alignment of Evidence Collection at the Patrol Level

While revising collection practices at the legislative level could be argued to be the most complicated of practical recommendations, re-appropriating forensic evidence collection at the officer level is the most complicated of philosophical recommendations. As the results of the NIJ study indicated, officers trained within evidence collection were capable of collecting the same quality of sample as a certified evidence technician (Roman et al., 2008). As indicated in the national survey and the interviews, officers are willing to take on the role and in many cases are currently trained to process minor level incidents. It is important to highlight that the alignment of forensic evidence collection within the patrol level is not designed to replace the civilian forensic technicians, who are trained and knowledgeable in the techniques and developments specific to violent crimes and evidence recovery, such as homicides, sexual assaults, and other high-level personal crime offenses. To expand evidence processing within property crime scenes and not align evidence collection of this crime type at the patrol level will require additional hiring of forensic technicians, who will not have the latitude that officers presently have within the organization.

In making this recommendation, it is important to highlight that in addition to improved training across all aspects of genetic evidence (a point officers noted within the research), it will prove necessary to revise the academy and police training commissions. To assign this task to officers and improve training within the agency is to miss the opportune moment to ensure that officers are as prepared to handle genetic scenes as they are in handling issues within search and seizure. Like issues within the Fourth Amendment, it is imperative that training commissions develop standard operating procedures for the handling of genetic evidence.

Implementation of the Body Worn Camera

At the time of this writing, I have spent nearly 2 years studying the specific implementation of the body worn camera (BWC) in a police agency, and have been enamored with the potential this single device brings to policing for nearly a decade, when I started researching cameras in patrol vehicles and became aware of the Plymouth Head Camera Project. For a bit of background, in 2007, the Home Office commissioned an evaluation of a pilot program involving the deployment of head camera devices. The device utilizes a small video camera that records to an internal compact computer drive (now available in a streaming format). The device does not impede officer mobility and records the officer's field of view. The report titled "The Plymouth Head Camera Project" noted several initial findings concerning officer safety, reduction in crime, improved crime detection, and increased prosecution. The initial and subsequent results from additional studies would establish that the device improved officer safety, but additionally what intrigued me was the accountability and transparency the device could provide, through improved documentation.

While photography has been standard practice in crime scene investigations, documentation of the collection practice was lacking. As discussed prior in the work, issues with training and pressures across the investigative stakeholder continuum have undermined forensics, fostering a state of training that is subpar and inhibiting high volume processing. While the Plymouth study was not concerned with documentation of forensic evidence, agencies deploying the device noted a 40% reduction in complaints, specifically for incivility and excessive use of force by officers (Somer, 2007). Having an entire video record of the collection process would prove immensely beneficial to challenges brought forth concerning collection, analysis, and issues of contamination.

Democratic Policing Theory and Officer Collection

In making this recommendation to expand the role of collection to officers, it is not without the consideration that the inclusion of forensic science within the police service was meant to epitomize democratic policing (and by extension criminal justice systems). This practice was meant to provide an accountable, verifiable, and reliable means of establishing innocence wherein abuse, misconduct, and corruption need not exist to see a successful resolution to a crime incident (Uildriks, 2009). Several scholars will likely argue that in doing so, the opportunity for vast abuses and corruption only increase. Their skepticism is both warranted and valid at the present state. To assign the task of evidence collection to officers certainly places great trust in officers. However, currently officers are engaged in these collection practices and in many areas, they exceed the collection beyond that of the civilian technician. As discussed within the prior chapter, the current cases of error are not at the officer level; rather, they are within the lab facility.

While forensics is said to epitomize democratic policing, it did so as a means of avoiding abuses, wherein the police could resort to abuse or at the end of the continuum unmitigated fraud to see a conviction. Technology continues to influence the police organization and while it has not transformed the day-to-day roles and responsibilities of officers, forensics has the capability of transforming the organization. In moving evidence collection to the officer level, it forces a national change within organizations, to align agencies with technology in a way that is not purely symbolic. Any organization that witnesses a twofold increase in clearance rates for property crime scenes will be viewed as not just effective, but progressive.

To counter the skepticism that making an officer responsible for evidence collection is unacceptable because of the potential for misconduct, I offer these points. (1) Officers are currently collecting evidence across the nation and by some accounts have been doing so for some time. Recognizing that officers are involved in this collection and that the issues present have been at the lab, suggests that officers are less likely to manufacture genetic evidence. I concede that the absence of widespread misconduct is not proof that it is not occurring but if it were occurring, it would be at present a considerable issue within research. (2) Officers have been collecting both fingerprints and blood and other fibers for decades and while we have examples of misconduct, those issues primarily reflected prosecutorial misconduct or forensic experts who were presenting opinion as fact. (3) Arguably, the most important point, forensic evidence is not proof. Forensic evidence is an investigative tool linking a person to a place or another person. It is not and should never be used as the sole source of evidence to see a conviction. In the criticisms offered by scholars, they universally forget that the argument they are making is not the misuse by officers, rather the misuse by the prosecutor, which is well beyond the scope of this research.

Recommendation: Ceasing Simulated Evidence Collection

In recommending that genetic evidence collection be aligned at the officer level, it must be stated that the practice of simulated evidence collection must cease. Regardless if it is for the benefit of the victim or the reinforcement of the professionalism of the officer, faking collection, collecting and discarding, or collecting and storing evidence with no evidentiary value is unethical, wasteful, and dangerous for the agency at a liability and community perception level.

As discussed within the earlier chapter, considerable research has been undertaken examining agency evidence room backlogs around the nation and considerable scene sample backlogs were discovered (see Strom and Hickman, 2010; Pratt et al., 2006; Home Office, 2005; Lovrich et al., 2004). If nearly a quarter of officers within this research and nearly all direct investigative stakeholders interviewed were familiar with the practice, it is valid to suggest that a portion of the evidence in an agency's backlog is benign evidence with no evidentiary value. Moreover, because of the lapse in time, officer turnover, and additional factors, evidence may likely see submission for processing as agencies address their backlog to find that it wastes valuable resources and perpetuates the belief that genetic evidence within property crime scenes is not advantageous.

Continuing on the issue of simulated evidence collection, credibility is tantamount to a successful career in the police service. When called into question, the value of that officer as a witness is harmed. Potential is the situation involving an officer who collects what he or she believes to be benign evidence, disposes of the evidence, and does not note that evidence was collected in the report to later be confronted with statements on the stand by the homeowner that the officer collected evidence. Such a situation, while hypothetical, would most certainly harm the credibility of the officer and call into question the forensic practices of the agency.

As introduced at the start of this research, inclusion of technology into the police service and the alignment of technology at the officer level are to improve confidence in the police. Simulated evidence collection undermines not only confidence in the agency but calls into question the bond between the community and the officer. Currently, civil rights groups and advocates have called into question the expanded genetic programs. Simulated evidence collection only provides additional points of critique.

Recommendation: Improved Dissemination of Training

The following recommendation originates from the disheartening findings that almost none of the officers were aware of the national study and subsequently the free training concerning genetic evidence specific to property crime scenes. Despite having spent millions of dollars to investigate and evaluate the feasibility of routine genetic analysis within property crime scenes, creating a training program dedicated to informing officers of the benefits, and publishing and delivering presentations across the nation, familiarity with those aspects was nearly nonexistent within the survey and interviews conducted.

There is no explanation as to why so few officers were aware of the national report or the free training offered to officers. It would be easy to place the blame squarely at the feet of command staff that saw little merit in exposing officers to training. However, none of the command staff interviewed were familiar with the training and as noted in the discussion with the Chief of Police, he requested I forward the information to him, so he could provide it to his officers.

RESEARCH STRENGTHS AND LIMITATIONS

As this is the first study into officer decision making specific to the treatment of genetic evidence and the first study to employ IPA within a mixed-method design, the strengths of this research directly reflect the research design. While the method alone is a strength because this is an original study with no prior guide, it is important to frame the study within the context of prior research. A similar study was the

PERF DNA study. As the survey design borrowed several elements from the PERF DNA study, it is an appropriate study to use as a source of comparison.

Concerning sample size, the PERF DNA survey used a sample of 216 respondents, while the present study obtained 441 respondents. The PERF study did not provide the response rate of their survey. Recognizing the results are similar to those within the PERF research, I highlight specially those reflecting decision making. PERF noted that 85% of agencies indicated that investigator discretion influenced the decision to collect DNA evidence, compared to 93% in the present study. In the present research project, 62% of respondents specified that the determination to process forensic evidence was at the request of the prosecutor, compared with 44% in the PERF study. Concerning policy treatment, 42% of officers in the present study indicated that they had a formal written agency policy, while 32% of agencies noted a standard operating procedure (SOP) in the PERF study. At the informal (discretionary) policy level, there is considerable variation in that PERF revealed that 30% of agencies utilize an informal policy on the treatment of genetic evidence but the present study found that 56% of officers are guided by an informal policy. While this is the most divergent of findings, all others mentioned above being more in agreement, it should be noted that the PERF study is 2 years old. As discussed prior there have been considerable changes in the treatment of genetic evidence at the legislative level that likely have come to influence agency treatment and thus informal policy development.

Further strengthening the results within the study is that the sample represented officers throughout the United States. The survey did not sample a single agency or interview officers from the same agency. All respondents, across both the national survey and IPA interviews, were from different agencies and states. By not selecting a single agency as a source of the research or relying upon a single agency as a focus group, the sample was fairly representative of all officers. A geoprofile of the survey respondents shows broad representation across the nation. However, as discussed prior, having no respondents from Texas or New York is not problematic but is worth noting.

Providing additional strength within this research is the inclusion of the entire stakeholder continuum as interview participants. As each stakeholder was measured within the national survey, it was important to speak to them, to use their knowledge and wealth of experience to better inform the national survey. Prior research had surveyed or obtained anecdotal statements from lab technicians or officers, but no study to date has included each role directly involved within the investigative process specific to the treatment of genetic evidence. Without their participation, results such as the moderate to high influence of the prosecutor would have no context as to how they influence collection. Moreover, an outcome that lab philosophy is a prominent inhibitor of collection would be important but would contribute little without the context provided by the forensic technicians and forensic experts interviewed. In this regard, the direct knowledge and experiences of those investigative stakeholders, those engaged in the use of this forensic evidence, is the research's greatest strength. While typically the qualitative supports the quantitative because of the depth provided by the IPA method, it could be offered that the national survey has come to support the IPA interviews.

Limitations

Despite the relative strengths of this research, several limitations are present. Arguably, the greatest limitation within the study is the response rate. A 15% response rate is low and while it is comparable to other similar studies, it does present a limitation. However, recognizing that internet based survey research often has limited response rates, the study incorporated a mixed-method design to balance what was known to be a low response rate. Regardless, the response rate is low for the study and despite the use of the IPA method, the TDM model for survey research, and the detailed analysis within the mixed-method research mode, there are issues of generalizability. An additional limitation is the use of the Southern Police Institutes database. A true national sample would prove to increase the reliability of the results.

A second limitation within the study reflects the findings in terms of officer age. The average age of the respondents in this study was 44, which does reduce the generalizability of the study to account for the influences for "all officers." Many of the respondents in this research were detectives or very seasoned patrol officers, which presents a limitation in that younger officers, fresh from the academy, may have a different outlook. This was an issue discussed at the command staff level within the IPA interviews. Moreover, the years of experience across all of the interviews were considerable, which provided tremendous depth to the research but potentially misses the younger officer perspective.

DIRECTION OF FUTURE RESEARCH

As this research was designed to be exploratory not explanatory, the opportunity for future research is both great and needed. First, the present study details factors that influence officer decision making with a limited sample. While national in design, the research lacks the necessary response rate to offer truly reliable findings at a national scale. Future research must seek to replicate this scale at a national level, obtaining the necessary response rates to improve the confidence in the factor ranking. Moreover, it is important for researchers to replicate the study also at the individual state level to ascertain best practices and to identify how agencies have adapted to overcome those actual and perceived challenges; for example, the police executive who reported the creation of an incentive program, understanding that innovations at the agency and lab level are imperative to a routine forensic practice.

Additionally, research must come to examine the labs, beyond expressing backlogs, and process mechanics to overcome backlogs. As expressed within the interviews and the national survey, all stakeholders rely upon informal working relationships to see their evidence processed. Understanding how these relationships form and how they benefit each party is important at a practical level and theoretically allows for continued development within organizational theory.

Routine forensics within property crime scenes will prove costly. For this reason, it is imperative that future research examines how to reallocate current funding programs. For example, Ewing (2011) uncovered nearly half a billion dollars that states spent meeting the Sex Offender Registration and Notification Act (SORNA) requirements. This is half a billion dollars in a single year to replicate a current database that has limited public benefit. An improved CODIS system with the capability of enhanced scene processing is likely more beneficial than a sex offender registry. However, as no research exists comparing the two, it is important to see research undertaken at this level. Moreover, as denoted in this research, states have come to transition costs of genetic processing to the offender level. Research must come to examine the potential disparate impact of this policy and the potential deterrent effect of this type of policy.

Future research must explore how common simulated evidence collection is within agencies and if or how that evidence is routinely stored. As discovered in this research, nearly a quarter of officers engaged in the practice or knew of another who had, but undiscovered were the rates at which this occurred. If this is a common practice, this could explain the astronomical number of samples untested within evidence storage rooms across the nation.

Practical research must concern itself with examining if the criminal justice system can accommodate the increase in burden that an additional 10−15% more offenders would present. Can the system support the change? As indicated in this research, there was a divergence at the prosecutor level in that there was a belief that an increase in forensics within property crimes scenes could facilitate a broader use of diversionary programs or simply result in more use of plea bargains. While the court will alleviate its burden, unexamined are the potential issues within corrections. At present, community corrections receives but a small portion of resources, some 10% of the 25% that corrections receives (Kleiman, 2009). As noted in the Denver study, prison sentences increased significantly for those cases involving genetic evidence, with a 10-fold increase to 13.9 years compared to 1.4 years without genetic evidence (Ashikhmin et al., ND). The question to be answered is not necessarily can the police or courts adjust, but can the correctional institution adapt to the influx of offenders.

Building on the increase in offenders is the potential deterrent effect that routine genetic processing can have at a general or specific deterrent level. Limited research has sought to examine the potential deterrent capability that routine processing could have within property crime scenes. Could it be said that an agency that routinely analyzes for genetic evidence in every automobile theft can cause a reduction in the number of thefts as the practice becomes known within the illicit economy? Does word of mouth about a forensic practice influence offenders, be they juvenile or adult?

Bayley and Dixon (2010) offered that the impact that a continued focus on forensic science has within a community-oriented policing model is unknown. Originally, the intent of this book was to examine this very question. Is community-oriented policing and a routine utilization of genetic evidence compatible? Researchers must continue to examine the impact of policing models within the treatment of forensic evidence. As discussed within the present study, the impact of the policing model did influence the treatment of genetic evidence and if only anecdotal, it certainly fits within the theory of what is known on processes like COMPSTAT. Future research must come to explore the relationship.

Comparatively, it is important for more research to replicate the study at an international level to understand those factors that facilitate or inhibit routine treatment of genetic evidence across nations. The importance of the comparative research is to understand better the treatment of genetic evidence, as there have been increased partnerships and expansions of analysis at international levels.

CONCLUSION

The skeptical reader is likely to reject the recommendation that agencies expand their forensic analysis into property crime scenes. After all, there are reports suggesting that many agencies have resorted to reducing significantly their handling of property crime scene calls. In closing this book, I want to present three schools of thought on the use of technology within the police service: (1) technology is modifying police practice; (2) technology is simply a ploy in power by administrators to display "professionalism" regardless of how the agencies use that technology; or (3) technology is used to replicate traditional police practice and has not brought about any substantive change.

Over a decade ago, the DNA working group imagined a system urging accountability, efficiency, and effectiveness to move forward the criminal justice system using a national identification system involving genetic evidence. The current use of CODIS is myopic at best, undermined by the legislative focus to expand offender processing at the harm of even slight gains in scene processing. The practical reality is that agencies are facing fiscal and personnel shortages. However, agencies are collecting this evidence within property crimes scenes. What remains the limiting factor is the processing of the evidence, which as suggested within this research is a product of forensic laboratory policy, philosophy, and budgets. For the police service to become more technology centric, to align full forensics within an agency is to address the processing issue. I have provided specific recommendations that I believe will provide the early steps in making the necessary transition but for technology to transform agencies and thus police practice, genetic evidence must move beyond symbolic capital. Integrated forensic collection and analysis, and aligning collection at the officer level can transform not just a single practice but can provide officers and the organization with new skills. The tangible and intangible benefits to an organization that is technology centric, in concert with over a century of institutional knowledge, is vast as is the reality that this focus can improve the quality of a police service.

There is no discounting that current treatment of forensic evidence is acceptable. However, to paraphrase and update what Kamien (1993) so eloquently stated decades earlier, we must ask ourselves if adequate is what we want in our police service and our integration of forensic technology into the agency.

CHAPTER 9

A Police Chief's Perspective

Gary Jenkins
Chief of Police, Pullman Police Department, Pullman, WA

"Plate spinning"

My contribution is that of a practitioner's perspective and my comments are based on my own experiences and observations in a law enforcement career that began in 1977. In that respect, what I present is anecdotal, miniscule and narrow when compared to research-based findings. I do not purport to represent all of law enforcement nor do I suggest that my views are representative of law enforcement leaders. I can describe, however, how I have come to view this topic after working in three law enforcement agencies in two states over the course of 37 years. I suspect that at least some of my perspectives will resonate with other law enforcement leaders, as well as provide pragmatic balance to research and theory.

As police chief, I am responsible to my community for public safety. The driving force of that responsibility is the prevention, mitigation, and investigation of crimes. Bringing offenders to justice is a paramount task of law enforcement. To carry out those responsibilities requires a significant balancing act that involves many moving parts.

Law enforcement has an obligation to conduct thorough investigations. Investigation is the collection of evidence to determine the truth. Evidence can consist of many things, but generally consists of observations, statements (observations or relevant information of others), and physical evidence. If we are not thorough, if we leave evidence behind, then we may compromise our search for the truth. There are many reasons evidence is "left on the table." Insufficient staffing requires law enforcement agencies to prioritize their work, leaving some tasks with little resources. Poorly trained staff, or staff that is inadequately equipped, can result in evidence that goes undetected, or mishandling that compromises the integrity of evidence.

Law enforcement tends to match resources to severity of crime. For example, I worked for a suburban law enforcement agency that was part of a large metropolitan area. The agency had adequate resources and experience to investigate most crimes in its jurisdiction. However, when an infrequent homicide occurred, the agency would request mutual aid from the homicide unit of a large metropolitan agency in the same county. That homicide unit had significant experience investigating homicides. They also brought with them an experienced crime scene investigation team consisting of crime scene technicians. That crime scene team had specialized training to identify and collect evidence that is not collected on a regular basis by police officers who are, for the most part, generalists. The need for specially trained crime scene technicians did not rise to the level to justify the significant additional expense by our agency, particularly when we could call upon local experts to assist us when needed. There was some mystique to the collection of blood samples or other genetic evidence by the experts, considered beyond the ability of our officers to collect and package. This perspective was supported by regular reports of high profile cases that drew criticism of the crime scene investigations and evidence mishandling, even when conducted by specially trained crime scene investigators and technicians.

If we utilize specialists to process a crime scene for a homicide, but a generalist police officer to process the crime scene of a burglary, are we not potentially leaving evidence behind at the burglary? As a law enforcement leader, should I not ensure that every crime is thoroughly investigated? With unlimited resources, I could. But I don't have unlimited resources. I have to allocate my resources. I determine this allocation based on a number of factors, which include severity of crime, solvability factors, and the level of threat to the public by the offender. Crimes against persons are prioritized over property crimes for the very simple reason that a threat of injury or death outweighs the loss or damage of property.

Many law enforcement agencies aim to employ "best practices" in policy and procedure. Best practices are the incorporation of evidence-based or experience-based methods to achieve a superior result. By their nature, best practices continually evolve. What was a best practice or state-of-the art method a few years ago may be outdated today. In the area of genetic evidence collection, the best practices evolution has continuously provided more clear and simplified methods of collection and packaging. The basics have not changed, such as preventing evidence contamination, but in some cases, the need for specialization has been "de-mystified." The generalist police officer is now able to successfully collect and package genetic evidence that was once reserved for specialists. This is not to say there is no need for crime scene technicians and specialists. Advancing technology is continually revealing new ways of identifying and collecting evidence, or even redefining what is considered evidence, requiring practices and technologies beyond the abilities of generalist police officers.

Best practices constantly evolve to keep pace with technological changes. Consequently, we find ourselves not just trying to keep pace so that we do not leave evidence "on the table," but we also need to project where best practices will lead in the future. It was not so long ago that the discovery of a fingerprint at a crime scene was a fantastic find, maybe. For a cold case with little leads and no potential suspects, a latent print was not helpful at all in the investigation; the print only had possible future worth. It was only after a set of fingerprints from a suspect was available for comparison that the latent print had any value. Now latent prints are used to identify suspects who have no prior investigative link to the case at all. Latent fingerprints can be submitted and checked against vast databases of criminals to link a potential suspect to the crime scene. What was once of limited value has evolved into enormous value. Because of the increased value of latent fingerprints, the expectations were raised for patrol officers to attempt to locate and lift latent prints. A latent print is now a much more valuable piece of evidence that has a higher likelihood of identifying a suspect.

DNA is a relative newcomer to the best practices of criminal investigations. We now frequently hear of decades old cold cases in which DNA was used to identify a suspect or to prove the innocence of someone wrongly convicted. These older cases were initially investigated at a time when DNA genetic profiling was not in our investigative vocabulary. But the collection and maintenance of DNA evidence, albeit unknowingly and unintentionally, has nonetheless benefited from the advancement of technology and best practices. The value of the evidence has increased exponentially from the time when the evidence was collected. We used to collect cigarette butts found at a crime scene as potential corroborating evidence that the suspect may smoke that particular brand of cigarette. The cigarette butts collected as evidence for that purpose decades ago can now be used to identify a suspect based on the saliva DNA. Consequently, just as we experienced with latent fingerprints, the expectation is for officers to attempt to locate and collect evidence for genetic forensic testing.

Progressive law enforcement leaders strive to maintain best practices. Law enforcement organizations provide resources for agencies to stay abreast of best practices. For example, the International Association of Chiefs of Police (IACP) provides to its members model policies that represent current best practices. Many state and regional law enforcement organizations provide similar support. However, keeping best practices current is becoming increasingly more difficult. The process of staying ahead of the best practices curve is exacerbated by the rate of change. The rate that technology advances, including those technologies that enhance abilities to collect evidence, continues to increase at an ever accelerated pace. I also have to ensure my organization does not change at an unmanageable or intolerable pace. To facilitate successful change, I have to ensure my personnel buy into my vision of the organizational future. Organizations, particularly public organizations such as law enforcement agencies, are not necessarily adept at successfully realizing rapid change. Typically, the larger the organization, the more bureaucracy there is, and the more slowly change occurs. Smaller agencies have their own inhibitors, which can include less available funding for new technology and to train staff to utilize that technology, or even not being able to employ enough staff to put that technology into practice.

A factor affecting the acceptance and implementation of new technologies by agencies is generational differences within those agencies. Conventional wisdom, research, and experience tell us that implementing change in an organization is difficult. There is an innate resistance to change. While many law enforcement leaders of today did not have a personal computer until they were adults, the younger generation has grown up with computers, cell phones, Facebook, and Twitter. They not only had a head start on "modern" technology, they have experienced change at a faster pace than my generation. The rapid pace of technological advancements is their "norm," while older generations may tend to be more cautious and intentional about adapting to changes, preferring a slower pace.

Funding and costs affect every organization. When the science of DNA identification first evolved to be an accepted practice in the US legal system, DNA testing was cost prohibitive for many law enforcement agencies. DNA evidence from only the most serious of crimes was sent to the lab, and that lab was probably a private lab. Then, as the technology continued to advance, testing costs declined and soon were within reach for local, regional, and state crime labs to conduct their own DNA tests. As DNA testing costs continued to decline, there was a proportional increase in the availability of DNA testing for law enforcement. The particular point in time when a law enforcement agency could engage in DNA testing was dependent on many factors. For those agencies that maintained their own crime lab, had the ability to fund associated equipment and personnel, and were inclined to be on the cutting edge of this technology, they engaged early on. At the other end of the spectrum, some agencies were dependent on their local, regional, or state crime lab that made the determination of when they would engage in DNA testing and under what circumstances. Even if DNA testing was available, the ability of an agency to make use of that testing was likely hampered by restrictive policy criteria for testing acceptance. Testing fees could also impede an agency's participation. I can recall many years ago, as the detective bureau commander, contemplating sending a DNA sample to a private lab to compare with possible suspect DNA. The cost would be in the thousands of dollars. I had no other testing options. Contrast that to present day where our agency recently sent to the state crime lab a necklace with possible suspect DNA found at the scene of a property crime that was linked to a series of other property crimes. Subsequent testing identified a suspect who has since been convicted. If we had sent that DNA to the lab for testing years ago, the lab would have likely rejected it because it did not meet their criteria for testing, which generally only accepted evidence from serious crimes against person felonies.

When we look solely at the capabilities of evidence collection and testing practices and what impact they can have on the identification and apprehension of criminals, of course law enforcement leaders should want to employ the latest available technologies. This would naturally be a component of a thorough investigation, and is consistent with adhering to a best practices model. To do otherwise would fall short of finding the truth and bringing offenders to justice. But is that all there is to it? If this technology will help us to catch more criminals, should we not be "all in"? As a law enforcement leader, I have to step back and look at the "big picture" to make sure I view this singular issue in full context.

When someone asks me how I would describe my job as a police chief, many thoughts and images come to mind. I used to describe it as comparable to a juggler, juggling a number of balls at once and making sure none of them drops. But I was never fully comfortable with this description because, well, I have never seen a juggler who could juggle enough balls to adequately depict the number of issues I have to "juggle." I think a more accurate analogy would be with a plate spinner; someone who spins plates on poles without the plates falling off. The spinner must constantly manage all of the poles to keep all of the plates spinning to keep any of them from falling. The plates represent various components of a law enforcement agency in which the failure of any one component can be significantly detrimental to the good order and viability of the agency.

Every law enforcement agency leader has "plates" to manage. Personnel related issues range from recruitment and hiring to discipline, termination, evaluation, promotion, recognition, training, personnel career development, job assignment, etc. Personnel allocation requires decisions with regard to the number and structure of personnel assigned to various functions: patrol, detectives, records, etc. Other areas to be managed include press, social media, information technology (IT), dispatch, records management, policies and procedures, external and internal complaints, use of force review, community relations, specialized teams (e.g., Special Weapons and Tactics (SWAT)), evidence and property management, budgeting, planning, reporting (local, state, and federal), motor fleet, equipment, etc. There are many "plates" that need to be simultaneously managed. Leaders need to ensure that each component contributes toward the public safety mission; otherwise, we can be distracted unnecessarily. Adequate resources must be allocated to support each of the components necessary for the agency to properly function.

With my finite amount of resources, comprised of funding, personnel and equipment, to what priority do I assign DNA testing? If I agree that I need to devote more resources toward that effort, either I need an increase of resources, or I "squeeze the balloon" and divert resources from one component to another. Should I divert resources from training? I could, but then I could risk increased liability exposure for officer actions, particularly in use of force events. Should I divert resources from the motor fleet, or will that negatively impact our ability to quickly and safely respond to emergencies, and increase risk to officer safety in unreliable vehicles?

As a law enforcement leader, I must view every issue in context of the organization and the community and I must assess potential consequences and impacts. One way to frame this is to examine the relationship between actual crime and public perceptions of crime. It has been my experience that the community's perception of crime is, in many cases, not necessarily related to how much crime there actually is. Even if a law enforcement agency can positively affect crime, or the crime rate is relatively low, the community may still not feel safe. Conversely, there could be an increase of crime, or the crime rate could be relatively high, and yet the community may feel safe. I see my responsibility to the community to not only actually address and positively impact crime, but also make the community feel safe. I could divert significant resources toward reducing crime, but that may have no impact on the community's perception of crime. Which is more important? I believe they both are. This does not relieve law enforcement of the obligation to address crime; rather addressing the public perception of safety is complementary to crime fighting efforts.

A question law enforcement leaders need to ask themselves regarding public perception about crime is: How does the community define "safe"? There is never a community expectation for law enforcement to completely eliminate crime; there seems to be consensus between law enforcement and the communities they serve that complete crime eradication is unrealistic. But how does each community determine their level of comfort, or the amount of crime that is "acceptable." There is no question that a certain level of property crime is generally "acceptable." The crimes against persons are those crimes that subject the public to the threat of injury or death, and are those that catch the attention of the media and the community. Law enforcement consequently prioritizes their resources accordingly.

However, there is something to be said for the public's perception of safety based on how they view law enforcement's efforts to solve their crimes, whether or not they are property or person crimes. If a resident believes their police department empathizes with their plight as a crime victim and works as hard to solve their minor crime as they would if it were a major crime, those efforts facilitate a feeling of safety in the community, even if those efforts prove to be futile in bringing the offender to justice. In this regard, I have seen officers attempt to collect evidence to pacify victims as well as to demonstrate their commitment to try to solve their crime. Note that I did not use the term "simulated evidence collection." I agree that actually collecting what is purported to be evidence, knowing that is has no evidentiary value, is counterproductive. The examples I have observed involve officers "throwing some fingerprint powder around" in an "attempt" to locate latent fingerprints. In other words, officers' attempt, half-hearted as it may be, to locate evidence, even when they believe their chances of success are minimal. I have seen, more than a few times, viable evidence collected because of some of these attempts.

Resource allocation to solve crime is a complex art that is not as obvious and straightforward as it may appear. There are many subtleties and nuances that can impact crime. The agencies where I have worked maintained a Drug Abuse Resistance Education (DARE) officer in the public schools. There has been some criticism of the DARE program and its effectiveness in affecting drug and alcohol use by participants. While this may be arguable, I believe there are other benefits of the program, such as valuable lessons on personal accountability and responsible decision making. However, my chief motivation for maintaining the DARE program is the far-reaching positive relationships developed in the community because of the program. Elementary school students, a future generation, form a positive relationship with a uniformed police officer. I have seen adults run up to an officer who served as their DARE officer 10 or 20 years prior, excited to see the officer that made such an impression in their life. Positive relationships are developed with parents and school officials. We have combined the DARE and School Resource Officer duties into one position, so the officer also handles criminal and pre-crime issues at the schools. What impact does this position have on both actual crime and the public's perception of crime? I believe it to be significant.

Then should I not look at diverting resources from another, "non-critical" area so I can put more resources into solving crime? How about records management? Those are just administrative duties that don't have any real impact on crime or the public's perception of crime, right? I would argue the opposite. In many departments, records personnel are the first contact the public has with the police department, either in person or on the phone. The public may gauge our agency's effectiveness and credibility on their contact with our records staff. Records staff perform a support function to the police officers by processing police reports and citations, prepare documents for the next step in the criminal justice system (district attorney or prosecuting attorney), issue various licenses and permits to the public, and respond to public records requests. The requirements of the public records laws, which have broadened over the years, have placed a substantial burden on governmental entities, particularly law enforcement. Responses to requests for information must be provided within a strict timeline. What must, may, and cannot be released is not always clear. Hours are spent redacting prohibited information from documents before release. Agencies can be sued for releasing what they shouldn't, and sued for not releasing what they should. Our agency has been defending for a number of years a public records lawsuit filed by a person who is serving time in prison because of an arrest by our agency. The cost has exceeded $100,000 to defend the suit in which our agency has prevailed. Even when the agency is completely compliant with the stringent public records laws, we are still subject to lawsuit. I definitely do not want to reduce resources from an area that would increase my liability exposure where we are obviously vulnerable.

The SWAT team is used in high-risk incidents. The SWAT team is specially trained to confront armed individuals who pose a potential threat to others. They also perform hostage rescue, are deployed to make high-risk arrests, and engage in other high-risk law enforcement operations. While they do arrest serious offenders, SWAT's impact on overall crime is arguably very low to non-existent. SWAT teams exist for the benefit of public safety. When an armed suspect is barricaded in a structure and is shooting at people, it is the obligation of law enforcement to neutralize the threat. Many agencies do not have their own SWAT team. It is a relatively expensive proposition to equip and train, and maintain adequate training for, a SWAT team. However most agencies have access to a SWAT team (or similarly functioning group) through participation in a multi-agency or regional SWAT team, or through an agreement with another agency to provide SWAT team assistance if needed. Since our regional SWAT team may only be called out a few times in a year, should I divert resources from that program toward the solving of crime? If I do, what will be the impact on the community when a critical event necessitating a SWAT team occurs and the closest team is hours away? As a law enforcement leader, I would have a lot of explaining to do, particularly to those who may have been injured, or family members of those killed, during such an event. Crime clearance rates are not too important during those conversations.

So now let me bring you back again to the plate spinner. Can you see the SWAT team plate spinning? Just underneath that plate is a basket labeled "loss of life and loss of agency credibility" waiting for that plate to fall. Can you see the records plate? Beneath that is the lawsuit basket. The rest of the spinning plates are just as critical to the agency: press, personnel, IT, dispatch, budgeting, equipment, training, etc. My goal is to keep all of my plates spinning all of the time. This is a complex balancing act.

When the collection of DNA at crime scenes for identification purposes (other than blood and sexual assault evidence, which was commonplace prior to DNA profiling) became viable, collection and handling integrity was of primary concern for first responders. Those agencies that employed specially trained crime scene technicians had the capacity to collect and package DNA evidence. Many law enforcement agencies did not possess that capacity. Mutual aid could be requested from agencies to provide this specialized assistance, but this was reserved for major crimes, certainly not for generic property crimes. As DNA collection became more widespread, police officers became more engaged in the collection and packaging while still meeting evidence integrity requirements of crime labs. This eliminated much of an agency's cost to collect DNA evidence other than training for the officers and collection equipment. Collection costs have become less of a barrier. Patrol officers can collect crime scene DNA evidence with relatively little training and expense, and genetic forensic evidence collection has consequently become common practice. In fact, I submit that a patrol force properly trained and backed by organizational policies and practices will collect more viable genetic evidence than if crime scene evidence technicians are utilized. Even though the crime scene technicians may be more adept at identifying and collecting genetic evidence, patrol officers can competently identify and collect the evidence. Moreover, the patrol officers are at every crime scene, while the evidence technicians will likely be called to a scene only after certain criteria are met. The evolution of DNA evidence collection has drastically changed the dynamic of genetic forensic evidence for most agencies.

I must admit that I, too, am not familiar with the national study and free training concerning genetic forensic evidence. I agree that providing this training to officers would increase identification, frequency, and competency of collecting genetic forensic evidence. However, I would have to add that state crime lab limitations are a much more significant barrier to the process. If officers knew their viable genetic evidence would be processed, then identification and collection of that evidence would become a higher priority. I believe that the processing backlog and resulting restrictive acceptance policies adopted by crime labs for DNA evidence is the most significant barrier to utilization of genetic evidence for property crimes. When evidence is not tested, or even accepted, by the crime lab, officers conclude that routine DNA evidence collection is pointless.

I currently work for a law enforcement agency in Washington State. Washington recently legalized recreational marijuana for persons 21 years of age and older. The new law also includes a per se DUI based on 5 ng/mL of THC, the active ingredient in marijuana. The specific legal definition of marijuana in the new law has presented challenges to the capabilities of the state crime lab. Legislation is pending to amend the definition to address that issue, but it is clear that the new law will impose an additional burden on the state crime lab. How this will ultimately play out is yet to be seen, but it certainly will not ease any DNA processing backlog.

I am not familiar with the details of the allegations against police officers in the United Kingdom who were accused of arresting individuals simply to obtain their genetic profile. However, with proper safeguards, this may not be indicative of abuse. As an example, let us say we are investigating a homicide and we lifted a latent fingerprint at the crime scene. Suppose our prime suspect has never been arrested for a crime so we do not have the suspect's fingerprints to compare. (I use the example of arrest here instead of conviction because we do obtain fingerprints of those arrested.) Also suppose we don't yet have enough evidence to meet the standard of proving beyond a reasonable doubt that is required to successfully prosecute the suspect in court, but we do have enough probable cause to make an arrest. So we arrest the suspect as a furtherance of the investigation; we can attempt to question the suspect and we can collect fingerprints. Now we have suspect fingerprints to compare with the latent prints found at the crime scene. We could be accused of arresting that person just for the purpose of obtaining their fingerprints. Of course we did; we would be negligent if we didn't. A reason the probable cause standard for arrest is less stringent than the beyond a reasonable doubt standard for conviction is that the courts recognize the need for law enforcement to make an arrest as a component of an investigation. I believe that standards that exist for obtaining fingerprints should also be applied to the collection of genetic profiles. Additionally, I believe we will experience advancements in DNA testing that will parallel what we have seen with fingerprints. Due to technological advancements in fingerprint processing, the labor and complexity to compare a latent print found at a crime scene with the national database has become so manageable that most viable latent prints are now processed quickly. In the meantime and until we realize those technological innovations in DNA testing, crime labs establish criteria for the acceptance and processing of DNA evidence to prioritize their work.

The truth is that I like to be on the cutting edge. I embrace new technology that will make our job more efficient and effective while maintaining responsiveness and connectedness with our community. I want to equip my officers with the tools that will best allow them to solve crime. Police officers want to catch the bad guys, put them in jail, and put them out of business. If there is a tool available to facilitate that process, officers will utilize that tool to achieve their goals. Identifying, collecting, and testing DNA at property crime scenes is clearly advantageous and fits within the best practices model of modern law enforcement. And don't forget about those other plates I have to keep spinning.

REFERENCES

Alder, K., 2007. The Lie Detectors: The History of an American Obsession. Free Press, New York.

Anderson, J., 1967. Crime control: task force urges use of science and technology. Science 1967 156 (3782), 1579–1582.

American Civil Liberties Union (ACLU), 2009. Statement of the American Civil Liberties Union (ACLU) for Hearing on "Ensuring the Effective Use of DNA Evidence to Solve Rape Cases Nationwide." American Civil Liberties Union (ACLU), Washington, DC.

Ashikhmin, S., Berdine, S.G., Morrissey, M.R., LaBerge, G.S., ND. Effectiveness and Cost Efficiency of DNA Evidence in Volume Crime. Denver, Colorado, Site Summary. Denver: Denver District Attorney's Office.

Asplen, C.H., 2004. The Application of DNA Technology in England and Wales, Final Report Submitted to NIJ. Available at http://www.ncjrs.gov/pdffiles1/nij/grants/203971.pdf. National Institute of Justice.

Associated Press, 2011. Idaho Senate passes bill to expand DNA database. March 2011. Retrieved May 27, 2011, from Idaho Press Tribune: http://www.idahopress.com/news/state/article_54a4f76f-5ccb-5bf9-bc2e-57dff8c2a622.html.

Attride-Stirling, J., 2001. Thematic networks: An analytic tool for qualitative research. Qual. Res. 1 (3), 385–405.

Baumgartner, F.R., De Boef, S.L., Boydstun, A.E., 2008. The Decline of the Death Penalty and the Discovery of Innocence. Cambridge University Press, Cambridge.

Bayley, D., 1994. Police for the Future. Oxford Univeristy Press, New York.

Bayley, D.H., Nixon, C., 2010. The Changing Environment for Policing, 1985–2008. National Institute of Justice and John F. Kennedy School of Government Program in Criminal Justice and Policy Management (New Perspectives in Policing Series). Cambridge, MA: National Institute of Justice. Retrieved July 22, 2011, from http://www.ojp.usdoj.gov/nij/pubs-sum/230576.htm.

BBC News, 2009. Police making arrests "just to gather DNA samples." November 24, 2009. Retrieved February 23, 2012, from BBC News: http://news.bbc.co.uk/2/hi/uk_news/8375567.stm.

Bell, S., 2008. Crime and Circumstance: Investigating the History of Forensic Science. Praeger, Westport.

Bhattacharya, S., 2004. Killer convicted thanks to relative's DNA. April 20, 2004. Retrieved May 25, 2011, from New Scientist: http://www.newscientist.com/article/dn4908-killer-convicted-thanks-to-relatives-dna.html.

Biancamano, J.D., 2009. Arresting DNA: the Evolving Nature of DNA Collection Statutes and Their Fourth Amendment Justifications. Ohio State Law J. 70 (3), 613–655.

Bond, J.W., Phil, D., Hammond, C., 2008. The Value of DNA Material Recovered from Crime Scenes. J. Forensic Sci. 53, 797–801.

Briody, M., 2004. The effects of DNA evidence on the criminal justice process. Retrieved from Dissertations and Theses Database (Australian Digital Theses Program).

Bruder, C.E., Piotrowski, A., Gijsbers, A.A., Andersson, R., Erickson, S., Diaz de Stahl, T., 2008. Phenotypically concordant and discordant monozygotic twins display different DNA copy-number-variation profiles. Am. J. Hum. Genet. 82, 763–771.

Calladine, C.R., 2004. Understanding DNA, Third Edition: The Molecule and How it Works. Elsevier/Academic Press, San Diego.

Campbell, D.T., Fiske, D.W., 1959. Convergent and discriminant validation by the multitrait-multimethod. Psychol. Bull. 56, 81–105.

Chaiken, M.R., Chaiken, J.M., 1982. Varieties of Criminal Behavior. Rand Corporation, Santa Monica.

Chaiken, M.R., Rolph, J.E., 1985. Identifying High-Rate Serious Offenders. Rand Corporation, Santa Monica.

Chan, J.B., 2001. The technological game: How information technology is transforming police practice. Crim. Justice 1, 139–159.

Chanen, D., 2005. Defense attorneys raise concerns about DNA sample mix-up. Star Tribune (Minneapolis, MN), May 20, 2005, p. 1B.
Clear, T.R., Cole, G.F., 2000. American Corrections. Wadsworth, Belmont.
Collins, J.J., 1977. Offender Careers and Restraint: Probabilities and Policy Implications. Final draft report. Law Enforcement Assistance Administration, US Department of Justice, Washington, DC.
Crank, J.P., 2004. Understanding Police Culture. Anderson, New York.
Creswell, J.W., 2009. Research Design: Qualitative, Quantitative, and Mixed Methods Approaches. Sage Publications, Thousand Oaks.
CriMNet Program Office, 2008. Criminal and Juvenile Justice Information Policy – Minnesota. Saint Paul: https://dps.mn.gov/divisions/bca/boards-committees/crimnet/Pages/governing-bodies-policy-group.aspx.
Cromwell, P.F., Olson, J.N., Wester Avary, D., 1991. Breaking and Entering: An Ethnographic Analysis of Burglary. Sage Publications, Newbury Park.
DeLisi, M., 2005. Career Criminals in Society. Sage Publications, Thousand Oaks.
DeLisi, M., 2006. Zeroing in on early arrest onset: Results from a population of extreme career criminals. J. Crim. Justice 34, 17–26.
Denver DNA Burglary Project., 2004. Retrieved April 20, 2011, from DenverDA: http://www.denverda.org/dna/Denver_DNA_Burglary_Project.htm.
Denzin, N.K., 1978. The Research Act: A Theoretical Introduction to Sociological Methods. Praeger, New York.
Derksen, L., 2010. Micro/macro translations: The production of new social structures in the case of DNA profiling. Sociol. Inq. 80, 214–240.
DiFonzo, H.J., 2005. The crimes of crime labs. Hofstra Law Rev. 34 (1), 1–11.
Dillman, D., 2000. Constructing the Questionnaire. Mail and Internet Surveys. John Wiley & Sons, New York.
Dillman, D.A., Smyth, J.D., Christian, L.M., 2009. Internet, Mail and Mixed-Mode Surveys. John Wiley and Sons, New Jersey.
DNA Initiative, 2010. Convicted Offender and/or Arrestee Backlog Reduction Funding Awards. Retrieved June 4, 2011, from DNA Initiative: http://www.nij.gov/topics/forensics/lab-operations/capacity/convicted-offender-funding.htm.
Dunsmuir, W.T., Tran, C., Weatherburn, D., 2008. Assessing the Impact of Mandatory DNA Testing of Prison Inmates in NSW on Clearance, Charge and Conviction Rates for Selected Crime Categories. Attorney General's Department of NSW, State of New South Wales.
Durose, M., 2008. Census of Publicly Funded Forensic Crime Laboratories. Bureau of Justice Statistics, Washington, DC.
Evans, C., 2007. The Casebook of Forensic Detection: How Science Solved 100 of the World's Most Baffling Crimes. Berkley Books, New York.
Ewing, C.P., 2011. Justice Perverted: Sex Offense Law, Psychology, and Public Policy. Oxford University Press, New York.
Fang, R., Liu, J.Y., Kijenski, H.L., Benfield, J., Wong, A., Lagace, R., 2010. The HID EVOlution System for Automation of DNA Quantification and Short Tandem Repeat Analysis. J. Assoc. Lab. Autom. 15, 65–73.
Federal Bureau of Investigation, 2009. Uniform Crime Reports for the United States: 2009. Government Printing Office, Washington, DC.
Federal Bureau of Investigation, 2011, March. CODIS—NDIS Statistics. Retrieved April 19, 2011, from Federal Bureau of Investigation: http://www.fbi.gov/about-us/lab/codis/ndis-statistics.
Fender, J.K., 2007. Probationers, parolees and DNA collection: is this "justice for all"? Seventh Circuit Rev. 3, 312–366.
Ford, R., 2009. Arrests are being made "to expand DNA files." November 24, 2009. Retrieved June 23, 2011, from The Times: http://www.timesonline.co.uk/tol/news/uk/crime/article6929017.ece.
Forst, B., Lucianovic, J., Cox, S., 1977. What Happens after Arrest? A Court Perspective of Police Operations in the District of Columbia. Institute for Law and Social Research, Washington, DC.
Garland, D., 1990. Punishment and Modern Society. University of Chicago Press, Chicago.
Garland, D., 2001. The Culture of Control: Crime and Social Order in Contemporary Society. University of Chicago Press, Chicago.
Garrett, B., 2008. Judging innocence. Columbia Law Rev. 108, 55–142.
Garrett, B.L., 2011. Convicting the Innocent: Where Criminal Prosecutions Go Wrong. Harvard University Press, Cambridge.

Gill, P., Jeffreys, A.K., Werrett, D.J., 1985. Forensic application of DNA fingerprinting. Nature 318, 577–579.

Gordon Thomas Honeywell Governmental Affairs, 2010. State DNA Database Laws Qualifying Offenses. September 2010. Retrieved June 2, 2011, from Gordon Thomas Honeywell Governmental Affairs: http://www.dnaresource.com/documents/statequalifyingoffenses2010.pdf.

Gordon Thomas Honeywell Governmental Affairs, 2011. 2011 DNA Database Legislation. March 30, 2011. Retrieved June 2, 2011, from DNA Resource: Forensics DNA: http://www.trendtrack.com/texis/app/viewrpt?event=495bdbf6ba.

Gould, J., 2007. The Innocence Commission: Preventing Wrongful Convictions and Restoring the Criminal Justice System. NYU Press, New York.

Goulka, J., Matthies, C., Disley, E., Steinberg, P., 2010. Toward a Comparison of DNA Profiling and Databases in the United States and England. Rand Corporation, Santa Monica, CA.

Greenwood, F., Chaiken, J., Petersilia, J., Prusoff, L., 1975. The Criminal Investigation Process, Volume III: Observations and Analysis. RAND, Chicago.

Griffin, G., 2009. Familial DNA Software May Catch On In Catching Criminals. November 17, 2009. Retrieved May 25, 2011, from The Denver Post: http://www.denverpost.com/news/ci_13804045.

Griswold, M. E., Murphy, G. R., Police Executive Research Forum (PERF), & United States of America, 2010. It's More Complex Than You Think: A chief's guide to DNA. Police Executive Research Forum.

Grubin, D., Gunn, J., 1990. The Imprisoned Rapist and Rape. Institute of Psychiatry, London.

Hanson, R.K., Bussiere, M.T., 1998. Predicting relapse: A meta-analysis of sexual offender recidivism studies. J. Consult. Clin. Psychol. 37, 348–362.

Harris, A.J., Hanson, R.K., 2004. Sex Offender Recidivism: A Simple Question. Public Safety and Emergency Preparedness Canada, Ottawa.

Harris, D.A., Smallbone, S., Dennison, S., Knight, R.A., 2009. Specialization and versatility in sexual offenders referred for civil commitment. J. Crim. Justice 37, 37–44.

Home Office, 2005. DNA Expansion Programme 2000–2005: Reporting achievement. Retrieved June 1, 2011, from Home Office: http://www.homeoffice.gov.uk/documents/DNAExpansion.pdf.

Horvath, F., Meesig, R., 1996. The criminal investigation process and the role of forensic evidence: A review of empirical findings. J. Forensic Sci. 41, 963–969.

Horvath, F., Meesig, R.T., Lee, Y.H., Michigan State University, 2001. National Survey of Police Policies and Practices Regarding the Criminal Investigations Process: Twenty-Five Years After Rand. National Institute of Justice, Washington DC.

Huff, R.C., Killias, M., 2008. Wrongful Conviction: International Perspectives on Miscarriages of Justice. Temple University Press, Philadelphia.

Huff, C.R., Rattner, A., 1988. Convicted but innocent: False positives and the criminal justice process. Controversial issues in crime and justice, 130–144.

Hurst, L., Lothridge, K., 2010. 2007 DNA Evidence and Offender Analysis Measurement: DNA Backlogs, Capacity, and Funding. Retrieved June 8, 2011, from National Criminal Justice Reference Service: http://www.ncjrs.gov/pdffiles1/nij/grants/230328.pdf.

International Association of Chiefs of Police (IACP), 2004. Police In-Car Video Camera Evaluation. IACP, Arlington.

Interstate Commission for Adult Offender Supervision (ICAOS), 2005. DNA Survey Results. January 2005. Retrieved June 7, 2011, from Interstate Commission for Adult Offender Supervision: http://www.interstatecompact.org/LinkClick.aspx?fileticket=wljMeaQ8X0Q%3D&tabid=105&mid=431.

Johnson, R.B., Onwuegbuzi, A.J., Turner, L.A., 2007. Toward a definition of mixed methods research. J. Mixed Methods Res. 16, 112–133.

Kamien, M., 1993. The reform of medical education. Med. J. Aust. 39, 226–227.

Kemp, S., Pinchin, R., 2007. Decreasing Turnaround Time of DNA Analysis by Improving Processes in the Laboratory. American Laboratory.

Keteyian, A., 2010. *Exclusive: Rape in America: Justice Denied.* Retrieved June 3, 2011, from CBS News: < http://www.cbsnews.com/stories/2009/11/09/cbsnews_investigates/main5590118.shtml >.

Kim, Y.S., Barak, G., Shelton, D.E., 2009. Examining the "CSI-effect" in the cases of circumstantial evidence and eyewitness testimony: Multivariate and path analyses. J. Crim. Justice 37, 452–460.

Kleiman, M.A., 2009. When Brute Force Fails: How to Have Less Crime and Less Punishment. Princeton University Press, Princeton.

Komarinski, P., 2005. Automated Fingerprint Identification Systems (AFIS). Elsevier/Academic Press, Burlington.

Krohn, M., Thornberry, T.P., Rivera, C., Le Blanc, M., 2001. Later delinquency careers. In: Loeber, R., Farrington, D.P. (Eds.), Child Delinquents: Development, Intervention, and Sevice Needs. Sage, Thousand Oaks, pp. 67–93.

Lazer, D., 2004. DNA and the Criminal Justice System: The Technology of Justice. MIT Press, Cambridge.

Lee, H.C., Tirnady, F., 2003. Blood Evidence: How DNA Is Revolutionizing the Way We Solve Crimes. Perseus Publishing, Cambridge, MA.

Leo, R.A., 2008. Police Interrogation and American Justice. Harvard University Press, Cambridge, MA.

Lincoln, Y.S., Guba, E.G., 1985. Naturalistic Inquiry. Sage Publications, Newbury Park.

Lipsky, M., 1980. Streel-Level Bureaucracy: Dilemmas of the Individual in Public Services. Harvester Wheatsheaf, London.

Loader, I., Walker, N., 2007. Civilizing Security. Cambridge, New York.

Lovrich, N.P., Pratt, T.C., Gaffney, M.J., Johnson, C.L., Asplen, C.H., Hurst, L.H., et al., 2004. National Forensic DNA Study Report, Final. National Institute of Justice.

MacNamara, D.E., 1969. Convicting the innocent. Crime Delinq. 15, 57–61.

Manning, P., 1992. Information technologies and the police. Crime Justice 349–398.

Manning, P.K., 2008. The Technology of Policing – Crime Mapping, Information Technology, and the Rationality of Crime Control. New York University Press, New York.

Manning, P.K., Van Maanen, J., 1978. Policing: A View from the Street. Random House, New York.

McCollister, K.E., French, M.T., Fang, H., 2010. The cost of crime to society: New crime-specific estimates for policy and program evaluation. Drug Alcohol Depend. 108, 98–109.

McCue, C., 2007. Data Mining and Predictive Analysis: Intelligence Gathering and Crime Analysis. Butterworth-Heinemann, Oxford.

McLean, N., Marshall, L.A., 2010. A front line police perspective of mental health issues and services. Crim. Behav. Ment. Health 20, 62–71.

Miller, M.T., 2003. Crime scene investigation. In: James, S.H., Nordby, J.J. (Eds.), Forensic Science: An Introduction to Scientific and Investigative Techniques. CRC Press, New York, pp. 115–136.

Moffitt, T.E., 1993. Adolescence-limited and life-course persistent antisocial behavior: A developmental taxonomy. Psychol. Rev. 100, 674–701.

Murphy, E., 2006. The new forensics: criminal justice, false certainty, and the second generation of scientific evidence. New Forensics 1–71.

Nelson, M., 2011. Making sense of DNA backlogs, 2010: Myths vs. reality. National Institute of Justice, Office of Justice Programs, US Department of Justice.

Office of State Budget and Management, 2006. Cost Study of DNA Testing and Analysis. Office of State Budget and Management, Raleigh.

Office of the Inspector General, 2009. US Department of Justice Audit of the Convicted Offender DNA Backlog Reduction Program. US Dep. Justice. http://www.justice.gov/oig/reports/OJP/a0923/final.pdf.

Peterson, J.L., Hickman, M.J., 2005. Census of Publicly Funded Forensic Crime Laboratories, 2002. Department of Justice, Office of Justice Programs, Bureau of Justice Statistics, Washington, DC.

Peterson, J., Leggett, A., 2007. The evolution of forensic science: Progress amid the pitfalls. Stetson Law Rev. 36, 621–660.

Peterson, J., Mihajlovic, S., Gilliland, M., 1984. Forensic Evidence and the Police: The Effects of Scientific Evidence on Criminal Investigations. National Institute of Justice, Washington.

Peterson, M., Braiker, H., Polich, S., 1980. Doing Crime: A Survey of California Inmates. The Rand Institute, Santa Monica.

Pokuchek, D.L., Ward, T., Hudson, S.M., 1997. Rape and rapists: Theory and treatment. Clin. Psychol. Rev. 17, 117–144.

Postman, N, 1992. Technopoly: The Surrender of Culture to Technology. Alfred A. Knopf, New York.

Pratt, T.C., Gaffney, M.J., Lovrich, N.P., Johnson, C.L., 2006. This Isn't CSI: Estimating the national backlog of forensic DNA cases and the barriers associated with case processing. Crim. Justice Policy Rev. 17, 32–47.

Pycroft, A., Gough, D., 2010. Multi-agency Working in Criminal Justice: Control and Care in Contemporary Correctional Practice. The Policy Press, Bristol.
Pyrek, K., 2007. Forensic Science Under Siege: The Challenges of Forensic Laboratories and the Medico-Legal Investigation System. Academic Press, San Diego.
Radelet, M.L., Bedau, H.A., Putman, C.E., 1992. In Spite of Innocence: Erroneous Convictions in Capital Cases. Northeastern University Press, Boston.
Radin, E.D., 1964. The Innocents. William Morrow, New York.
Rafter, N., 1997. Creating Born Criminals. University of Illinois Press, Chicago.
Rago, J.T., 2005. Forensic science and law-revealing truth and freedom in a single light. In: Wecht, C.H., Rago, J.T. (Eds.), Forensic Science and Law: Investigative Applications in Criminal, Civil and Family Justice. CRC Press, Boca Raton, pp. 35–66.
Roman, J.K., Reid, S., Reid, J., Chalfin, A., Adams, W., Knight, C., 2008. The DNA Field Experiment: Cost-Effectiveness Analysis of the Use of DNA in the Investigation of High-Volume Crimes. Natl. Crim. Justice Ref. Serv.
Roman, J.K., Reid, S.E., Chalfin, A.J., Knight, C.R., 2009. The DNA field experiment: A randomized trial of the cost-effectiveness of using DNA to solve property crimes. J. Exp. Criminol. 5, 345–369.
Rosenbaum, D.P., Schuck, A.M., Costello, S.K., Hawkins, D.F., Ring, M.K., 2005. Attitudes toward the police: The effects of direct and vicarious experience. Police Q. 80, 343–365.
Rubin, J., 2010. Grim Sleeper: How LAPD followed the DNA to an arrest. July 8, 2010. Retrieved May 25, 2011, from Los Angeles Times: http://latimesblogs.latimes.com/lanow/2010/07/how-dna-led-to-the-arrest-of-the-grim-sleeper.html.
Rudin, N., Inman, K., 2002. An Introduction to Forensic DNA Analysis, Second Edition. CRC Press, Boca Raton.
Ryan, C., 2011. Bill requiring DNA testing after certain arrests dies in committee. June 6, 2011. Retrieved June 7, 2011, from Las Vegas Sun: http://www.lasvegassun.com/news/2011/jun/06/bill-requiring-dna-testing-dies-committee/.
Sample, L.L., Bray, T.M., 2003. Are sex offenders dangerous? Criminol. Public Policy 3, 59–82.
Sample, L.L., Bray, T.M., 2006. Are sex offenders different? An examination of rearrest patterns. Crim. Justice Policy Rev. 17, 83–102.
Saxena, A.K., 1997. Professionalism in Indian Police. Efficient Offset Printers, New Delhi.
Scheck, B., Neufeld, P., Dwyer, J., 2000. Actual Innocence. Doubleday, Garden City.
Schwardt, T., Lincoln, Y.S., Guba, E.G., 2007. Judging interpretations: But is it rigorous? Trustworthiness and authenticity in naturalistic evaluation. New Dir. Eval. 114, 11–25.
Scully, D., 1990. Understanding Sexual Violence: A Study of Convicted Rapists. Unwin Hyman, Boston.
Shannon, L.W., 1980. Assessing the Relationship of Adult Criminal Careers to Juvenile Careers. US Government Printing Office, Washington, DC.
Sherman, L.W., 1978. Scandal and Reform: Controlling Police Corruption. University of California Press, Berkeley.
Simoncelli, T., 2006. Dangerous excursions: The case against expanding forensic DNA databases to innocent persons. J. Law Med. Ethics 34, 390–397.
Skinner, C., 2010. Clients or offenders? The case for clarity of purpose in multi-agency working. In: Pycroft, A., Gough, D. (Eds.), Multi-Agency Working in Criminal Justice: Control and Care in Contemporary Correctional Practice. The Policy Press, Bristol, pp. 35–50.
Smallbone, S., Wortley, R., 2004. Onset, persistence, and versatility of offending among adult males convicted of sexual offenses against children. Sex. Abuse 16, 285–298.
Smith Alling Lane, 2000. DNA Legislation and News. July 21, 2000. Retrieved June 4, 2011, from DNA Resource: http://www.dnaresource.com/documents/2000_07_21.pdf.
Smith Alling Lane, 2003. DNA Resource Report. March 14, 2003. Retrieved June 20, 2011, from DNA Reource: http://www.dnaresource.com/documents/2003_3_14.pdf.
Smith Alling Lane, 2004a. DNA Resource Report. December, 2004. Retrieved June 20, 2011, from DNA Resource: http://www.dnaresource.com/documents/2004_12_3.pdf.
Smith Alling Lane, 2004b. DNA Resource Report. Janurary 30, 2004. Retrieved June 27, 2011, from DNA Resource: http://www.dnaresource.com/documents/2004_1_30.pdf.
Smith Alling Lane, 2004c. DNA Resource Report. July 30, 2004. Retrieved June 20, 2011, from DNA Resource: http://www.dnaresource.com/documents/2004_7_30.pdf.
Smith Alling Lane, 2005. DNA Resource Report. August, 2005. Retrieved June 20, 2011, from DNA Resource: http://www.dnaresource.com/documents/2005_8_26.pdf.

Smith Alling Lane, 2006. DNA Legislation and News. September, 2006. Retrieved June 12, 2011, from DNA Resource: http://www.dnaresource.com/documents/2006_9.pdf.

Smith Alling Lane, 2007. DNA Resource Report. June 2007. Retrieved June 20, 2011, from DNA Resource: http://www.dnaresource.com/documents/2007_6.pdf.

Smith Alling Lane, 2008a. DNA Legislation & News. August, 2008. Retrieved June 20, 2011, from DNA Resource: http://www.dnaresource.com/documents/2008_8.pdf.

Smith Alling Lane, 2008b. DNA Legislation and News. January, 2008. Retrieved June 20, 2011, from DNA Resource: http://www.dnaresource.com/documents/2008_1.pdf.

Smith, F.M., Marshall, L.A., 2007. Barriers to effective drug addiction treatment for women involved in street-level prostitution: A qualitative investigation. Crim. Behav. Ment. Health 17, 163–170.

Smith, J.A., Osborn, M., 2003. Interpretative phenomenological analysis. In: Smith, J.A. (Ed.), Qualitative psychology: A practical guide to research methods. Sage, London, pp. 51–80.

Somer, R., 2007. Body Worn Digital Recording System: Interim Report. Retrieved from http://police.homeoffice.gov.uk/publications/operational-policing/Plymouth_Head_Camera_Project.pdf.

Soullière, N., 1999. Police and Technology: Historical Review and Current Status. Canadian Police College, Ottawa.

Southey, P., Braybrook, B., Spier, P., 1994. Rape Recidivism and Sexual Violation. Department of Justice, Wellington.

Staley, K., 2005. The Police National DNA Database Balancing Crime Detection, Human Rights, and Privacy. GeneWatch UK, Derbyshire.

Stevens, D.J., 2011. Media and Criminal Justice: The CSI Effect. Jones & Bartlett Publishers, Sudbury.

Strom, K.J., Hickman, M.J., 2010. Unanalyzed evidence in law enforcement agencies: A national examination of forensic processing in police departments. Am. Soc. Criminol. 9, 381–404.

Teichroeb, R., 2004. Rare Look Inside State Crime Labs Reveals Recurring Problems; 23 Cases in 3 Years Had DNA Test Errors. Seattle Post-Intelligencer, July 22, 2004, p. A1.

US Department of Justice, 2000. The Future of Forensic DNA Testing: Predictions of the Research and Development Working Group. National Institute of Justice, Washington, DC.

US Department of Justice, 2009. Forensic DNA Backlog Reduction Program: Fiscal Year 2009 Awards and Abstracts. National Institute of Justice, Washington, DC.

US Department of Justice, 2010a. Forensic DNA Backlog Reduction Program: Fiscal Year 2010 Awards and Abstracts. National Institute of Justice, Washington, DC.

US Department of Justice, 2010b. Solicitation: FY 2010 Forensic DNA Backlog Reduction Program. National Institute of Justice, Washington, DC.

Uildriks, N.A., 2009. Policing Insecurity: Police Reform, Security, and Human Rights in Latin America. Lexington Books, Plymouth.

Visher, C., 1986. The Rand Inmate Survey: A reanalysis. In: Blumstein, A., Cohen, J., Roth, J.A., Visher, C.A. (Eds.), Criminal Careers and Career Criminals, vol. 2. National Academy Press, Washington, DC, pp. 161–211.

Walsh, S.J., Moss, D.S., Kliem, C., Vintiner, G.M., 2002. The collation of forensic DNA case data into a multi-dimensional intelligence database. Sci. Justice 42 (4), 205–214.

Warr, M., 1980. The accuracy of public beliefs about crime. Social Forces 59 (2), 456–470.

Watson, A., 2000. A new breed of high-tech detectives. Science 289 (5481), 850–854.

Webb, B., Smith, C., Brock, A., Townsley, M., 2005. DNA fast-tracking. In: Smith, M.J., Tilley, N. (Eds.), Crime Science: New Approaches to Preventing and Detecting Crime. Willan, England, pp. 167–190.

Webb, E.J., Campbell, D.T., Schwartz, R.D., Sechrest, L., 1966. Unobtrusive Measures. Rand McNally, Chicago.

Weinrib, E.J., 1992. Law as idea of reason. In: Williams, H.L. (Ed.), Essays on Kant's Political Philosophy. University of Chicago Press, Chicago, pp. 15–49.

White, M.D., 2007. Current Issues and Controversies in Policing. Pearson Education, Boston.

Whitney, D.M., Trosten-Bloom, A., 2003. The Power of Appreciative Inquiry. Berrett-Koehler, San Francisco.

Williams, R., Hammond, S., 2009. Building Forensic Technology Capacity. National Conference of State Legislatures, Washington, DC.

Willing, R., 2003. USA Today. April 30, 2003. Retrieved June 12, 2011, from Mueller defends crime lab after questionable DNA tests: http://www.usatoday.com/news/washington/2003-04-30-lab-usat_x.htm.

Wolfe, D., 1967. Technology and control of crime. Science 156 (3783), 1687.

CASES

Andrews v. State, 533 So. 2d 841 (Fla. Dist. Ct. App 1988).

INDEX

Note: Page numbers followed by "*f*" and "*t*" refers to figures and tables respectively.

V

W